D0291075

BENEFIT
of the
DOUBT

BREAKING *the* IDOL *of* CERTAINTY

Gregory A. Boyd

BakerBooks

a division of Baker Publishing Group
Grand Rapids, Michigan

Published by Baker Books
a division of Baker Publishing Group
P.O. Box 6287, Grand Rapids, MI 49516-6287
www.bakerbooks.com

Printed in the United States of America

Library of Congress Cataloging-in-Publication Data
Boyd, Gregory A., 1957–
    Benefit of the doubt : breaking the idol of certainty / Gregory A. Boyd
       pages cm
    Includes bibliographical references.
    ISBN 978-0-8010-1492-5 (pbk.)
    1. Faith. 2. Belief and doubt. 3. Certainty. 4. Knowledge, Theory of (Religion)
  I. Title.
  BT771.3.B69 2013
  234'.23—dc23   2013016850

13   14   15   16   17   18   19   7   6   5   4   3   2   1

"Even when certainty is inaccessible, commitment remains an option. Greg Boyd is incapable of uninteresting thoughts. And this book is not merely thoughtful; it will be a tremendous help to doubters (and non-doubters) everywhere."

—**John C. Ortberg,** author of *Who Is This Man?*;
pastor of Menlo Park Presbyterian Church

"Sometimes I feel like Greg Boyd is a 'brother-from-another-mother.' I try to read everything he writes. Sometimes I find him articulating things I haven't been able to put the words to. He's one of the great thinkers of the contemporary church. He's gotten used to exploring new territory, and in this book he dives into the issue of doubt and certainty—and recovers the lost treasure of Christlike humility and childlike wonder. Enjoy."

—**Shane Claiborne,** author, activist, and lover of Jesus;
www.thesimpleway.org

"*Benefit of the Doubt* is a deeply personal yet profoundly theological look at the important role of doubt in the Christian faith. I found myself underlining entire chapters and tucking away favorite quotes in my journal. This is a book I suspect I will return to again and again. Prepare to feel a little less crazy, a little less alone, and a lot more challenged to take the risk of following Jesus with your head and heart engaged. Boyd is the best sort of company for the journey."

—**Rachel Held Evans,** blogger at www.rachelheldevans.com;
author of *Evolving in Monkey Town*
and *A Year of Biblical Womanhood*

"Prolific author and speaker Greg Boyd has crafted a tour de force that will help countless Christians who are struggling with their faith. Like a fine surgeon, Boyd takes dead aim at numerous misconceptions about faith that are in the drinking water of evangelical Christianity today. He then presents a strikingly beautiful and solidly biblical portrait of what believing faith looks like on the ground and how it's *not* incompatible with the struggle against doubt. If you're a Christian who wrestles with doubt or you know someone who does, *Benefit of the Doubt* is one of the best books ever written on the subject. It's an important work whose time has come."

"If I was one of Jesus's first disciples, I would be doubting Thomas. My mind naturally questions everything and faith never feels simple. *Benefit of the Doubt* was written for me. Thank you Greg Boyd! If you ever wrestle with an inner skeptic (like me) or regularly interact with skeptics, this book offers hugely helpful insight into the benefits of doubt and how to leverage doubt in deepening our trust in God. I predict many people who read *Benefit of the Doubt* will find it profoundly life-changing."

"As usual, Greg Boyd has hit a home run. *Benefit of the Doubt* is brutally honest, thought provoking, and creative. If I could require all conservative Christians to read one book (besides the Bible!) it would be this one. It would liberate them from fear-based theology and spirituality. As good as the title is, it doesn't begin to describe this book that ranges far and wide over many issues of fear-based theology and liberating faith."

I'd like to dedicate this book to my dear, artistic, super-creative, and highly gifted friend, Terri Churchill. Terri worked as my editor throughout the duration of this project, and her feedback, corrections, and insights have made it a much better work than it would have otherwise been.

Contents

Abbreviations

ASV	American Standard Version
CEB	Common English Bible
CEV	Contemporary English Version
ESV	English Standard Version
GNT	Good News Translation
GW	GOD'S WORD Translation
HCSB	Holman Christian Standard Bible
KJV	King James Version
Message	The Message
NASB	New American Standard Bible
NCV	New Century Version
NIV	New International Version
NIV 1984	New International Version, 1984 edition
NLT	New Living Translation
NRSV	New Revised Standard Version
Phillips	*The New Testament in Modern English*, J. B. Phillips
RSV	Revised Standard Version
TNIV	Today's New International Version
WEB	Webster's Bible
YLT	Young's Literal Translation

Introduction

Certainty Lost

I encountered Christ in a very powerful way when I was seventeen years old. The experience was so overwhelming that for about a year I felt absolutely certain that everything this Pentecostal church taught me was true. Unfortunately, as is so often the case with Pentecostal or charismatic churches, this church valued emotional experiences over reason. In fact, questioning matters of faith was viewed with suspicion, and expressing outright doubt was considered positively immoral.

This didn't bode well for me, for up until my conversion I'd always been a questioner. Since childhood I had found it hard to accept things just because someone told me it was so. I recall the nun who taught my second-grade catechism class angrily reprimanding me because I kept asking "why?" and "how do you know?" She said something like, "Mr. Boyd [the nuns always addressed me this way for some reason], too much questioning does not please God! *Faith* pleases God!"

In any event, my initial experience with Christ, combined with several subsequent powerful experiences, sufficed to keep my questions and doubts at bay for almost an entire blissful year. Despite the fact that I struggled with a particular nagging sin that I at the time believed required me to get "resaved" several times a week (I'll say more about this in chap. 5), I for the most part enjoyed the euphoria of feeling absolutely certain I had found "the truth" through my senior year of high school. I was absolutely *certain* I had one single eternally important purpose in life, which was to help others discover "the truth."

Though I now see my state of mind during this brief period as childishly naive, I can't deny that part of me has a sort of nostalgic longing for it. I know I'll never again enjoy such bliss this side of death. And while I think this mind-set is misguided, self-indulgent, idolatrous, and even dangerous, as I'll argue later, I completely understand why a multitude of believers try to cling to it. *It feels good!*

For me, such certitude was destined to crash. As I'll share in this book, it took just one university course in evolutionary biology and one course in the critical study of the Bible to blow my blissful certainty sky-high. I obviously managed to piece my faith back together eventually, but my yearlong vacation from my incessantly questioning brain was over for good.

The faith I eventually recovered and have struggled to grow in ever since has been anything but certain. My core commitment to Christ has been mostly unwavering, but I've had questions, doubts, and confusions about most of the beliefs Christians typically espouse. Not surprisingly, my beliefs have changed quite a bit over the years, with the number of convictions I have a fair degree of confidence in dwindling throughout the process. At the same time, however, the number of things I feel I *need* to remain fairly confident about has dwindled along with them.

In fact, if I'm totally honest with you—something I promise to be throughout this book—I am now persuaded that, at the end of the day, there is only *one* thing I *really* need to remain confident about, and that is "Jesus Christ and him crucified" (1 Cor. 2:2). As I'll discuss in the latter part of this book, there are a number of beliefs that are important, for one reason or another. But this one conviction is all I need—and all I believe any of us should truly need—to feel secure in my relationship with God, my identity, and my place in the world.

What's Up with Faith?

In any event, one of the things that Christians typically believe in and that I've struggled a great deal with is the concept of faith itself.

Like most Christians, I once assumed a person's faith is as *strong* as that person is *certain*. And, accordingly, I assumed that doubt is the enemy of faith. This is, after all, how Christians generally talk. And there are, in fact, some verses in the Bible that can be cited in support of this assumption. "When you ask," James says, for example, "you must believe and not doubt. . . . Those who doubt should not think they will receive anything from the Lord" (James 1:6–7 TNIV). In chapter 10, I'll offer an alternative interpretation of this and another passage that is commonly used to support this understanding of faith, which I label "certainty-seeking faith."

Yet, as commonsensical as this view of faith is for Christians, I have to confess that it has always bothered me. I admit that it's possible that part of my frustration is personal, if not prideful. For if this understanding of faith is correct, it means my faith has always been weak (with the exception of the above-mentioned year of bliss). This no longer bothers me, but it certainly used to. Early on in my walk with Christ there were times when I wondered if my limping faith would keep me from being "raptured" if the Lord returned in my lifetime.[1] Over the years I've encountered multitudes of unfortunate Christians whose doubts give them similar concerns. If any readers struggle with this, I am confident that by the end of this book they will clearly see that their concern is absolutely unnecessary.

My personal frustrations aside, however, this conception of faith raises a number of perfectly legitimate questions—questions we will be exploring throughout part 1 of this book. For example, Scripture teaches us that we are saved by faith and that the power of prayer, whether for healing or for some other blessing, is directly connected to a person's faith. But I've always wondered, why would God place a premium on one's ability to convince oneself that something is true? What is particularly virtuous about one's ability to push doubt aside and make oneself feel certain?

Let's be honest: some people are naturally good at doing this and some are not, but this ability has nothing to do with their *character*. Whether a person is good at this is simply a function of how the person's brain is wired. Some people's brains are naturally inquisitive and others' are not. And to be frank, the people who are best at convincing themselves that something is true, beyond what a rational assessment of evidence warrants, are most often people who are either self-delusional or intellectually dull.

Now, I've got nothing against self-delusional or intellectually dull people. God bless them! But why would God unfairly advantage them over rationally balanced and naturally inquisitive people? Why would God leverage whether a person is healed, let alone saved, on this ability—which, if anything, seems to be more of a *disability*? Why did God even bother to create minds that naturally gauge their level of confidence in a belief on the evidence and arguments for and against it if he's only pleased with minds that can make themselves *more certain* than the evidence and arguments for it warrant? I just don't get it!

Here's another example of the sort of problems I've had with most people's concept of faith. If God is pleased by our ability to make ourselves feel certain that a particular set of beliefs is true, then a person is going to be pretty much locked into whatever beliefs they were initially taught to believe. Think about it. How likely is it that people will change their beliefs if they think salvation and damnation depend on whether they can remain as certain as possible that what they *already* believe is true? Not much. But this means that a person's set of beliefs will be determined *by circumstance*—where they were born, who raised them, what proselytizer first persuaded them, and so on. Is this really how our beliefs should be determined?

Over the years I became increasingly convinced that there is something seriously screwed up about this certainty-seeking concept of faith. Look, what it means to believe in something is that you believe it is *true*. But if you're really concerned that what you believe is *true*, then you *can't* leave this belief to chance. The only way to determine if a belief is true is to *rationally investigate it*. Which means you *have* to doubt it. It's simply impossible for people to be concerned that their beliefs *are true* unless they're genuinely open to the possibility that their current beliefs *are false*. There are no two ways around it. But this is precisely what certainty-seeking faith discourages.

A closely related aspect of this common view of faith that has troubled me concerns the way we who consider ourselves evangelicals are typically encouraged to hold it. As my work as a scholar progressed, I grew increasingly uncomfortable with the fact that my faith depended on so many things. Like most evangelicals, for example, I assumed that believing the Bible to be the inspired Word of God meant I was supposed to trust that every one of its stories was historically accurate. To doubt any one story was to call into question the inspiration of the whole book, including the good news of God becoming a human and dying to save humanity.

As I studied issues surrounding Scripture, however, I occasionally encountered data that seemed to undermine the historical veracity of certain narratives. When this happened, I would feel pressured by my belief in inspiration to spin the data in a way that would instead support the narrative's historical accuracy. While I was aware that evangelical and non-evangelical scholars frequently do this, it felt disingenuous to me. *Is this really what God would want me to do?* I wondered.

Over the years, I have increasingly felt there is something amiss with a concept of faith that inclines me to be anything but totally honest with whatever my research uncovers. At the same time, I have gradually seen less and less reason why my belief in inspiration should require that every story conform to our modern concept of historical veracity, and even less reason why my life-giving relationship with Christ, which has come to form the very core of my being, should be affected by how I evaluate the evidence for any particular biblical story.[2] There is, I concluded, something fundamentally wrong with this "house-of-cards" model of faith, as I shall call it.

The Harm Our "Faith" Causes

It's my conviction that this certainty-seeking concept of faith is causing a great deal of harm to the church today that most are not aware of. For example, as I'll argue in chapter 8, I believe this model of faith has led many to mistakenly interpret the doctrine that we're "saved by faith" to mean we're "saved by feeling certain about particular beliefs"—most importantly, the belief that Jesus is Lord. This, I shall argue, largely explains why studies show that the faith of most Americans has next to no impact on how they live.

Against this, I will argue that salvation involves a real, marriage-like relationship with Christ that cannot help but radically affect every area of our life.

On top of this, I'm convinced that the idea that faith is as strong as a person is certain, combined with the house-of-cards way of embracing this faith, is behind most of the faith struggles Christians have today. In fact, I am convinced it is the main reason so many of our young people abandon the Christian faith and the main reason most nonbelievers today don't take Christian truth claims very seriously. Among other things, certainty-seeking faith, combined with the all-or-nothing way evangelicals typically embrace it, is simply no longer viable in the postmodern world in which we live.

Owing to technology, the increased pluralism of Western culture, and a host of other considerations, the world we find ourselves in is far more complex and ambiguous than it was even fifty years ago. Whereas the majority of people in the past could go their entire life without having their faith seriously challenged by alternative truth claims, people today are confronted at every turn with the widest array of mutually exclusive and equally compelling truth claims. It's much easier to remain certain of your beliefs when you are not in personal contact with people who believe differently. But when you encounter people with different beliefs, and when those people's sincerity and devotion possibly put yours to shame, things become quite a bit more difficult.

The confusion this intense pluralism has created is such that many today struggle with the very concept of "objective truth." And in this highly ambiguous environment, the invitation to embrace a faith that asks us to *try* to be *certain* about *anything*—let alone certain about a multitude of things, including the accuracy of every biblical story—is unattractive at best, a complete nonstarter at worst.

Now, I am not suggesting we modify our concept of faith simply to make it conform to the zeitgeist of our age. But the unviability of this prevalent understanding of faith, combined with the multitude of problems it creates, as I'll later discuss, should certainly give us pause. It was considerations such as these that began to lead me, around twenty years ago, to begin to seriously wonder if our understanding of faith is correct.

The Message of This Book

My reexamination of the biblical concept of faith led me to the conclusion that the concept of faith that equates strength with certainty and that views doubt as an enemy is, in fact, significantly different from the biblical model. As we'll explore throughout part 2 of this book, while the certainty-seeking model of faith is *psychological* in nature, the biblical concept is *covenantal*. That is, while the former is focused on a person's *mental state*, the latter is focused on how a person demonstrates a commitment by how they *live*.

I hope to show that this model of faith allows us to embrace a rationally anchored faith that is nevertheless compatible with whatever level of doubt, and however many unresolved questions, a person may have. Unlike the house-of-cards approach to faith, this model of faith does not incline one toward an all or-nothing mind-set, and thus isn't shaken if a person feels compelled by evidence to accept that one, or any number of biblical narratives, are not rooted in history. For while this model yet looks to the Bible as God's Word as the foundation for *what* we believe, it doesn't lean on it as the rational foundation for *why* we believe.

I am convinced that by returning to the biblical model of faith, many if not most of the struggles that thoughtful believers have with their faith, as well as the struggles that cause so many to abandon their faith, can be altogether avoided. And because the biblical model doesn't demand or expect certainty, let alone certainty about a large number of beliefs, and because it is perfectly at home with ambiguity, doubts, and unanswered questions, I also believe this model will be much more plausible to nonbelievers in our postmodern age than are the certainty-seeking and house-of-cards models of faith.

One final thing that I hope returning to the biblical model of faith accomplishes is that it will disturb believers who may be too comfortable in their feeling of certainty. By orienting us away from our subjective mental states and toward how we actually live, I trust my discussion of biblical faith will confront those who have assumed that they are "saved" by virtue of the fact they feel relatively certain that Jesus is Lord, though this feeling has no discernible impact on their life. These misguided believers will see that, while it is unequivocally true that we're "saved by faith alone," *real* faith can't help but impact our day-to-day lives, and do so in a radically Jesus-looking way.

The only other thing I will say about the message of this book—and this has already been reflected in this introduction—is that readers will find that this book is much more autobiographical than anything I have ever written before. Given the personal nature of faith, it seemed appropriate for me to flesh out my ideas by weaving them into the events in my life that inspired them. A more autobiographical approach also seemed appropriate inasmuch as faith is a gift that God delivers to us by working through the people and events of our lives. As I look back on the winding road that has brought me to where I am today, I can discern the hand of God at every turn. And it just seemed like it would be irresponsible of me not to seize this wonderful opportunity to brag about what Abba Father has done in my life.

The Outline

Before going on a journey, it's always helpful to have a glimpse of the map. So here's an overview of how this book will unfold. It's divided into three parts. Part 1 ("False Faith"), which covers the first three chapters, aims at refuting the mistaken assumption that one's faith is as strong as one is free of doubt. Part 2 ("True Faith"), which covers chapters 4 through 7, aims at unpacking the biblical understanding of faith. And part 3 ("Exercising Faith"), which comprises the last five chapters of this book, is intended to offer insights from Scripture and from my own experience that I hope will help readers exercise their faith in a rationally grounded, yet appropriately flexible, way.

It may help readers to know ahead of time that part 3 of this work builds on insights gleaned from parts 1 and 2 and is the practical goal of this book. My aim in writing this book, in other words, is not merely to dispel a false view of faith and offer readers information on the biblical view, though I think this is important in and of itself. My ultimate goal, however, is to help readers *apply* this information and embrace a kind of faith that is intellectually compelling, passionately centered on Christ, and fearlessly efficient in negotiating the complexity and ambiguity of our postmodern age. To be frank, I have been driven by my grief over seeing so many walk away from the faith, or stay away from the faith, for reasons that are entirely avoidable.

And just to tip my hand a little regarding the thesis around which this last section is woven, I will argue that the most biblical and intellectually viable way of constructing and exercising faith is to make "Jesus Christ and him crucified" (1 Cor. 2:2) the center of every aspect of our faith. More specifically, I believe that Christ crucified should be the center that intellectually grounds our faith as well as the center that meets every core need in our life (chap. 8), the center of our interpretation of Scripture as well as our theology (chap. 9), the center of our imaginative world, which, we shall see, is the "substance" of faith (chap. 10), and the center of all that we trust God for (chaps. 11 and 12). As Paul confessed, if we know "Jesus Christ and him crucified," we essentially know all we need to know about God, ourselves, and our world.

So long as we remain confident enough to commit our lives to God on that basis, we need not fear any doubt or confusion about any matter that may come our way, regardless of how wide or how deep it may run. Indeed, so long as we have Christ crucified to cling to, instead of running from the doubt that plagues us, we can embrace our doubt and calmly seek our Father for how to grow and benefit from our doubt.

May the Lord bless you as you read this book, and as you apply whatever insights you glean from it to your life.

Part 1

FALSE FAITH

Embracing the Pain

Doubt is a pain too lonely to know that faith is his twin brother.

—KHALIL GIBRAN

Be merciful to those who doubt.
—JUDE 22

Certainty-Seeking Faith

Jacobson-Sized Faith

In the Pentecostal church I served while in seminary, Sunday night services always included a time for testimonies. No one was more consistent in sharing than an eighty-some-year-old saint I'll refer to as "Brother Jacobson" (everyone was referred to as "brother" and "sister" in this church).[1] The trouble was that Brother Jacobson almost always gave a version of the same testimony. Standing with his Bible raised in his right hand, he'd typically begin by saying something like, "I've walked with my Lord for over eighty years, and I thank God that, by his grace, my faith in God's Word has never for one moment wavered, *never*!" "Amen!" the church would respond, though I never knew if this meant that their faith also had never wavered, or if it rather meant something like, "Yes, Brother, we've heard that before."

Either way, this church often talked about how strong Brother Jacobson's faith was. Every now and then I'd hear someone encouraging somebody by saying something like, "You need a Jacobson-sized faith!" The assumption of this church—and I've found it's shared by most Christians—is that the more psychologically certain you are, the stronger your faith is. In this conception of faith, therefore, doubt is an enemy.

Despite its popularity, and despite the fact that there are a dozen or so verses that can be marshaled in its support (the most important of which I'll address in chap. 10), this is the conception of faith I will be arguing *against* in this book. It's not just that I think this model of faith is mistaken. As will become clear over the next two chapters, I believe this model is *gravely* mistaken inasmuch as it can have negative consequences in the lives of believers and for the kingdom movement as a whole.

How Much Faith Is "Enough"?

Not too long ago a middle-aged lady who looked rather distressed approached me after a church service. She explained to me that, while she sincerely tried to believe in the Bible, she struggled with some of its stories. With a worried tone in her voice, she asked, "Why on earth would God include in his Holy Word a story about a poor young girl getting gang-raped, murdered, and dismembered?" She was referring to a story in Judges 19, and it is indeed a truly horrible account. "It's not exactly the kind of story you'd want to read in children's church, is it?" I replied. "And pastor," she continued,

> I have a degree in ancient literature, and if I'm honest with myself, I just can't deny that some Bible stories sound like folklore, not history. Like the one about Lot's wife turning to a pillar of salt, just because she was curious! Would God really do such a thing? Do we *have* to believe these stories are all literal?

I thought she wanted me to respond, but before I could open my mouth she jumped back in.

> And the stories of Samson getting strong when his hair grew long, killing a lion with his bare hands, slaying one thousand Philistines with the jawbone of an ass, and sending two hundred foxes into some fields with their tails tied together around a torch? Come on! I'm sorry, pastor, but I just can't keep myself from doubting stories like this. If God knows I'm sincerely trying to believe, do you think that is enough for me to still be saved?

My heart went out to this dear woman. I reassured her that God knows her heart and that she needn't worry about her salvation. And as it concerns her questions about various Bible stories, I shared with her some of the things I'll be sharing with you later on in this book (especially chap. 9). My reason for mentioning her now, however, is because she illustrates the conception of faith I'm going to be talking about. Her question was basically about whether she had *enough* faith to be "saved."[2] For her, this was really a question of whether her *level of certainty* was adequate to be saved.

As I suspect is true of most pastors, I get questions along these lines quite often.

- Do my doubts disqualify me from "salvation"?
- If I'm fairly sure that Jesus is the Son of God—but not 100 percent certain—am I still "saved"?
- Are my doubts about God's willingness to heal my child the reason she is not healed?
- How much faith do I need to get God to change the heart of my husband?
- I struggle with the idea that God really cares about my family and me. Do you think this is why I can't find a job?

Questions such as these are predicated on the assumption that one's faith is as strong as it is certain. And they each assume that, whether we're talking about salvation, getting healed, or keeping a job, the more certain we are, the more God will be involved in our lives.

Slamming for the Certainty Bell

If you've ever gone to a carnival or fair, I'm sure you've seen that game where people test their strength by trying to ring a bell at the top of a pole with a metal puck by striking a lever with a mallet as hard as they can. It's sometimes called the "Strength Tester." I believe it provides a fair analogy of what goes on inside people's heads when they assume that their faith is as strong as they are psychologically certain.

Think about it. If the strength of your faith is measured by the intensity of your psychological certainty, then the way to increase your faith is to *try to push doubt aside* in order to *make yourself certain*. And in this sense, exercising faith is something like a psychological version of the Strength Tester game. You are, in essence, trying to hit a faith mallet as hard as you can in order to send the faith puck up the faith pole to get as close to the certainty bell as you possibly can.

In this certainty-seeking model, when Jesus said, "according to your faith let it be done to you" (Matt. 9:29), he was saying, "the more certain you are that God will do things, the more you'll see God do those things." So too, when the man said to Jesus, "I do believe; help me overcome my unbelief" (Mark 9:24), within this paradigm, the man was asking, "Lord, I can only hit the faith puck a little way up the faith pole, but please help me to ring the certainty bell."

Along the same lines, when Jesus praised the centurion for having "great faith" (Matt. 8:10), the certainty-seeking model would have us understand that Jesus was praising his psychological certainty that Jesus could and would do what he needed him to do. By contrast, when Jesus reprimanded his disciples for having "little faith" (Matt. 14:31), he was, according to this model, expressing his anger that they wavered in their certainty about what he could and would do.

The Level of Required Certainty

With this interpretation of these verses, it's no wonder pastors regularly get the sort of questions I mentioned above. Related to this, it's also no wonder that Christians often instinctively rank things in terms of how much faith they will require. It's like this lady who spoke with me recently about her troubled marriage. In the course of sharing her problems, she mentioned that she was a heavy smoker who wanted to quit. But, she said, "I'm afraid I don't have nearly enough faith for *that* one yet." Quitting smoking would require a greater act of faith than healing her marriage, she assumed, and this meant she would need a Jacobson-sized faith, which she was convinced she lacked. (Truth be told, once this lady told me about the full extent of her marital problems, it seemed to me her ranking system was upside down—assuming faith worked that way.)

The closer to the certainty bell you send your faith puck, the prevailing assumption goes, the greater the blessing you'll receive from God. I suspect most Christians would agree that you only need a minimally acceptable level of faith to be "saved." We might say that to get "saved," you only need enough psychological certainty to get the faith puck 25 percent of the way up the faith pole. If you're able to muster up more certainty and slam the faith puck (say) 50 percent of the way up the faith pole, then we might say you've entered the "basic blessing" zone. Here God may grant you success in your relationships or finances, and you may experience small supernatural interventions like having a headache or toothache disappear or gaining the strength to quit smoking.

If you are able to push doubts away further, however, thereby mustering up the psychological certainty to get the faith puck (say) three-quarters of the way toward the certainty bell, well, then you've entered what we might call the "super-blessed" zone. God will now answer your prayers in rather spectacular ways, and you just might experience more impressive, Jesus-type miracles. But if anyone is ever able to vanquish *all* doubt, become *completely* certain, and thereby actually ring the certainty bell with that faith puck, then they presumably could have "whatever they ask for," which is how people who hold to this certainty-seeking understanding of faith interpret passages such as Matthew 21:22: "If you believe, you will receive whatever you ask for in prayer."

The fact that we still don't have peace in the Middle East can only mean that either no one has yet rung that bell or, if they have, they were too self-centered to think about this ongoing atrocious conflict and chose instead to acquire a Mercedes for themselves.

In the next chapter I'm going to offer eight arguments as to why I believe certainty-seeking faith is misguided, unhealthy, and dangerous. I will follow this in chapter 3 with a discussion of the ninth, and the most serious, objection to this model, for I'll contend that this conception of faith tends to make an idol out of certainty. And then, throughout the three chapters that comprise part 2 of this work, I'll argue that this psychological conception of faith contrasts with the covenantal concept of faith found in Scripture. In part 3 we'll flesh out some more practical and helpful ways of thinking about and living out our faith.

Before we turn to this, however, I'd like to say something about one of the most common and powerful motivators for this popular conception of faith. It is, in a word, the desire to avoid the pain of cognitive dissonance. To get at this, I'd like to share a little bit of the story of how I found, and lost, my faith.

From Blissful Certainty to Excruciating Doubt

A Lost Certainty and Purpose

As I mentioned in the introduction, I came to Christ at the age of seventeen after having spent several years in the "drugs, sex, and rock-n-roll" culture of the early '70s. While I had a lot of fun, I also felt a painful emptiness that intensified over the two years leading up to my conversion. Despite the fact that the Pentecostal church in which I met Christ was legalistic to the extreme and theologically aberrant in a number of ways, my encounter with Jesus was undeniably real and powerfully life changing. Words can't describe how good it felt to have the gnawing ache of emptiness in my soul replaced with a sense of joy and purpose.

For a little more than a year I enjoyed the bliss of feeling absolutely certain my newfound faith was true. I felt like I knew what life was about, was sure about where I was going when I died (or when I was "raptured"), and had a strong sense of mission and purpose to motivate me to live passionately in the meantime.

Then I enrolled in the University of Minnesota.

Perhaps it was because I felt I had a duty to save people, or maybe it was to impress my atheistic father, whom I'd been debating since my conversion (he couldn't believe his own son had become one of those "born-again nitwits"), but for whatever reason, I decided to jump-start my university career by taking a summer school course titled Introduction to Evolutionary Biology. I didn't tell any of my Christian friends about my decision because I knew they'd try to talk me out of it. (They'd already tried to talk me out of going to a secular university in the first place.)

As you probably could guess, the Pentecostal church I was saved in believed in "young-earth creationism," which means they interpreted Genesis 1 literally and held that the earth was less than ten thousand years old. In fact, I recall our pastor teaching that, if Genesis 1 wasn't literally true, then "the whole Bible is a book of lies!" So, as far as I was concerned, my entire faith was leveraged on my ability to survive this class with my faith in young-earth creationism intact. To prepare myself, and with rather megalomaniacal dreams of converting the entire class, I read three whole books (yes, *three*!) defending creationism and refuting evolution. I'd never before read so much on a single subject. I felt like a bona fide expert.

Things didn't go quite as I had planned. From the start I took every opportunity to interrupt the lecture, raise objections, and offer counterinterpretations. The professor, who was always very gracious and seemed to welcome my enthusiastic pushbacks, would gently proceed to show how my objections and counterinterpretations were misinformed and/or wildly implausible. This clearly was not his first run-in with a young-earth creationist. When the class would chuckle after I'd been once again silenced, the professor would quickly come to my defense and praise my willingness to question things. It almost bothered me that this pagan opponent of Christ (so I viewed him) was so nice to me, even as he diced me up!

I'd come home discouraged after each class and would spend the remainder of the day poring over the notes I'd taken from my three books, trying to find better lines of attack. After this arsenal was depleted, I went to several libraries and Christian bookstores to find better material, once even gaining some hope from a book I found (called *Fish to Gish*, by Duane Gish) that anticipated one of the professor's counterpoints. But without fail, the patient professor managed to gently expose the weakness of my objections.

By the time we had reached the midterm, I had begun to doubt my one-year-old faith.

The pain of the cognitive dissonance this doubt created in me was like nothing I'd ever experienced before. I wanted so desperately to believe my experience with Christ wasn't an illusion and my sense of purpose a false dream. I desperately wanted to reexperience that delightful feeling of certainty I'd enjoyed throughout the previous year.

I eventually shared my pain with some of my Pentecostal friends who, after chastising me for "playing the devil's poker" by taking this class, would tell me that my doubt was from Satan and that I needed to let it go and "just believe." I so badly wanted to return to the joy of feeling certain that I actually tried this several times, but it frankly felt artificial. For a while I even tried to rationalize suppressing doubt by appealing to (and, I now see, grossly misapplying) an idea I'd gotten from Søren Kierkegaard, whom I'd been reading and whom I'd come to deeply respect. In several books he talks about faith as a "leap" that involves passionately grabbing hold of something that is absurd to our reason—namely, the incarnation and crucifixion.[3] I recall thinking to myself that, if taking an absurd leap of faith was good enough for a guy as smart as Kierkegaard, it should be good enough for me.

It didn't work. My brain would not let me forget the troubling questions evolution posed.

By the end of the summer school course on evolution, I was a tormented young man who was being slowly ripped in two, with my longing for faith and the evidence for evolution pulling me in opposite directions. Within another half semester—one that included a course that examined the Bible from a historical-critical perspective—I concluded my fight was hopeless. The obstacles to my faith were too formidable, and I could not, for the life of me, find an intelligent and informed Christian to help me work through them. I finally concluded that evolution was true and that the Bible was no different from other ancient works. As real as my experience with Christ had seemed, I concluded that it must have been some sort of strange psychological phenomenon I didn't yet understand. And this, in turn, meant that the joyful sense of purpose I had experienced for a year was nothing more than an illusory oasis in the desert of a meaningless world.

I returned to the atheism I'd embraced in the four years leading up to my conversion. My father was overjoyed. But I had just entered what proved to be the most depressing year of my life.

The Necessity of Pain

The fact that I'm writing this book obviously means I eventually managed to find my way back into the Christian faith. It was a long and arduous journey we need not go into right now. It also began a new journey of faith that was also long and arduous, about which I'll have more to say later on. My present goal is to simply convey to you that I understand how painful doubt can be when it concerns the things that matter the most to us—and there is nothing that matters more than the sense of identity, worth, purpose, and security that is associated with our faith. On the register of things that create pain, seriously doubting one's faith is right up there toward the top, at least for people such as myself who make faith the foundation for their life.

The truth is, the process of learning and growing almost always involves a certain amount of pain. Perhaps you, like me, were a child who found it very hard to accept that Santa Claus wasn't real. I fought my doubt for at least a year, and when my older brother finally convinced me, I cried. Then I got angry—*very* angry. Feeling I'd been duped, I vowed I'd never believe anything anyone ever told me again. While this pledge thankfully didn't stick, I sometimes wonder if this experience is part of the reason I have always had a skeptical streak. I don't like being fooled.

This experience illustrates how painful growing out of old, cherished beliefs can be, which is why we sometimes fight tenaciously, and often irrationally, to resist letting them go, or even letting go of our certainty about them. And yet, if we want to continue to grow, and if we are genuinely concerned with believing the truth, there is no way to avoid this pain. Indeed, having the courage to embrace the pain of doubt and to face unpleasant facts, as well as to embrace challenging questions and to live with ambiguity, is the hallmark of a mature and responsible human being. As we'll see in the next chapter, one of the unfortunate consequences of the certainty-seeking model of faith is that it encourages pain-avoidance and thus keeps people from learning, growing, and maturing.

To put all my cards on the table, I'm going to be asking you to reconsider this certainty-seeking model of faith, along with a number of other beliefs and assumptions that I'm sure many of you hold dear. And I'm going to be inviting you into a way of embracing faith that accepts that our world is filled with complexity, ambiguity, and unanswerable questions. It's a kind of faith that accepts that there is no absolutely certain place to stand, but that also sees that there is no need for such a place, so long as we have *reason enough* to place all our trust in Christ.

It is thus more than likely that this book will at times be painful, as well as aggravating, for many readers. You may already be fighting an urge to put this book down. Yet the fact that you were interested in this book and haven't yet closed it means that you're open to being challenged, and I applaud you for that. And if you experience some level of pain and aggravation as you move through this book, I want to encourage you to embrace the pain and continue to press on. Remind yourself that this is what learning and growth are all about.

You may end up disagreeing with me, which is fine, but your convictions will be more refined and stronger for having done so. On the other hand, you may end up embracing a kind of faith that is more secure precisely *because* it is free of the need to feel certain. You may discover a way of exercising faith that is more vibrant precisely *because* it empowers you to fearlessly question, to accept ambiguity, and to embrace doubt. And you may end up agreeing with me that this way of doing faith is not only more plausible in our contemporary world and more effective in advancing the kingdom, but it is also more *biblical*.

In fact, for reasons that I'll begin fleshing out in the next chapter, I am convinced that, as widespread as certainty-seeking faith is, it is absolutely unbiblical and even idolatrous.

Whether my arguments that lead to this conclusion are compelling, however, is something that you will have to decide.

2

Hooked on a Feeling

Doubt is not a pleasant condition, but certainty is absurd.
—Voltaire

This is what the Lord says: Do not deceive yourselves.
—Jeremiah 37:9

I began to sense something was fundamentally wrong with certainty-seeking faith around twenty years ago. One of the first times I recall sensing this took place at a prayer meeting I attended for a young man I'll call Brian. Brian and his lovely wife and two young children began attending my newly planted church soon after the doctors had informed him and his wife that they could do nothing more to treat the spreading cancer in his brain that they'd discovered about two years earlier.

We met at the home of a friend of Brian and his wife. Before we began praying, this friend, whom I had never met before, read a passage of Scripture in which Jesus said, "According to your faith be it unto you" (Matt. 9:29 KJV). She and several others then talked for a moment about how God rewards those who have faith and how we therefore needed to push all doubts aside, "stand on the promises of God," and believe and confess that Brian was certainly going to be healed. We then formed a circle around Brian and began engaging in passionate prayer.

As some cried out to God and others rebuked the cancer, I suddenly realized that I, probably like everyone else in the room, was *trying to convince myself* that Brian *would be* healed. I found myself *fighting* the perfectly reasonable awareness that, for all I or anyone else knew, Brian might die. It was almost as if I was fighting this awareness like it was a demon that would prevent Brian from being healed if it wasn't slain. I was, in effect, trying to hit the faith puck up the faith pole, believing—or at least *trying* to believe—that if I and everyone else could just get this puck far enough up the pole, our brother would be spared.

And then, as my eyes remained closed and with my hands raised, the cowardly lion in *The Wizard of Oz* suddenly popped into my imagination! As happened in the movie, the lion had his eyes closed and was reciting in an intense voice, "I *do* believe, I *do* believe, I *do*, I *do*, I *do* believe!"

While this prayer meeting was as serious as any prayer meeting could be, this way of exercising faith suddenly struck me as rather silly. We were all behaving like the cowardly lion! To the best of my recollection, it was this experience that started me down a trail that eventually led me to open the Pandora's box of problems with the certainty-seeking model of faith.

In this chapter I'm going to raise eight objections against this model of faith, and this story will serve to illustrate the first three of them.

The Virtue of Irrationality

The Reasonable Way to Assess Beliefs

The moment the cowardly lion popped into my imagination, it struck me that this way of exercising faith was completely irrational. The way reasonable people go about forming beliefs is that they base them on *rational considerations*. A reasonable person's confidence that a potential belief is true is in *proportion to* the strength of the evidence and arguments that support the belief compared to the strength of the evidence and arguments that count against the belief. What a reasonable person does *not* do is *try* to increase their level of certainty by *talking themselves into believing* something is true!

What rational grounds did we have for believing Brian would certainly be healed? I couldn't identify any. Even if you (mistakenly) hold that this model of faith is taught in the Bible while arguing (correctly) that we have rational grounds for believing Scripture (a point I'll discuss in chap. 8), you *still* couldn't be certain Brian would be healed. For even if you somehow managed to convince yourself of this, how could you know everyone else in the room had adequately convinced themselves?

Faith versus the Real World

The assumption that exercising faith requires us to try to be more certain than evidence rationally warrants is also irrational because it conflicts with the way the real world works. If God interacts with our life to the degree that we make ourselves certain, shouldn't we find that people of faith are generally healthier, wealthier, and safer than unbelievers? If we are honest, however, we have to admit that, if there is any discernible difference in these matters, it is meager.

Not only this, but every tombstone of people of faith who died before reaching an old age is evidence of prayers that "didn't work." In this light, trying to make ourselves certain that a friend will be healed because of our prayers when there is such overwhelming evidence of people who were *not* healed by the prayers of their friends is, frankly, the height of irrationality.

Please don't get me wrong. On the authority of God's Word, I believe praying with faith is "powerful and effective" (James 5:16). But we'll see later that the biblical understanding of faith doesn't require us to irrationally try to convince ourselves of something that is, in reality, impossible to be certain of. And we'll see that the way prayer is "powerful and effective" doesn't necessarily involve seeing the outcome that you're praying for.

The Virtue of Gullibility?

A final aspect of the irrationality of certainty-seeking faith is that it requires us to accept something as virtuous that is, in truth, not at all virtuous. The Bible uniformly treats faith as an all-important virtue, without which it is impossible to please God (Heb.11:6). But what is virtuous about a person's ability to make themselves certain about their beliefs? What is it about the ability to be free of doubt that God deems so valuable?

Like most of you, I've known people who were able to easily accept whatever they're told "on faith." To be frank, these kinds of people tend to have very simple ways of understanding the world. There is, of course, nothing wrong with being simple or even gullible, if this is the way you were born. But why would God think it virtuous for people who are not created with simple minds to *try* to believe this way? Even more puzzling, why would God leverage everything from people's salvation to their being healed from cancer on their ability to believe in this way?

Along the same lines, if God is so enamored with the ability to not doubt, why on earth did he bother to create critical minds that instinctively doubt truth claims and that are unable to believe anything until they've thoroughly examined the matter? While we should of course always be on guard against intellectual pride, and while we are to aspire to trust God like little children (Matt. 18:3), why would God want his people to aspire to *believing* as uncritically as children? The all-too-common model of faith that makes a virtue out of certainty and an enemy out of doubt has the effect of making critical thinking a supreme liability.

Come Let Us Reason

This way of exercising faith is not only irrational; it's unbiblical. Throughout Scripture, the Creator, who gave us our minds, encourages us to *use* them in our relationship with him. "Come now, let us reason together," the Lord says to the Israelites (Isa. 1:18 TNIV). "Present your case," he elsewhere says, "set forth your arguments" (Isa. 41:21). The Creator of the mind clearly expects us to *use it*.

Throughout Scripture we find a multitude of passages encouraging people to seek wisdom, to search for truth, and to rationally consider matters. In fact, Proverbs 8 is about nothing other than this (cf. also Prov. 2:3–5; 18:15; 25:2). So too, Luke declares that Jesus gave "many convincing proofs" to people that he had in fact risen from the dead (Acts 1:3). God clearly does not expect people to embrace beliefs without sufficient reason or to try to convince themselves of things beyond what the evidence warrants.

Along the same lines, Jesus frequently encouraged people to carefully search for truth and to rationally consider matters (e.g., Matt. 7:7–8; Mark 4:24; Luke 8:18; 12:24, 27; 14:28 33). He told challenging parables that require people to think and figure things out. He also called on us to worship God with *all* our mind (Matt. 22:37) and commissioned his disciples to be "shrewd as snakes" as they go out into the world, even as their character is to be "innocent as doves" (Matt. 10:16). None of this sounds like a clarion call for God's people to try to dumb down, shut off our critical brains, and try to convince ourselves of beliefs beyond what our reason warrants.

An Un-Christlike God

A Sadistic Game

My second objection arises from the fact that one of the most important questions to ask when considering the truth of any belief or practice is, what picture of God does it presuppose? More specifically, since Jesus is the ultimate revelation of God's true character (Heb. 1:3), we need to always ask whether the picture of God presupposed by a particular belief or practice is consistent with what we learn about God in Christ.

Not long after I had gotten the image of the cowardly lion out of my mind on the night we prayed for Brian, another bizarre image popped into it. It was an image of God up in heaven looking down on us and saying, "If you convince yourself that I'll heal Brian, he lives. If not, he dies." This wasn't far off the mark of the kind of God reflected in the theology of the lady who opened this prayer meeting! It was as if God was holding Brian hostage with a gun to his head, and for his ransom he was demanding that we convince ourselves he wasn't going to kill him.

As I struggled to get this bizarre image out of my head, it occurred to me that this didn't seem like something Jesus would do. To be frank, this rather seemed like an image of a cruel, demented deity engaging in psychological torture! Think about it. God is leveraging our friend's life on whether we can successfully engage in what amounts to nothing more than an impossible mental gimmick. If we can muster up enough certainty to get the faith puck far enough up the faith pole, our friend lives; if not, he dies. Is this not sadistic?

The "Al Capone God"

I debated an atheist on a university campus a number of years ago who was objecting to the notion—which he wrongly assumed all Christians shared—that God answers prayers based on how much faith people can muster. He told a story of a woman his wife knew who blamed herself for her daughter's severe mental and physical disabilities because, she assumed, if she had enough faith, her daughter would be healed. He then claimed that any deity who would withhold healing and even salvation from people on this basis was "an Al Capone god."

I applauded the accuracy of my opponent's label. "Any deity who refused to heal a mother's daughter because she doubted him," I said, "would indeed be an Al Capone sort of monster." Fortunately, I was able to point out to him and the audience that not all Christians embrace this twisted conception of God or this misguided understanding of faith. I then gave a brief description of the biblical model of faith, which we'll be exploring in part 2 of this book, and I pointed him and the audience to the beautiful God of the New Testament, the God who looks like Jesus, dying out of love for his enemies, rather than like Al Capone, subjecting people to psychological torture.

Faith versus Magic

My third objection to the certainty-seeking model of faith is that it replaces biblical faith with magic. Magic is generally understood to involve people engaging in special behaviors that empower them to gain favor with, or to otherwise influence, the spiritual realm in order to get it to work to their advantage. Depending on the culture or religious system, the "spiritual realm" a magical practitioner seeks to influence may be anything from an impersonal force (e.g., the Tao), to particular angels, to the God who created and sustains all things. Also depending on the culture or religious system, the relevant magical behaviors the practitioner engages in may be chants, spells, sacrifices, or other sorts of rituals. Or the practitioner may simply court the favor of God or angels by obediently embracing revealed truths or by obediently engaging in specific acts that align the practitioner with the will of God or angels.

I will postpone a discussion of the nature of biblical faith until part 2 of this work, but for now I'll simply highlight the fact that one of the many differences between "magic" and biblical faith is that magic is about engaging in *behaviors* that ultimately *benefit the practitioner,* while biblical faith is about cultivating a *covenantal relationship* with God that is built on *mutual trust.* And while the God-human relationship, like all trusting human-to-human relationships, benefits both God and the person of faith, it is not entered into *as a means to some other end.* We might say that magical faith is *utilitarian* while biblical faith is simply *faithful.*

In this light, it seems apparent that we were engaging in a Christianized form of magic when we were praying for Brian. The assumption was that if we engaged in a certain behavior—namely, making ourselves sufficiently certain our friend would be healed—then we could influence the spiritual realm—in this case, God—to act in a way that would benefit our friend and therefore us. While this might on the surface appear very similar to how a person with a biblical understanding of faith might pray, the assumption about what is going on is, I submit, much closer to magic.

Even more troubling, I believe something similar could be said about the way many, if not most, evangelical Christians understand salvation. The prevailing understanding is that for a person to be "saved," they must believe those doctrines that are "essential to salvation." And as we've seen, for most Christians, to "believe" means that a person has become sufficiently certain that a doctrine is true. In other words, it means the person has hit the faith puck past the minimum required level of certainty regarding the "essential for salvation" doctrines.

Along the same lines, many, if not most, evangelical Christians assume that, while all Christians sin, there are certain "deal-breaker" sins that, if not repented of, will cause a person to lose their salvation (or which, for Calvinists, indicate that a person has never "really" been saved). So, for example, I've never heard an evangelical say that greed, gluttony, or gossip that is not repented of will keep a person from being "saved." But I've frequently heard and read evangelicals say that homosexuality will certainly do this, even if practiced in the context of a lifelong monogamous relationship, and even when the couple sincerely believes it's not sin in God's eyes.

My point in raising these beliefs and behaviors is not at all to comment on how they compare to one another in terms of the severity of their sinfulness. It is rather to ask: Is this way of thinking about beliefs and behaviors reflecting a *biblical* or a magical understanding of faith? It seems to me, quite frankly, that it's much closer to the latter.

With all sincerity, people who have the latter type of understanding are trying to attain a sufficient level of certainty about particular doctrines and are avoiding particular "deal-breaker" sins *in order* to get God to "save" them (or, for Calvinists, to feel secure God has elected them for salvation). How is this significantly different from those who engage in magic by performing certain behaviors to get the spiritual realm to benefit them?

The content of what these Christians believe is obviously different from pagan practitioners of magic, of course. But *the way* they believe, and the *motive* they have for believing, seems to me very similar. And for this reason I stand by my claim that the notion that God grants healing or salvation or anything else on the basis of how certain people can make themselves about particular beliefs or on the basis of any other behavior is closer to magic than it is to biblical faith.

The Need for Flexibility

My fourth objection to the assumption that doubt is the enemy of faith is that it requires people to hold their faith in an inflexible way. Unfortunately, in the complex and ambiguous world in which we live today, this way of holding faith is, at least for thinking people, no longer viable.

Just ask Pete.

The Outsider

Pete is a supersmart, good-looking, and incredibly funny young man whom I met in a bar several months ago. My twenty-six-year-old son, Nathan, and I spend almost every Wednesday night at this place. It's his favorite "hang out." Pete had recently moved into the apartment complex where Nathan lives, and they had spoken earlier that day. Pete had heard of me, and when he found out I was Nathan's dad, he asked if he could meet me because, as Nathan put it, "he said he loves theology and has tons of questions."

Now, my son has high-functioning autism and a learning disability, so while he believes in Jesus, he has absolutely no interest in trying to discuss theology. "To me," he's told me, "it's all boring 'gobbledy-gook.'" But he was happy to have something to offer his new friend, so he promptly invited Pete along on our weekly get-together so we could discuss some "boring gobbledygook."

I told Nathan he was an "evangelist," and he beamed with a proud smile. Then he asked me what an "evangelist" is.

As the three of us sat around a table sharing a pitcher of Miller, Pete shared how he had accepted Christ at the age of sixteen and was "on fire" for about two years. As happened with me and so many others, his faith began to unravel when he entered college. Pete was fortunate to find a group of Christians on campus who embraced him and who were initially happy to discuss his questions. But by the end of his freshmen year, Pete told me, "The well of thoughtful answers as well as the patience of my friends started drying up."

With increasing frequency, his friends "began to play their faith-mystery card," he said. And before long, he continued, "I began to be viewed as an outsider." Pete said that this is what he's consistently found with Christians. "They'll tolerate your questions for a while, but sooner or later you hit a wall," he said. "That's when they throw down their faith-mystery card, and if you don't acquiesce, you become an outsider." He chugged the last bit of beer in his glass before mumbling, "It pisses me off!" I could relate.

By his junior year in college, Pete's unanswered questions had led him to become "a Christian agnostic," as he called it. In the ten years since he'd graduated, he told me he'd lived in a murky world suspended between faith and doubt. He wished he could believe, he told me, but too many aspects of the Christian faith conflicted with his learning and his experience of the world.

When a Small Faith Meets a Big World

The primary problem that Pete and others like him struggle with is not that they can't find answers to their legitimate questions, though that is unfortunate. The biggest problem is rather that they have inherited a model of faith that is, by its very nature, *inflexible*.

The Christianity that Pete inherited as a sixteen-year-old was a fixed set of eternal truths you either accept or reject as a package deal. And, not surprisingly, the understanding of faith he inherited was thought of as the opposite of doubt. It's not okay in this all-or-nothing model of the Christian faith to be *inclined* toward believing one doctrine or another or to accept a central belief *to a degree*, let alone to have *significant reservations* about any aspect of the package that defines "orthodoxy." Faith isn't viewed as a journey in which one explores and possibly changes beliefs along the way in this inflexible understanding of Christianity. It's a fixed package about which one must strive to be certain.

There was a time when this inflexible understanding of the Christian faith was viable, at least for most people, but that world has long since passed. As I mentioned in the introduction, the world we live in today is much smaller, more pluralistic, more complex, and much more ambiguous than it was even fifty years ago. A person would have to be remarkably secluded, have a remarkable lack of intellectual curiosity, or have a remarkable fear of change to maintain this sort of inflexible faith today. Yet it is this model that the church by and large continues to give young people, which goes a long way in explaining why roughly sixty percent of young people walk away from their faith sometime after high school.[1]

The fact of the matter is that the faith that accommodates the worldview of a young person will likely, at some point, start to conflict with their ever-expanding worldview once they encounter the pluralistic and ambiguous world of today. And if the faith a young person inherited is assumed to be an inflexible package of true beliefs that must be embraced in an all-or-nothing fashion, then, as happened with Pete, the whole package will likely begin to feel implausible and eventually get jettisoned when parts of it begin to conflict with their ever-expanding learning and experience of the world.

Pete, Nathan, and I spent the remainder of the evening going through another pitcher of Miller and talking "gobbledygook," with Nathan occasionally blurting out with a big smile, "I have absolutely NO idea what you guys are talking about!" Pete unloaded many of the questions he'd been churning in his brain over the last ten years, and I did my best to answer them. More importantly, however, I tried to show Pete a way of thinking about the Christian faith in which it is possible to be a passionate disciple of Jesus without feeling the need to suppress doubt or to try to be certain about everything, or anything. As we'll see in part 3 of this book, it's a faith that has flexibility built into it and that can thus continually grow and change with our ever-expanding experience of the world.

The fact that the all-or-nothing and certainty-seeking model of faith can't adjust to accommodate the complex ambiguity of our contemporary world is yet another reason for thinking it's mistaken.

A Faith-Based Learning Phobia

My fifth problem with this model of faith is closely related to the fourth. Because it has inflexibility built into it, I contend that certainty-seeking faith tends to inflict a selective learning phobia on those who hold to it.

What's at Stake?

It's no secret that, at least in America, evangelical Christians sort of have a reputation of being narrow-minded and intolerant. Deny it though we may, research has established it.[2] There are a number of plausible explanations for this, but I believe one of the main reasons has to do with the widespread assumption that a person's faith is as strong as they are certain.

Imagine a Christian I'll call Bob. Like most other conservative Christians, Bob believes that he is saved by believing the doctrines that are "necessary for salvation." And, like most others, Bob assumes that his faith is as strong as he is free of doubt.

It's apparent that for Christians like Bob, one's sense of security is anchored in their level of confidence that their beliefs are correct. If Bob were to lose confidence or change his mind about any of these things, his salvation, as well as his acceptance as a fellow "saved" believer in his church, would at least be thrown into question, if not absolutely denied. Not only this, but Bob's sense of identity, purpose, and well-being is wrapped up in his remaining convinced his beliefs are correct. With so much at stake, how open do you really think Bob would be to seriously studying books and dialoguing with people who might pose strong challenges to his core convictions? And how capable do you suppose Bob would be at objectively assessing the merits of points of view that disagree with his own, were he to somehow muster the courage to examine them? The answer, I think, is obvious.

The Pain We'd Rather Avoid

Not only this, but neurological studies have shown that the pleasure centers of our brain are activated whenever we encounter facts or opinions that confirm beliefs that are important to us. Conversely, they also reveal that our amygdala, which controls our "fight or flight" reflex, is activated when we initially confront facts or opinions that conflict with these beliefs. And, as we noted in the previous chapter, most of us know firsthand, to one degree or another, how painful it is to doubt beliefs that are important to us. Cognitive dissonance over important matters can be excruciating!

So everybody experiences pleasure when important beliefs are confirmed, anger when they are threatened, and pain when they are doubted. This is what makes learning, as well as teaching, a challenging endeavor. But the situation is much worse for those who embrace certainty-seeking faith. For people like Bob, his eternal destiny, his fellowship, his identity, and his sense of purpose and well-being depend on his ability to remain confident he's right, not just about one or two beliefs, but about the entire package of beliefs he and his church identify as "orthodox." For people like Bob, these beliefs are not only important; they define people to the core of their being, and they do so with an eternal intensity.

This is why I claim that certainty-seeking faith tends to inflict people with a learning phobia. Learning requires students to be willing and able to allow their beliefs to be challenged and to experience cognitive dissonance. Learning requires students to at least hypothetically suspend their beliefs to objectively consider other points of view. And learning demands that students sincerely consider the possibility that they're wrong when assessing perspectives that conflict with their own. With so much riding on his remaining convinced that the beliefs in his fixed package are all true, how could Bob *not* fear this process?

From personal experience as well as my interactions with conservative Christians over the years, I'm convinced that one of the main selling points of the model of faith that declares war on doubt is that it allows people to feel justified indulging in the pleasure of feeling certain and avoiding the pain of doubt. In fact, it not only allows for this: it declares it a supreme virtue! Unfortunately, the price one pays is that they must insulate themselves from everything that might threaten this certainty, which means it installs a phobia of learning in areas that could potentially conflict with their beliefs.

And when they do confront challenges to their faith, their amygdala is triggered. Indeed, since the stakes could not be higher, it is triggered *with a vengeance*. If you're looking for an explanation for why conservative Christians in America have a reputation for being narrow and intolerant, I submit you've just found it. In fact, as we'll discuss in a moment, if you're looking for an explanation for why religion has, in one fashion or another, been behind so much of the bloodshed throughout history, I submit that you've found your answer for this as well.

What's Good for the Goose

My sixth objection to the common identification of faith with psychological certainty is that it tends toward hypocrisy.

The Arrogance of Assumed Rightness

I attended an apologetics conference years ago in which a speaker was offering a critique of the Qur'an. In the discussion that followed, someone asked a question about the difficulty he'd experienced sharing the gospel with his Muslim neighbor. "He's so dang convinced he's right," the man said. The speaker empathized with the complaint and at one point stated: "No one can rationally consider a belief that conflicts with their own unless they are willing to grant the possibility that they're wrong. So pray that God frees your neighbor from his arrogant assumed rightness."

No one? I remember thinking. If no one can rationally consider a belief without considering the possibility that they're wrong, I wondered if this apologist or anyone else in the room, including myself, had ever *really* considered Islam in a rational way? *What's good for the goose is good for the gander.*

As is true of most Muslims, as well as many devotees of other religions and cults, evangelical Christians generally assume that it's arrogant, if not sinful, for people *of other faiths* to refuse to doubt their beliefs. And I think we'd all agree that it is arrogant for anyone to simply assume their views are right and to refuse to question them. But is this not how Christians who embrace certainty-seeking faith tend to hold on to their beliefs? If people are trying to remain as free of doubt as possible, how could it be otherwise?

But this means that these Christians are claiming that it's arrogant, if not sinful, for other people to assume they're correct, but not for them. It's wrong for others to refuse to doubt, but not for them. And while it's sinful for others to try to remain as certain as possible about the assumed rightness of their views, it's positively virtuous for Christians to do so, as we saw above.

This strikes me as blatantly hypocritical. What else can you call it when people apply a standard to others that they aren't willing to apply to themselves? The model of faith that is at war with doubt essentially claims that what's good for the Christian goose is *not* good for the non-Christian gander.

The Unexamined Faith

My conviction is that it is good for non-Christians and Christians *alike* to question their beliefs. I'm not suggesting people in either group should live in a perpetual state of doubt. The mistake agnostics make is that they fail to see that to choose *not* to commit to any belief about spiritual matters is itself a choice *to commit* to a belief about spiritual matters. That is, the belief that it is appropriate to perpetually suspend committing to a belief about spiritual matters is itself *a belief*, and they are committed to it! And I, for one, think the faith of agnostics is misplaced.

In every area of our lives we find we must commit to a course of action without absolute proof that it's the right course of action. When you board a plane, for example, you are exercising faith that the pilots are not drunk, the mechanics have done their job, and there isn't a terrorist on board. You can't be certain of this, of course, but given the fact that flight travel is usually safe, it's rational to act on the faith that the plane is safe.

The truth is we could do very little if we weren't willing to act on faith, and this is one compelling reason to accept that the world is such that it is *not* appropriate to perpetually suspend belief about spiritual matters.

At the same time, to grant that people shouldn't perpetually suspend committing to a faith is not to say that they should commit to a faith *unthinkingly*. Nor is it to say that even after we've committed, we can't remain open to the possibility that we're mistaken. I'm thus suggesting that, at the very least, it would be good if Christians and non-Christians *alike* critically examined their beliefs by entertaining the possibility that they're wrong from time to time.

I, of course, know this will never actually happen, if only because people enjoy the blissful feeling of being certain they're right and hate the pain of feeling they may be wrong, as we noted earlier. It takes a courage that is not at all common to seriously question cherished beliefs. But this doesn't negate the fact that it would be good if people would occasionally choose the discomfort of doubt over the comfort of certainty and critically examine their beliefs. For it is, as a matter of fact, arrogant, if not sinful, for *anyone* to *assume* their beliefs are true and all others wrong, simply because they enjoy feeling certain they're right and would rather avoid the pain of thinking they may be wrong.

Socrates said that the unexamined life is not worth living. I think it applies to faith as well. The unexamined faith is *not worth believing*.

The Danger of Feeling Certain

I'm particularly passionate about my seventh objection to any understanding of faith that encourages people to strive for the feeling
of being certain. I'm writing this sentence about thirty minutes after
watching a news story reporting that the United States Embassy in
Libya was attacked yesterday and that several United States officials
were murdered, including Chris Stevens, the chief ambassador to
Libya. It is reported that the attack was carried out by Muslims who
were outraged about a movie, made and produced by an American,
which painted the prophet Mohammed in a negative light. (It was
later discovered that the attack was orchestrated by Islamic terrorists.)

There's no question but that those who carried out this savagery
were utterly convinced they were carrying out God's will. This illustrates the point that any religion, including Christianity, that encourages people to strive for a feeling of certainty and to therefore
suppress doubt is a potentially dangerous religion.

If the followers of Jim Jones would just have been willing to forgo
the nice comfort of feeling certain and to endure the pain of doubt,
it's highly unlikely the 908 disciples who followed his orders and
killed their children before committing suicide would have met such
a tragic fate. And wouldn't it have been wonderful if the blissfully
certain Islamists who flew planes into the World Trade Center on 9/11
had had the courage to doubt the rightness of their extremist beliefs
about jihad and the rightness of obeying their murderous leaders in
Al Qaeda?

I'm willing to bet that the vast majority of the bloodshed in religious conflicts throughout history could have been avoided if people
had simply chosen the discomfort of doubting their beliefs over the
pleasure of feeling certain.

So, if we agree it's dangerous and wrong to never doubt, what
does this say about a model of faith that transforms this wrong into
a chief virtue?

I can imagine that some of you are thinking at this point that Christianity is the one exception. Our religion *is* true, so in this one case
it's virtuous to fight doubt and be as certain as possible. Of course,
this is what every other religious devotee thinks about *their* religion.

And, in any case, if a religion is indeed true, why should anyone have to try to convince themselves of this rather than letting the evidence speak for itself?

At the same time, history provides unambiguous proof that unquestioned certainty is no less dangerous for Christians than it is for anyone else. To give just one illustration, between 1618 and 1648 Protestants and Catholics throughout Europe massacred one another over the religious and political differences between their various "Christian" states (with a lot of economic motives mixed in, as usual). This was the infamous Thirty Years War. These inter-Christian wars were so brutal that the male population of Germany and several other countries was reduced by half, with civilian casualties reducing the general population by 25 to 40 percent. All told, it's estimated that upwards of 11 million people perished, and this at a time when the total population on earth was only around 500 million!

It's rather astonishing when you consider that all this slaughtering was done by people who ostensibly professed Christ as Lord—the one who modeled how we are to treat enemies by swearing off violence and allowing himself to be killed on their behalf, and the one who explicitly made refusing violence and loving enemies the precondition for being considered a child of the Father in heaven (Matt. 5:44–45; Luke 6:35; cf. 1 Pet. 3:9)!

As has been true of every war ever fought, the vast majority of those who fought in the Thirty Years War were absolutely certain their killing was justified and that God was on their side. The fact is that it is hard to motivate most people to kill and risk being killed unless they're pretty certain their cause is justified and that God (or the gods) is on their side. Though Americans seem to think it's unique to them, wars have almost always been fought under some version of the slogan "for God and country."

I'd like to suggest that a little humility and doubt might have gone a long way during this and every other Christian bloodbath. For example, what if some of these soldiers would only have questioned the curious coincidence that, without giving it a second thought, every solider is certain that the country they were born into "happens" to be on the side of right in this conflict? And since all these warriors were professing Christians, what if some would have dared to wonder how their orders to kill other professing Christians could be reconciled with Jesus's call to love and bless one's enemies?

To the extent that leaders and soldiers on both sides would have doubted, the bloodshed could have been avoided. And this confirms that the quest to feel certain by Christians is just as dangerous as it is by Muslims, Hindus, or anybody else. Conversely, doubt can be as beneficial for Christians as it is for anybody else. And this is one of the reasons why, though I am a passionate follower of Jesus, I am also a passionate advocate of the benefit of doubt and a passionate opponent of the aspiration to feel certain.

A Quest in the Wrong Direction

I suspect that my eighth objection to certainty-seeking faith may, for some, be the most surprising, though I believe my point is indisputable if you will hear me out. It is that those who strive to feel certain that their beliefs are true are not, in fact, primarily concerned about the truth of their beliefs.

The Rational Way to Seek Truth

As I mentioned earlier, the rational way to go about deciding whether something is true is to assess the evidence and arguments for and against a truth claim and to base your level of confidence in its truth or falsity on the weight of these considerations. There really is no other way of rationally deciding what's true or false. Of course, the prompting of the Holy Spirit and the testimony of others whom we trust also play an important role in the formation of our beliefs, but these factors should complement rather than replace our rational assessment of truth claims. There really is no other way of rationally deciding what's true or false than by carefully weighing the evidence and arguments.

Suppose you're in the market to buy a car. You go to a used-car dealer and find a car that you like, though the dealer is asking more money for it than you think this particular car should go for. But the dealer adamantly defends his hefty price tag by making a number of impressive-sounding claims about the car.

Before you put your hard-earned cash down, you understandably are going to want to determine if the claims this dealer is making are true. And how would you go about this? You'd begin by entertaining the possibility that the dealer's claims are false, either because he's sincerely mistaken or (God forbid) because he is lying. And then, if you didn't know how to do it yourself, you'd get a friend or hire a mechanic to open the hood, get underneath the car, and do everything that was necessary to thoroughly check the car out.

Now suppose a lot more than your money depended on accurately assessing this dealer's claims. Suppose your *eternal welfare* hung in the balance. In this case, wouldn't you go even further and perhaps get *five* friends or hire *five* mechanics to check the car out? The more that is at stake in assessing a truth claim, the more intensely we work to determine if the truth claim is, in fact, true.

A Curious Lack of Reason

So how is it that, when it comes to believing the truth claims of Christianity, those who hold the kind of faith we're talking about do the *exact opposite* of what they would when asked by a dealer to believe his claims about a car? *Precisely because* so much hangs in the balance on believing the truth, these people try not to doubt the beliefs they've been given and instead try to be as certain as they can be that these beliefs are true without exposing them to any challenges. Doesn't this strike you as peculiar?

I don't mean to sound disrespectful, but the only conclusion I can draw from this peculiar behavior is that these people are not concerned with believing *the truth* as much as they are concerned with *feeling certain* they already believe the truth while avoiding the pain of thinking *they might not*. I'm not questioning the sincerity of these people when they claim they want to believe the truth. But I also see no way of avoiding the conclusion that they're sincerely deluding themselves.

The truth is that there simply is no way for a person to be concerned that what they believe *is true* if they're at the same time trying to feel certain that *what they already believe* is true. The goal of believing *the truth* and the goal of *feeling certain* you already believe the truth are mutually exclusive.

A Self-Serving Quest

If my assessment is correct, it means that the quest to feel certain is a fundamentally self-serving quest. Though certainty-seeking believers claim to care about believing the truth, they are actually only concerned with enjoying the secure feeling of being certain while avoiding the pain of doubt. They can *hope* they believe the truth, but if they were actually *concerned* with this, they'd act the way they do when they are thinking about purchasing a car that a dealer claims is worth more than they'd expected to put down.

I want to be clear: I'm not blaming anyone for declaring war on doubt and craving the feeling of certainty. The world is a complex, confusing, scary, and often painful place. Who can be blamed for longing to feel certain about the things that matter most? Add to this the fact that many conservative Christians embrace a picture of God who will damn people to eternal hell if they hold wrong beliefs, sometimes even on relatively minor points, regardless of how sincere they are. It's an extreme example, for sure, but the odd church I originally found Christ in taught that a person's sins weren't forgiven and they were destined to hell if the *exact right words* weren't spoken over them when they were baptized.[3] That's a frightful view of God, to say the least!

Yet that image of God is actually pretty tame compared to what some others imagine. Many Christians believe God has already predestined (before birth) who will believe the right and wrong things and thus who will end up in heaven or hell! With such a terrifying image of God, who could blame anyone for wanting to feel certain they believe the right things or for needing to feel certain that they're one of "God's elect"?

Getting Honest

At the same time, I think it important to strive to be as honest with ourselves as possible about what we are doing and why we are doing it. As I see it, we are all just little, ignorant, and fallen humans living in a highly ambiguous world doing the best we can to figure out what the heck the whole thing is about. Not everyone shares the same degree of passion about this, and many have simply given up. But many of us are simply trying to work through the fog to arrive at beliefs we think, or at least suspect, are true. And we each defend these beliefs as best we can in the face of objections and competing beliefs, often revising and/or abandoning beliefs along the way. (If I had a quarter for every belief I've changed, I'd be a rich man.)

As we work to see through the fog, along comes a vast multitude of Christians and Muslims and others in different religions and cults who are convinced that God thinks it's a virtue to become as certain as possible that their beliefs are right and to doubt them as little as possible. They choose, for whatever reason, to enjoy the secure feeling of being certain their beliefs are right over the uncomfortable feeling of possibly being wrong. And as history and recent events make painfully clear, these folks with their unquestioned certainty sometimes slaughter each other along with other innocent people, all in the name of their God.

Given the scary uncertainty of our world and the frightful images of God some of these people have, we can understand and empathize with their longing to feel certain. But we should also be forthright about what is going on. These people, whether Christian, Muslim, or members of the Jim Jones cult, *hope* they're believing the truth, but they aren't *trying* to believe the truth. They're instead *trying to feel certain* that the belief they *hope* is true *is* true.

And that is why they can be very dangerous.

Also in the interest of being honest about what is going on, it needs to be said, and demonstrated, that the self-serving, doubt-quenching, certainty-seeking faith that these folks are choosing to pursue is not faith as it's taught in Scripture. As we'll see throughout part 2 of this book, the faith that God's people are called to embrace is one that encourages people to wrestle with God, to not be afraid of questions, and to act faithfully in the face of uncertainty.

Before turning to this, however, there is one final point to be made about the kind of faith that certainty-seekers embrace, and, frankly, it's the most important criticism of all.

The Idol of Certainty

You have made us for yourself,
and our hearts are restless
till they find their rest in you.

—St. Augustine

Dear children, keep yourselves from idols.

—1 John 5:21

So far we've explored eight questionable aspects of the all-too-common certainty-seeking model of faith. Now it's time to explore what is without question the most serious problem of this model. In this chapter I'm going to have the audacity to argue that this model is guilty of the number one sin in Scripture: idolatry. In the process, I'll be discussing a concept that will be centrally important throughout the remainder of this book. It concerns a hunger in the core of our being and how we satisfy it.

I want to be perfectly clear at the start that I'm not at all suggesting that the scores of sincere people who exercise faith in this certainty-seeking way are intentionally engaging in idolatry. Still less am I calling into question anyone's salvation (as though anyone other than God could speak about *that*). But we are going to see that this certainty-seeking, doubt-shunning view of faith makes an idol of certainty.

To see this, however, we have to back up quite a bit and look at why God made humans in the first place, why we now feel so empty, and where we are supposed to get full.

Everybody's Got a Hungry Heart

I've Got to Get Out of Here

"The Boss" nailed it when he sang, "Everybody's Got a Hungry Heart." A guy with a wife and kids in Baltimore goes out for a ride, makes a wrong turn, and just decides to never go back. What would lead a man to make a cold-hearted on-the-spot decision to abandon his wife and kids? It's terrible, but also not at all hard to understand. We all have hungry hearts, and sometimes they drive us to do some crazy things.

We can imagine the guy Bruce sang about is thirty-five years old and has been married for five to ten years. He feels empty, unloved, unappreciated, and unhappy. He's starting to face the frightening reality that time flows in one direction, and it is not kind. His decision to get married and raise a family contributed to the fact that he now suspects he'll never be the huge success he once dreamed he'd be. He's resenting his decision to marry and feels trapped. He wanted to be special, but he finds himself bound in a life that is just like everyone else's.

This man knows there must be more. And as he drives, his mind wanders to fantasies of a "better" life. What if he was freed from this enslavement to paying the bills? What if he was freed from always having to say "no" to bar buddies because he has to spend time with his family? What if he was freed from the fatigue of working through the endless conflicts in his marriage? What if he met "the girl of his dreams"—a woman who loved him better than he believes his wife ever could, who found him sexually irresistible, who laughed at all his jokes, and who encouraged him to pursue his dreams? He's hungry for something just out of reach.

His daydreaming comes to an abrupt end as he realizes he's made a wrong turn. Frustrated, he starts to figure out how to get back on course when he suddenly hears himself mutter—almost as if someone else were speaking through him—"I've got to get out of here."

Like a river that doesn't know where it's flowing, Bruce sang, he took a wrong turn and he just keeps on going.

Everybody's got a hungry heart.

Sehnsucht

Bruce Springsteen knows what all of us on some level know: deep down, *we're hungry*. Every human being with normal mental and emotional faculties *longs for more*. People typically associate their longing for more with a desire to somehow improve their lot in life—to get a better job, a nicer house, a more loving spouse, become famous, and so on. *If only* this, that, or some other thing were different, we say to ourselves, then we'd feel complete and happy.

Some chase this "if only" all their lives. For others, the "if only" turns into resentment when they lose hope of ever acquiring completeness. But even if we get lucky and acquire our "if only," it never quite satisfies. Acquiring the better job, the bigger house, the new spouse, or world fame we longed for may provide a temporary sense of happiness and completeness, but it never lasts. Sooner or later, the hunger returns.

The best word in any language that captures this vague, unquenchable yearning, according to C. S. Lewis and other writers, is the German word *Sehnsucht* (pronounced "zane-zookt").[1] It's an unusual word that is hard to translate, for it expresses a deep longing or craving for something that you can't quite identify and that always feels just out of reach. Some have described *Sehnsucht* as a vague and bittersweet nostalgia and/or longing for a distant country, but one that cannot be found on earth. Others have described it as a quasi-mystical sense that we (and our present world) are incomplete, combined with an unattainable yearning for whatever it is that would complete it.

Scientists have offered several different explanations for this puzzling phenomenon—puzzling, because it's hard to understand how natural processes alone could have evolved beings that hunger for something nature itself doesn't provide.[2] But this longing is not puzzling from a biblical perspective, for Scripture teaches us that humans and the entire creation are fallen and estranged from God.

Lewis saw *Sehnsucht* as reflective of our "pilgrim status." It indicates that we are not where we were meant to be, where we are destined to be; we are not *home*. Lewis once wrote to a friend that "our best havings are wantings," for our "wantings" are reminders that humans are meant for a different and better state.[3] In another place he wrote:

> Our lifelong nostalgia, our longing to be reunited with something in the universe from which we now feel cut off, to be on the inside of some door which we have always seen from the outside is . . . the truest index of our real situation.[4]

With Lewis, Christians have always identified this *Sehnsucht* that resides in the human heart as a yearning for God. As St. Augustine famously prayed, "You have made us for yourself, and our hearts are restless till they find their rest in you."[5] In this light, we might think of *Sehnsucht* as a sort of homing device placed in us by our Creator to lead us into a passionate relationship with him.

Our Hunger for Life

As I've pulled together insights from Scripture, the social sciences, and my own experience, I've come to the conclusion that the most important aspect of our inner longing is a need to experience God's *perfect, unconditional love*. A central aspect of what this means is that we long to know, in an experiential way, that we have *unlimited* or *unsurpassable worth* to God and that we are *absolutely secure* in this love and worth.

Whether a person knows God or not, the degree to which we feel anything approximating this unconditional love, unsurpassable worth, and absolute security is the degree to which we feel *fully alive* and *at home* in the world. To the degree we don't experience this, however, we remain hungry, out of place, and less than fully alive. For this reason, I find it helpful to refer to *Sehnsucht* as a hunger for *life*. (I will henceforth italicize "life" when expressing what we hunger for in order to distinguish it from mere biological "life.")

It's my conviction that we are made to perpetually share in a *life* in which we are perfectly and unconditionally loved, in which we experientially know we could not matter more to God than we already do, and in which we feel absolutely secure in this love and worth, for we know that nothing—including the loss of our biological life—could cause us to lose this *life*.

Throughout the remainder of this book, you're going to find that the question of what it is we hunger for and how we should go about satisfying it lies at the foundation of everything I'll discuss, for it's my conviction that our hunger for *life* is the most fundamental driving force in our lives. What follows is my understanding of why God placed this hunger within us.

The Opening of the Triune Community

As Augustine and many others in church history have in various ways said, the unquenchable yearning in our hearts is really a yearning for nothing less than to share in God's own eternally full *life*. This is why our *Sehnsucht* cannot be permanently satisfied by anything in this world. More specifically, as the New Testament and the church tradition teach, the *life* of God is nothing other than the perfect love that eternally unites the Father, Son, and Holy Spirit, and this Triune God spoke creation into being with the ultimate goal of inviting humans to share in this *life*. *This* is what God created us to long for!

The great Puritan theologian and pastor Jonathan Edwards expressed this concept in a powerful way in his famous work *The End for Which God Created the World*.[6] Edwards painted a portrait of the Trinity in which the love and joy of the three divine persons was so full and intense, it simply could not be contained. God's fullness thus yearned to be expressed and replicated by sharing it with others. So this fullness overflowed, as it were, as God brought forth a creation that mirrored his triune beauty. And the pinnacle of this creation is created beings whose yearning for God mirrors, in a small way, his yearning for them. But whereas God's yearning comes out of his fullness, our yearning comes out of emptiness.

It's a beautiful arrangement. The God of overflowing love longs to pour his love into others, so he creates beings that long for his love to be poured into them.

But in my opinion (not Edwards's), it wasn't God's original intention for us to ever go a moment with this longing unsatisfied. Living without the fullness of God's love is a reality *we* have brought on ourselves through our rebellion, and it's completely unnatural to us. And try as we may to run from it or numb it, the pain of our unnatural emptiness is acute and incurable. The profundity of our emptiness is the negative reflection of the profundity of the fullness of the One we long for.

A Replicated Oneness

I think Edwards's understanding of why God created the world is on the money![7] We can see a reflection of this perspective in what I consider to be the most profound prayer in Scripture, found in John 17:20–26. Jesus prays to the Father that his disciples and "those who will believe in me through their message" (which I think he hopes will include all humans) would be "one as we are one" (v. 22). Then he prays that *he* would be in *us* in the same way the *Father* is in *him* (v. 23). God apparently wants the loving unity of his own triune being to be replicated in the way we relate *to one another* as well as in the way he relates *to* us and dwells *within* us!

But it gets even better, for Jesus then proclaims to the Father that he "will continue to make you [the Father] known in order that *the love you have for me* may be *in them* and *I myself* may be *in them*" (v. 26, emphasis added). And he essentially says the same thing when he says to the Father, "I have given them the glory that you gave me" (v. 22), for the "glory" that the Father gives the Son and that the Son shares with us is simply the weighty, brilliant radiance of the self-giving love of the three persons of the Trinity.

This means that God's ultimate goal in creation is nothing less than for the *very same perfect love* that the Father has for his own Son to be given *to us* and to be placed *within us*. Not only this, but his goal is for *Jesus himself* to dwell in us and, as we read throughout the New Testament, for us to dwell in him (e.g., John 15:4–5). We become the recipients of the Father's eternal love *for* the Son because we are *in* the Son as he is perfectly loved, and the Son *is in us*, as he is perfectly loved. This is how God graciously allows us to *"partici-pate* in the divine nature" (2 Pet. 1:4), for as I've said, the "nature" and "unity" of the three divine persons is nothing other than their perfect, eternal love.

It's clear that God's plan is to *completely envelope* everyone who is willing into the threefold loving eternal dance of the Father, Son, and Holy Spirit. And as a result, the love of the Triune God will be replicated *toward* us, *in* us, and *through* us as we love God and one another. I can't imagine a loftier and more beautiful goal for human-ity than this!

This is the true *life* our hearts are desperately thirsty for. And in this light, it's hardly surprising that nothing in this world can quench it. While some of us may be blessed with loving people in our life, with worthwhile work to engage us, and with some measure of security, no one, and nothing, could come close to permanently meeting this need. Only God himself can satisfy our longing for *perfect, unconditional* love, *unsurpassable* worth, and *absolute* security.

It's All about the Crucified Christ

If our hunger is for the *life* of God, the next question we need to ask is, where do we go to find this *life*? And the answer, of course, is Jesus Christ. The world was created "by him" and "for him" (Col. 1:16; cf. Heb. 1:3). At the center of "the purpose for which God created the world" was his plan to unite himself to us in Christ, reveal himself to us through Christ, and share his *life* with us by incorporating us into Christ.

We don't know what it might have looked like for God to share his *life* with us had we not fallen (about which more will be said below). But we do know how it is communicated and shared now that we *are* fallen. In a word, it looks like *the cross*. Every aspect of Jesus's life reveals God's loving character, of course. But it is first and foremost on the cross that we see the fullness of God's love demonstrated (Rom. 5:8). Indeed, John *defines* the love that is God's eternal nature

(1 John 4:8) by pointing us to the cross (1 John 3:16). Everything Jesus was about is thematically summed up on the cross, which is why we find the cross holding center stage whenever the meaning of Christ's coming is touched on throughout the New Testament, as a number of scholars have argued.[8]

The fact that the self-sacrificial love of God revealed on the cross is the thematic center of Jesus's identity and mission is further reflected in the fact that each of the four Gospel narratives has the cross as its focal point. As the prominent New Testament scholar Martin Kähler famously put it, "one could call the Gospels passion narratives with an extended introduction."[9] This centrality is also reflected in the fact that Jesus highlights the cross as the event that most glorifies the Father (John 12:27–28, 31–33; cf. 13:31–32), while Paul highlights it as the event that most decisively reveals God's wisdom and power (1 Cor. 1:17–18, 24).[10] So too, its centrality is evident in the fact that the cross forms the centerpiece of all of Paul's summaries of the gospel.[11]

For Paul, to preach the gospel was simply to preach "the message of the cross" (1 Cor. 1:18, 23), so all who opposed the gospel could be described as persecuting the cross (Phil. 3:18; cf. Gal. 6:12). And so it's not surprising that for Paul, as well as for Jesus, what it means to be a follower of Jesus is that we participate in, and therefore imitate, the self-sacrificial love manifested on the cross (e.g., Matt. 10:38; Luke 14:27; Rom. 8:17; 2 Cor. 1:5, 7; Phil. 3:10). Nor is it surprising that the ceremony that we shall see joins us to the bride of Christ (chap. 7) is baptism, whereby we own Christ's death and resurrection as our own (Rom. 6:3).

When it comes to understanding what God is like and what he thinks of us, we ought to adopt the same attitude Paul expressed when he resolved "to know nothing . . . except Jesus Christ and him crucified" (1 Cor. 2:2). Set aside all you thought you knew about God and about yourself and keep your eyes fixed on Calvary. So too, in order to begin to experience the full *life* God planned for us before he created the world—the *life* that is nothing less than participating in the eternal love of the Triune God—I recommend we resolve to look nowhere else than to "Jesus Christ and him crucified."

We'll explore the remarkable significance that a cross-centered approach to Scripture has for the way we interpret the Old Testament in chapter 9, and we'll explore more deeply how the cross is the center around which everything pertaining to the kingdom revolves in chapter 12. For now, however, the only important thing for us to embrace is the realization that our deepest longings and hungers are meant to drive us to the one and only source of true *life*, whose self-sacrificial character was fully disclosed on the cross. Anything other than the love of God revealed on Calvary that we turn to for *life* is an idol that eventually ends up *sucking life from us* rather than *giving life to us*.

Idolatrous Cravings

The World Gone Astray

You've probably noticed that the world we find ourselves in doesn't exactly reflect the beauty of God or of his glorious plan for humanity that we've just laid out. The sad truth is that human history has been a veritable merry-go-round of hatred, violence, injustice, deception, and rank immorality. Even nature has been corrupted. Sure, we can still see something of the glory of God in creation (Rom. 1:20), but a lot of it seems frankly diabolical. A creation filled with deadly parasites, viruses, and diseases that is also plagued with famines, drought, hurricanes, and a host of other natural disasters isn't exactly a world that puts on display the perfect, other-oriented, self-giving love of the Creator that we've been talking about![12]

What happened? I alluded to it above. We rebelled. We catch a little glimpse of how this happened in the story of Adam and Eve in Genesis 3.[13] As far as we're told, the problem began when the serpent, which the New Testament identifies as Satan (Rev. 12:9; 20:2; cf. 2 Cor. 11:3), planted an ugly, petty picture of God in Eve's mind. Make a note of that. It will become important later on. At the root of all that is wrong with humans is a false and ugly mental image of God.

The serpent made it look like God was forbidding Eve to eat from the tree of the knowledge of good and evil because he didn't want any competitors in the knowing-all-things department. "God knows that when you eat from it," he said, "your eyes will be opened, and you will be like God, knowing good and evil" (v. 5).

Setting aside the less important issue of how literally or figuratively we understand this account, the way I interpret it is that the forbidden tree was meant to serve as a sort of "No Trespassing" sign. It was God's warning, placed in the garden out of love, not to try to take on God's role of defining and judging good and evil.[14] God was essentially saying, "Your job is to love like I love, *not judge like only I can judge*. And to do the first, *you can't do the second*." When non-omniscient beings like us start to judge, we stop loving and begin to look more like Pharisees, who reflect the character of their "father," "the Accuser" (Rev. 12:10, cf. John 8:44), than like Jesus, who reflects the loving character of his Father and the character that all humans are *supposed to* reflect.

Once Eve believed the serpent's false picture, she stopped trusting God and thus no longer leaned on God to be her source of *life*. And since God was no longer her source of *life*, she had to look for it elsewhere. Looking at the forbidden tree with hungry eyes, it looked "good for food and pleasing to the eye, and also desirable for gaining wisdom" (v. 6). I'm convinced that if Eve had continued to get *life* from God, the prospect of violating God's "No Trespassing" sign wouldn't have looked appetizing at all. But just as insects can begin to look tasty to people who are starving to death, just about anything can begin to look like potential food for a starving soul. And so Eve took the bait, and so did Adam.

Idol Addiction

This inspired account is not only about a tragic event in the past; it's also the story of every human (except Jesus) who has ever lived. To one degree or another, we have all internalized lies about God that have caused us to mistrust him and therefore to look elsewhere to find *life*. Looking at the world through hungry eyes, we, like our primordial parents, have come to see various versions of the forbidden tree as potential sources of *life*.[15]

This is what an idol is. It's anything we try to use to *fill what only God can fill*, which means, it's anything we use to *replace God*. When anything or anyone becomes the means by which we try to fill our innermost need for unconditional love, unsurpassable worth, and absolute security, it becomes an idol.

I'm of course not suggesting there's anything wrong with feeling loved by people or wanting to do things that are worthwhile. Nor am I suggesting there's anything wrong with wanting to feel secure in your home, with your retirement, or in your relationships. To the contrary, God always intended us to be loved by people, to do worthwhile things, and to feel secure. This is how things were *supposed* to work. But God never intended anyone or anything other than Jesus Christ to meet our *core need* for unconditional love, unsurpassable worth, and absolute security. And, as I've already noted, the fact of the matter is that no one and nothing can come close to meeting this need.

Augustine spoke a profound truth when he said our hearts are restless until we rest in God. So long as we try to meet our core needs with idols, we experience disappointment, frustration, and a host of other negative emotions. Yet we find ourselves unable to discontinue our searching, for our hunger never dissipates. We may try to numb it with the novocaine of alcohol, drugs, or pornography. Or we may try to forget about it by distracting ourselves with work, television, movies, sports, politics, and the like. But the novocaine eventually wears off and the distractions are only momentary.

Until we learn how to find our *life* from God, we are incurable idol addicts.

The Variety of the Idols We Crave

There are an endless variety of idols people use to satisfy their hunger. Secular Western people today typically try to get *life* from what they achieve, what they possess, or whom they impress. The misdirected homing device of some leads them to work eighty hours a week, sometimes sacrificing family and friends in the process of climbing the ladder of success to achieve "the American dream." Others strive to gain the applause of the crowd, performing or achieving their way to fame.

And then there are the multitudes that tend to experience the inner void as a gnawing boredom with life. They chase after peak experiences, believing that the next risk-taking adventure, the next experience of falling in love, the next lurid sexual experience, or the next drug-induced high will make them feel fully alive. At best, however, these merely provide a momentary diversion from their emptiness.

For more spiritually inclined people, however, religious idols carry far more appeal than secular ones. In fact, in contrast to the modern, materialistic West, most people throughout history have been far more tempted by religious idols than by worldly idols.

Now, when Western Christians think of religious idols, they typically think of people praying to golden calves, statues, shrines, sacred trees, or the like. These have certainly been common idols throughout history, but they are by no means the only ones. An idol, recall, is *anything* we use to meet the core need that only God can meet.

Some religious people have tried to find their ultimate worth and security in special rituals they believe will win God's approval, or at least appease God's wrath. (By the way, when I refer to "God" in this section, I'd like readers to remember that many who have embraced these forms of idolatry were focused on *a god* or on a number of *gods*.) Some have tried to feel loved, esteemed, and assured by God by believing that their righteous behaviors have secured God's favor. And others have tried to feel these things by trusting that their tribe or religion was superior to others because their distinctive beliefs and practices were the ones that God revealed or at least that God favored the most.

These are all forms of idolatry, for people are trying to feel accepted, worthwhile, and secure before God through things they *do for* God or *believe about* God rather than *receiving from* God the *life* God wants to share with them for free.

This, in fact, was precisely the kind of idolatry many religious leaders in Jesus's time were involved in. And it's why they and Jesus didn't get along well.

The Idol of Theology and Scripture

A particularly instructive example of this is found in John 5. As Jesus confronted some religious leaders, he said, "You study the Scriptures diligently because you think that in them you have eternal life. These are the very Scriptures that testify about me, yet you refuse to come to me to have life" (John 5:39–40). These leaders thought they possessed *life* by diligently studying Scripture. What made these leaders feel accepted, worthwhile, and secure before God was that they knew their Bible and were confident they embraced only true Bible-based beliefs. Jesus, of course, wasn't suggesting there was anything wrong with their diligent study of Scripture or with the rightness of their Bible-based conclusions. As a matter of fact, these leaders were more or less orthodox by first-century Jewish standards. More importantly, however, Jesus didn't dispute the rightness or wrongness of their beliefs, because the issue wasn't about *what* these leaders believed: he disputed the *way* they believed it.

Jesus responded to them by pointing out that all Scripture is intended to point to him (cf. v. 46), the one true source of *life*. He was trying to get them to see that there is no *life* in knowing the Bible and embracing Bible-based beliefs *unless they lead to him*. Yet by trying to wring *life* out of things that have no *life* apart from Christ, these leaders made an idol out of the Bible and their Bible-based beliefs.

I'd like us to notice a demonic self-reinforcing quality about idolatry that can be discerned in these leaders. By trying to derive false *life* from their confident knowledge of Scripture instead of the One Scripture points to, these leaders had made an idol of their knowledge of Scripture. But the river also flowed in the other direction. Precisely because these leaders had made an idol of their knowledge of Scripture, they would not come to the true source of *life* to which Scripture points. So these leaders were not hungry for the true bread of *life* (John 6:32–58) because they had already stuffed themselves with the false *life* of their idol. And they had to stuff themselves with the false *life* of their idol because they would not come to the true bread of *life*. It's a vicious, idolatrous, self-reinforcing cycle that these religious experts were caught in. And the idols that trapped them, we must remember, were something that looked very spiritual: they diligently studied Scripture. They believed the right things. This is what made them confident they were okay with God.

This episode demonstrates that the *way* we believe *what* we believe can transform *what* we believe into an idol that actually blocks us from getting *life* from Christ—*even when* what we believe is completely true! And this happens *whenever* we are confident we're okay with God because of what we believe rather than because of our relationship with the one true source of *life*. If what makes us feel okay with God is our confidence in the correctness of our beliefs, then our confidence in our beliefs is, in effect, our god. *This* is what gives us our false sense of *life*.

The Foundation of All Idolatry

I'd like us to notice one final thing about the idolatry of these leaders: *it was all predicated on a false picture of God*. Their assumption that they were accepted, worthwhile, and secure before God on the basis of how well they knew their Bible presupposed an image of God who loves diligent Bible study and accurate Bible knowledge more than people. Whatever else may be said about this picture, it is certainly less beautiful and less life-giving than the true God revealed on the cross. As we noted above, at the root of all idolatry and sin is a false and untrustworthy picture of God that does not give *life*, which is why those who believe the false picture remain hungry and are driven to their idolatry and sin.

This reflects another dimension of the demonic, self-reinforcing quality of idolatry that we noted above. The inability of their false image of God to give them *life* is what pushed these leaders to try to find *life* in the idol of diligent Bible study. Yet their idol of diligent Bible study presupposed this false image of God that was not able to give them *life*. In other words, their *life*-less idol pointed them to a *life*-less image of God that drove them to their *life*-less idol, and so on. This is another dimension of the vicious, self-reinforcing, idolatrous cycle that these leaders, like everybody else who hasn't been set free by the revelation of the true God who alone gives *life*, were trapped in.

Marriage Lessons

I want to be clear that I am not in any way minimizing the importance of diligent Bible study or of aspiring to embrace only true, Bible-based beliefs. Neither was Jesus. But we must remember that studying Scripture and holding true, Bible-based beliefs are not ends in and of themselves. The ultimate purpose of studying Scripture and of holding true beliefs is to lead us to, and to help us sustain, a relationship with God through Jesus, our one true source of *life*.

It's not unlike getting married, which is a particularly appropriate analogy since followers of Jesus are called the "bride of Christ" (about which we'll have a lot to say in coming chapters). When Shelley and I exchanged our vows thirty-four years ago, we obviously held beliefs about each other and about our future life together that we were confident were true. I believed (and still believe) she was a wonderful, loving, kind, generous, godly, fun, and drop-dead gorgeous woman (that last one took *zero* faith on my part!). I've never quite understood what Shelley believed about me, but she must have believed *something* since she was willing to take the plunge!

We, of course, could not be *certain* our beliefs were true. But we were *confident enough* to make a lifelong commitment to each other. We'll see later that this is the nature of biblical faith. It's not about striving for certainty; it's about a willingness to commit in the face of uncertainty (chap. 7). The point right now, however, is that although we had to be confident enough about our beliefs to commit to each other, our focus wasn't on *our beliefs*. It was on *the person* our beliefs were *about*.

So too, we obviously need to believe certain things to become betrothed to Christ. And we need to be confident enough about the truthfulness of these beliefs to make this commitment. But the purpose of our beliefs is not for us to feel good about how certain we are that they're all true. The purpose is rather to point us to, and to help sustain, a *life*-giving relationship with the One our beliefs are *about*.

The trouble with the way the religious leaders of Jesus's day believed, however, was that their confidence in their beliefs didn't point them to the source of *life*. Instead, their confidence in their beliefs *was itself* their source of *life*. It was an idol, because it was the confidence in their diligent Bible study that made them feel they were accepted, worthwhile, and secure before God.

Instead of marrying *God* on the basis of their confident beliefs, they married *their confident beliefs* about God.

The Idolatry of the Certainty Quest

What Is Your Actual God?

In light of all this, what should be said about the certainty-seeking model of faith? To put it bluntly, I find it hard to avoid the conclusion that, for all its sincerity, the certainty-seeking, doubt-shunning understanding of faith reflects the same religious idolatry that entrapped the religious leaders of Jesus's day. The things that make certainty-seeking Christians feel loved, worthwhile, and secure before God—that is, the thing that assures them they are "saved"—is that they feel confident *they believe the right things with a sufficient level of certainty*. Doesn't this mean that it is their certainty in what they believe *about* God, rather than *God himself*, that is their source of *life*?

Is this honestly any different from the idolatry that Jesus confronted in the religious leaders of his day?

The Evidence of How We Live

If further proof is needed, consider this. As long as a person remained confident enough in the belief that Jesus is the true revelation of God that they can get their *life* from him (about which I'll say more below), would they ever be afraid of confronting ideas that might cause them to doubt any of their other beliefs? I, for one, don't see how it is possible.

Think about it. If I am confident that God unconditionally loves me because of what he did for me on Calvary, then wouldn't I be confident that his love for me does not increase or decrease based on how accurate or inaccurate my other beliefs are? So too, if I am confident God ascribes unsurpassable worth to me on the basis of Calvary, then wouldn't I be confident that my worth can't be increased because I hold correct beliefs and can't be decreased because I hold mistaken beliefs? These questions answer themselves.

But the opposite would seem to apply as well. If I am anxiously striving to make myself feel certain that all my beliefs are true, fearfully avoiding anything that might cause me to doubt them, and fearfully suppressing any doubts I may already be experiencing, doesn't this indicate that I am *not* getting my core need for love, worth, and security from the God who is revealed on the cross? This question also answers itself.

We can get at the same point from another direction by asking this question: Could a person who feels secure in their salvation because they have placed their trust in the loving character of God revealed on the cross also be driven to try to feel secure in their salvation by convincing themselves they believe the true "saving" doctrines? I think it is self-evident that the answer to this question is "no," for the God

revealed on the cross is a God who loves people more than right doctrines. He's the God who welcomes the repentant criminal dying next
to him into his kingdom without asking a single theological question (Luke 23:43)! For the same reason, I think it is self-evident that
a person who is compelled to try to feel secure in their salvation by
convincing themselves they believe the true "saving" doctrines cannot
also be a person who feels secure in their salvation because they have
placed their trust in the loving character of God revealed on the cross.

I will say again that I firmly believe it is important for a number
of reasons that we aspire to embrace true beliefs. But never should
we do so as a means of trying to satisfy our hunger for *life*, including
our need to feel secure in our relationship with God. Only the perfect
love of God that is displayed on the cross can satisfy this need, and
looking to *any* other source, however good and holy it may be, is
nothing short of idolatry.

How to Seek Truth

Not only should we not try to find life by convincing ourselves that
the beliefs we embrace are all true, but as I mentioned in the previous
chapter, if we are really interested in embracing *true* beliefs, then the
last thing we would ever do is to try to convince ourselves that we
already embrace true beliefs. A genuine concern for truth is simply
incompatible with a concern to *feel certain* that one *already* believes
the truth. If a person is *really* concerned with truth, they will try to
examine their beliefs critically and go out of their way to confront
evidence that has the potential to make them doubt their beliefs.

But this is very hard, if not impossible, to do if a person is getting
any aspect of their fullness of *life* from feeling certain their beliefs are
already true. It's apparent, therefore, that getting all our *life* from the
love that is showered on us from the cross not only frees us from the
need to convince ourselves that our beliefs are true, but it also frees
us to genuinely explore whether our beliefs are true.

What about the Belief in the Cross?

One final question needs to be addressed before we turn in part 2
to explore the biblical concept of faith. I've been saying we should

get all our *life* from God, as revealed on the cross, not from our feeling certain we believe all the things necessary to be "saved." But as I mentioned above, this obviously presupposes that the belief that God is fully revealed on the cross is true. And so, one could legitimately ask, doesn't this mean you're getting *life* from feeling certain that at least one belief is true, just as those who embrace certainty-seeking faith do?

Obviously, in order to get *life* from the God who is revealed on the cross, one must believe it's true that God was in fact revealed on the cross. As I'll discuss at length later on (chap. 8), I believe this is the one belief we should leverage everything on, precisely because the God revealed on the cross is to be our one and only source of *life*. I could be wrong about every other thing I believe and it would not substantially affect my relationship with God or, therefore, the sense of *life* I get from this relationship. With Paul, the only thing I *really* need to know is "Jesus Christ and him crucified" (1 Cor. 2:2). If I were ever convinced this belief is wrong, however, I would be completely lost.

Having said this, I'll respond to the above question by saying three things.

First, to get *life* from the God revealed on the cross is not the same as getting *life* by feeling certain I'm right in my belief that God is revealed on the cross. To illustrate, for me to enjoy the committed relationship I have with my wife, I need to be confident that certain beliefs I have about her are true. But this doesn't mean I am enjoying a relationship *with my beliefs*. As I said above, the beliefs that are involved in our relationship with God, just like the beliefs involved in our relationships with people, are not an end in and of themselves. They should rather point beyond themselves to bring us into, and help us sustain, a relationship with the one our beliefs are about. And it's the *relationship* with God that gives us *life*, not *the beliefs* that got us into the relationship.

Second, precisely because the belief that God is revealed on the cross is not an end in and of itself, and precisely because I don't get *life* from being right about this belief, I don't need to feel certain this belief is true. As with my relationship with my wife, I only need to feel *confident enough* to act on the belief, *as if* it's true, in order to enter into the committed relationship with God. And again, it's the relationship, not the belief, that got me there, that gives me *life*.

And third, precisely because I need to be confident enough to act on this belief, but do not need to feel certain of this belief, I will not try to *convince myself* this belief is true. I will rather do what all rational people do when deciding whether something is true or not, as we discussed in the previous chapter. I will carefully consider all the evidence and arguments that can be marshaled for and against this belief. (I will share some of these in chap. 8.)

In light of these three considerations, I hope it's clear how getting all our *life* from "Jesus Christ and him crucified" is radically different from the certainty-seeking faith we've been discussing in the last two chapters.

Conclusion

The last two chapters have been a review of the Pandora's box that I began to open twenty-some years ago when the cowardly lion popped into my head at a prayer meeting. I understand that this may have brought you to an unpleasant place if you have embraced the certainty-seeking model of faith, depending on how important this model has been to you. To the degree that your *life* was derived from your confidence that you believed the right things, you are likely experiencing the pain of cognitive dissonance that doubt creates.

My heart goes out to you. Believe me, I've been in your shoes. I applaud your courage and encourage you to stay with your discomfort and honestly follow where it leads. The truth is, there is simply no other way to be concerned with truth and to grow except by walking through this door.

Throughout part 2 of this work, we will see that, in sharp contrast to certainty-seeking faith, the kind of faith Scripture encourages us to embrace is a faith that invites us to boldly raise questions, to honestly embrace ambiguity, and to fearlessly entertain doubt. And it does so precisely because it frees us from the need to be certain about anything, so long as we are confident enough to act on a belief about the "one thing [that] is needful" (Luke 10:42 KJV)—Jesus Christ, and him crucified.

Part 2

TRUE FAITH

Wrestling with God

It seemed to me certain, and I still think so today, that one can never wrestle enough with God if one does so out of pure regard for the truth.

—SIMONE WEIL

But I desire to speak to the Almighty and to argue my case with God.

—JOB 13:3

Before we embark on a discussion of the biblical model of faith, it might help to briefly review what we've covered and outline where we're going. Here, in a nutshell, is what I've argued is wrong with the certainty-seeking model of faith.

- There is nothing virtuous about the ability to make yourself feel certain of things. The more rational a person is, the less they have this ability. The more simple or gullible they are, the better they'll be. God loves simple and gullible people, but there's no reason to think they're saints! Trying to feel certain your beliefs are right and trying to avoid doubt is irrational and reduces faith to a form of mental gimmickry.

- Having people believe that their salvation and other things—like whether your friend lives or dies—hang upon how certain you feel about things is psychologically torturous and presupposes an ugly, Al Capone-ish mental picture of God.

- Certainty-seeking faith looks more like magic than biblical, covenantal faith in that it depends upon doing and believing certain things in order to gain God's favor and manipulate God to benefit ourselves and others.

- The certainty-seeking model of faith leaves us with an inflexible way of approaching our beliefs and makes us vulnerable to various challenges to our belief system. Since everything is a package deal that we must buy into in order to feel loved, worthwhile, and secure, we cannot afford to think flexibly and therefore are left with a faith that is brittle and easily broken.

- Believing that one's salvation depends on remaining sufficiently certain about right beliefs can cause people to fear learning things that might make them doubt the rightness of their beliefs. It thus creates a learning phobia that in turn leads many to remain immature in their capacity to objectively, calmly, and lovingly reflect on and debate their beliefs.

- Doubt-shunning faith tends to be hypocritical in that Christians see it as sinful for them to doubt but virtuous for non-Christians to do so.

- Certainty-seeking faith can be dangerous, as it discourages us from seriously questioning our assumptions even when we are asked to engage in questionable behaviors, such as killing people, in the service of our beliefs.

- It's self-serving and self-deceptive to strive to feel certain while also telling yourself you're concerned with truth. A concern for believing the truth requires us to take seriously the possibility that our current beliefs are mistaken.

- Finally, and most seriously, trying to convince ourselves that we embrace true beliefs can be idolatrous. When people feel they are loved, have worth, and are secure before God (they are "saved") because they embrace the right beliefs, they are getting their *life* from their confidence in their *beliefs about* God rather than from *a relationship with* God.

My hope is that this material has helped readers become aware of whether they've been holding to a version of the certainty-seeking model of faith and to seriously call it into question. While I've offered an array of arguments against certainty-seeking faith, however, I have not yet considered the argument that should carry the most weight for Bible-believing Jesus-followers: namely, the argument that this model of faith is simply *not biblical*. So over the course of the next four chapters I'm going to unpack this argument.

In this and the next chapter I'll demonstrate that biblical faith is grounded in authenticity. In chapter 6, I'll argue that biblical faith is covenantal. And in chapter 7, I'll show that biblical faith is not about striving for certainty, but about faithful living in the face of uncertainty.

As we proceed, it will become increasingly obvious how different this model is from the certainty-seeking model so many embrace today.

The Faith of an "Israelite"

We've seen that the assumption that a person's faith is as strong as they are certain motivates people to try to suppress doubt. The first thing we need to say about the biblical model of faith is that it holds an almost opposite attitude toward doubt. It's not that the biblical view encourages us to try to doubt. Indeed, we'll later see that there is a healthy place in the life of faith to put questions and doubts aside for a time. But we're now going to see that biblical faith is grounded in a willingness to be honest with ourselves and with God about whatever questions, doubts, or complaints we may have.

The biblical understanding of faith even encourages us to go to the mat with God when it's necessary for us to do so.

Wrestling to a Deeper Relationship

One of the most important biblical teachings on the nature of faith comes from the famous—and famously odd—story of Jacob wrestling with the Lord all night long (Gen. 32:22–32). As the story unfolds, Jacob is resting alone by a riverbed when, for reasons not supplied in the narrative, we suddenly find him wrestling with a man in the middle of the night. We soon learn that this man happens to be none other than *God* (vv. 28, 30)! The narrative reports that when this man "saw that he could not overpower" Jacob, he "touched the socket of Jacob's hip so that his hip was wrenched as he wrestled with the man" (v. 25).

It says something about the biblical nature of faith that this narrative, like so many narratives in Scripture, raises questions it doesn't answer. This narrative invites us to wrestle with it. For example, the narrative leaves us wondering how it is that Jacob's wrestling partner had the power to give himself a wrestling advantage by dislodging Jacob's hip with a mere tap of his finger and yet wasn't able to "overpower him" whenever he wanted to. The fact that we're then let in on the secret that this man was the almighty God makes his professed inability to overpower Jacob more puzzling still.

I'm inclined to doubt that the author of this narrative simply missed this obvious inconsistency. A more likely explanation, in my opinion, is that this story is being told from the perspective of Jacob. *Of course* the omnipotent Lord could have overpowered Jacob anytime he wanted to—*if this is what he had wanted to do*. As I interpret it, however, this wasn't what the Lord wanted to do. The very fact that the Lord showed up as a regular man suggests to me that the Lord wanted to *appear to Jacob* to be a wrestling foe he could conceivably defeat.

Maybe what the Lord was up to was something like this.

I frequently engage in wrestling matches with my mousey little five-year-old grandson, Soel. Out of nowhere, Soel will suddenly be transformed into "Wolverine" (Soel's favorite X-Men superhero). This is my cue to instantly become "an evil mutant" (one of the many foes that I'm told fight the X-Men). As I seek to destroy the universe for no apparent reason, Wolverine attacks me, and we tumble around on the floor in a life-and-death struggle with the fate of the universe at stake. In the course of our cosmic battle, I yell out things like, "You are so powerful, Wolverine, but I shall defeat you!" Wolverine will then lift his mighty arms and declare, "No evil mutant can defeat the mighty Wolverine!"

Wolverine then proceeds to strike me with a mighty blow or to zap me with the whatever-it-is zapper energy that comes out of his fingers and eyes. (Soel's version of Wolverine is clearly a composite of *all* X-men—the little cheater!) I, of course, resist his mighty blows and zapper energy with my magical force field as long as I can, but it invariably fails me and I dramatically fly backward on the couch in a dazed state. (Pacifist readers need not be concerned: I always remind Soel afterward that Jesus would never want us to engage in violence against *real* people, good or bad.) There are times when I come very close to defeating him, but in the end, it is always I, the evil mutant, that ends up pleading for mercy.

Now, while I'm not the athletic specimen I once was, I'm pretty sure I could pin my mousey grandson in about a half-second if I wanted to. But what grandpa on the planet would want to do that? Wrestling is a good way for Soel and I to bond together. This is made all the more important by the fact that as Soel grows up, he is buying into our culture's nonsense about "big boys" not giving grandpas or dads long, hard hugs! As Soel and I toil over the fate of the universe, I'm cleverly stealing the long, hard hugs he would otherwise hesitate giving me, and we are, in fact, wrestling our way into a closer relationship.

I strongly suspect this is something like what was going on when the Lord acted like he couldn't overpower Jacob throughout their night of wrestling. His goal in coming down to Jacob's level was to display just enough strength to motivate Jacob to display the stubborn tenacity he knew was in him. And he wanted to engage in this long wrestling match as a means of revealing the unique, "face to face" (v. 30), willing-to-go-to-the-mat relationship he wanted to have with Jacob.

From "Jacob" to "Israel"

Returning to our story, Jacob and the Lord wrestle throughout the night when suddenly the Lord says he has to call it quits because the sun is rising (v. 26). What the coming of dawn has to do with anything at all is yet another mystery that the narrative does not reveal. One almost gets the impression that Jacob's wrestling partner is a sort of vampire who is afraid of daylight!

The oddness of this narrative intensifies as we find Jacob refusing to let the man go until he receives a blessing from him. We again aren't told why Jacob makes this random request or even what the blessing is that he wants. But the Lord responds by asking what seems to be an equally random question, What is your name?—as if the all-knowing God wouldn't already know this.

The request for Jacob's name leads us to the punch line of this story. Apparently willing to do whatever it takes to receive a "blessing" from his wrestling partner, Jacob gives him his name, at which point the Lord immediately informs him that his name is about to change. It seems likely that this is the "blessing" he is giving to Jacob as a reward for his tenacious wrestling. From now on, the Lord says, Jacob will be called "Israel" (*Yisra'el*). And the reason for this change, the Lord tells Jacob, is "because you have struggled with God and with human beings and have overcome."[1]

"Jacob" obviously didn't become "Israel" because he had "overcome" the Lord in the sense of *overpowering* him. He became "Israel" and had "overcome" because *he had the audacity to wrestle with God* and not let him go until he received the "blessing" he was wrestling for.

What's in a Name?

Among ancient Jews—and this is true for most ancient cultures—a person's name revealed their core identity and character. So, by giving Jacob the name of "Israel," the Lord was revealing something profoundly important about Jacob and his descendants, "the Israelites." He was revealing that a distinctive characteristic of these people—the ones he called his "chosen people"—would be that they would be willing to struggle with God and with other humans, as their forefather had done.

The "blessing" Jacob received, in other words, was that his descendants would be known for possessing the same tenacity their forefather had demonstrated in his struggle to receive it.

Of course, as wise people throughout history have often reiterated, a person's greatest potential strength is also their greatest potential

weakness. It's not surprising, therefore, that much of Israel's struggling with God and with others throughout the Old Testament was
anything but godly. When we repeatedly read about how "stiff-necked"
the Israelites were in resisting God's will and about how quick they
were to mistrust God and to instead rely on their own human kings
and armies—things that usually caused them to wrestle with other
nations and lose—we are seeing the negative side of their greatest
potential strength.

But these negative illustrations simply confirm the fact that the
willingness of Jacob's descendants to struggle with God and with
others as they tried to follow God was also the distinctive *positive*
attribute that God conferred on them as a blessing to their forefather
who first demonstrated the tenacious audacity that was to be the
hallmark of their unique faith.

From a "Jacob"-like Faith to an "Israelite" Faith

The meaning of "Jacob" may also be significant for our purposes.
In the popular etymology of this name that is reflected in the narrative, it literally means "heel catcher," for Jacob was born grabbing
the heel of his twin brother, Esau (Gen. 25.26). But this name has
the connotation of one who connives to supplant another, and this
is certainly borne out by the way Jacob behaved toward others. He
was a true trickster!

I mention this because, as I argued in chapter 2, certainty-seeking
faith has a certain conniving quality to it.[2] Though the people who
exercise this faith are perfectly sincere, this model of faith motivates
them to engage in a form of mental trickery as they artificially try
to convince themselves of certain beliefs instead of basing their level
of confidence on an honest and rational evaluation of the merits of
these beliefs. It also causes some to avoid, or to at least not honestly
wrestle with, facts or arguments that might shake their faith. And,
as we've seen, this model motivates people to act this way in order to
get something from God, whether it be salvation or healing or some
other blessing.

In this light, it doesn't strike me as too much of a stretch to see in
this narrative a call of God to relinquish our "Jacob"-like faith, with

its conniving qualities, and to instead embrace an "Israelite" faith, which calls on us to have the courage to honestly struggle with issues before God and to even have the audacity to wrestle with God.

The "Israelite" Faith of Job

The Uncomfortable Faith of Biblical Heroes

In sharp contrast to many today who seek the comfortable feeling of certainty as a way of feeling at peace with God, biblical heroes are better known for their willingness to be uncomfortable and to honestly wrestle with God. The most powerful illustration of this, in my opinion, is Job. But before turning to him, I'd like to warm up by briefly looking at several other classic heroes of the faith.

We see a Jacob-like wrestling match in the Bible's account of Abraham questioning God's justice when he announced his plans to destroy Sodom and Gomorrah (Gen. 18:20–33). We see the same several times in the life of Moses. For example, he once boldly objected when God privately told him he was so angry with the Israelites that he planned on destroying them to start over with Moses alone. Moses's bold intercession succeeded in changing God's mind and thereby spared the nation (Exod. 32:10–14). In fact, we find dozens of examples in the Old Testament of people responding to God's announced plans by interceding and changing his plans.[3]

Biblical heroes of faith frequently objected to God's actions—or at least what they *thought* were his actions.[4] One of the greatest prophets in the history of Israel, for example, was Jeremiah. Yet throughout the book of Jeremiah, as well as its sequel, Lamentations, we find Jeremiah complaining of God's apparently unjust treatment of him and God's people as a whole while the wicked have it easy (e.g., Jer. 12:1; 14:8–9; 15:18). His bewilderment and honest objections become especially acute and are mixed with anger and sorrow in Lamentations, written in the wake of Babylon's seizure of Judah. Read this brief work, and you'll find Jeremiah sorrowfully crying out that God has acted like an enemy and a vicious predator (e.g., 2:4–5; 3:1–21) and ascribing to God absolutely barbaric behavior such as ruthlessly slaying young people (Lam. 2:21) and causing mothers to eat their own babies (2:20; 4:10–11)!

The prophet Habakkuk also is a great example of a man with a strong "Israelite" faith. Habakkuk acknowledges to God that "your eyes are too pure to look on evil" and that "you cannot tolerate wrong-doing" (1:13). But precisely because he believes this, he raises this complaint.

> Why then do you tolerate the treacherous?
>   Why are you silent while the wicked
>   swallow up those more righteous than themselves? (1:13)

Sprinkled throughout this book are expressions of anger and confusion about God's apparent inconsistency, especially as he allows pagans to conquer and abuse his own people.

As is apparent in so many Old Testament heroes, the faith of Habakkuk was obviously nothing like the certainty-seeking, doubt-shunning faith of so many today. Instead of avoiding cognitive dissonance by piously slapping the "mystery" label on an apparent contradiction, Habakkuk boldly goes to the mat with God. This is the kind of faith these descendants of Jacob were "blessed" with. And far from being offended by this raw honesty, God is the One who blessed them with it! This apparently is precisely the kind of honest relationship, and the kind of honest faith, God is looking for!

Caught in the Crossfire of Warfare

The most poignant example of Israelite faith in the Old Testament, in my opinion, is Job, a man who wasn't even a descendent of Jacob. In this epic poem, Job gets caught in the cross fire of a verbal form of spiritual warfare that is taking place in the Lord's court.[5] Making an unexpected appearance in the heavenly council (notice, God is *surprised* to see him, 1:7), Satan assails God's character and his way of running the universe (1:9–10).[6] Before the heavenly council, he alleges that no one, including Job, worships God of his or her own free will and for God's own sake. They are rather manipulated into doing so by the benefits God dangles before them. "Does Job fear God for nothing?" Satan says (1:9). He's essentially accusing God of being a Machiavellian type of deity, just as he originally did when he deceived Eve in the garden (Gen. 3:1–5).

In the context of this masterful tale, Satan's challenge is one that can only be refuted by being put to the test. And because the challenge is made publicly, before all the heavenly hosts (and, of course, the intended audience of this book), it must be responded to publicly. Were God to simply incinerate or ignore Satan, this would only serve to confirm Satan's allegation. No, the challenge must be refuted in a non-Machiavellian way.

And so, precisely because Job is "blameless and upright" and "the greatest man among all the people of the East" (1:1–3), Job becomes the means by which God's character and way of running the universe are to be vindicated.

When Piety Gets Thrown Aside

Satan first destroys Job's home and family. Because he's unaware of the satanic challenge that has necessitated his tragic losses, Job assumes that God must have arbitrarily decided to turn against him. Job initially expresses this conviction in pious-sounding language that doesn't attribute to God any "wrongdoing" (1:22).

> The LORD gave and the LORD has taken away; may the name of the LORD be praised. (1:21)

After a second assault in which he is afflicted with an excruciating skin disease, he expresses the same conviction, but a little less piously.

> Shall we accept good from God, and not trouble? (2:10)

The tinge of impiety in Job's statement is clearer in the Hebrew, for the word for "trouble" (*rah*) can be translated "adversity" and even "evil." Job is coming close to attributing "wrongdoing" to God.

As Job's pain increases and his energy begins to wane, however, his declarations become much less flowery, and he begins to charge God with "wrongdoing" in no uncertain terms. He continues to express his conviction that God arbitrarily gives and takes away, but in language that is much more raw. For example, at one point he tells his friends:

> All was well with me, but he [God] shattered me;
> he seized me by the neck and crushed me.

He has made me his target;
    his archers surround me.
Without pity, he pierces my kidneys
    and spills my gall on the ground. (16:12–13)

And a little while later he says to God:

I cry out to you, God, but you do not answer;
    I stand up, but you merely look at me.
You turn on me ruthlessly;
    with the might of your hand you attack me.
You snatch me up and drive me before the wind;
    you toss me about in the storm. (30:20–22)

Job is *still* confessing that the "Lord takes away," but in his increasing despair he doesn't couch his misguided conviction in pious terms. God is acting ruthlessly and capriciously, in his view, and that is all there is to be said about it. He is, in fact, espousing a theology that places God at the helm of all suffering and blessing.

Meanwhile, Job's "friends" share Job's mistaken conviction that God is directly involved in Job's afflictions, but they also believe, rightly, that God is just. So, like all too many sincere Christians today, they assume that Job must deserve the suffering he's enduring. They don't realize it, but Job's friends, and these Christians, are essentially defending Satan's Machiavellian view of God. It's just that, unlike Satan, they insist this Machiavellian providence is just.

The result is that while Satan and Job accuse God, Job's friends accuse Job.

When Job insists on his innocence, his friends are enraged—and terrified. Job correctly points out that they are like caravans of people who get caught in a terrible drought and leave their route to travel to a place that once held water, only to find it parched (6:15–19). "They are distressed," Job says, "because they had been confident" but are now "disappointed." So too, Job says, his friends "see something dreadful and are afraid" (6:20–21).

It is threatening to them, as it is for many today, to think we might live in a cosmos where righteous people can randomly suffer. And so, while both Job and his friends share the mistaken view that God

causes all suffering, his friends are as vigorous in arguing that Job
is guilty and his suffering is just as Job is in defending his innocence
and arguing that God is capricious.

God's Answer to Job and His Friends

When God finally shows up and speaks out of the whirlwind toward the close of this epic poem, he makes it clear to both Job and
his friends that they don't know what they're talking about. God first
points out that Job doesn't know anything about the unfathomable
complexity of creation (chap. 39). He then points out that Job and
all other humans are ignorant and helpless in the face of the forces
of evil that God must contend with, forces that Job and his contem-
poraries conceive of as cosmic monsters (Leviathan and Behemoth,
chaps. 40–41). In this way the Lord is letting Job and his friends know
that things are not as simple as their simplistic theologies and naive
moral equations suggest.

Along the same lines, it's highly significant that God never lets Job
or his friends in on the secret that the heavenly council, along with
the audience, has known all along: namely, that Job is caught in the
cross fire of a random conflict in the unseen realm. By leaving Job
and his friends in the dark about the ultimate cause of his misery, the
author of this masterpiece is reinforcing the theme that humans are
far too ignorant about the spiritual realm, the complex cosmos, and
the warfare that engulfs it to ever know why things unfold the way
they do and why good and evil take place so randomly. But for this
very reason, this book teaches us that we are arrogantly misguided if
we ever blame God (as Job did) or blame people (as Job's "friends"
did) when tragedy strikes someone.[7]

Job gets the point, for after God's speech, he says, "Surely I spoke
of things I did not understand, things too wonderful for me to know"
(42:3), and he repents "in dust and ashes" (42:6). His professed igno-
rance surely includes his first pious-sounding statement, "The Lord
gives and the Lord takes away," which we've seen is repeated in various
ways, and with increasing harshness, throughout this book.

This is why I frankly get a little crazy when I hear this passage re-
cited over and over again at funerals, as if it was God's definitive word

on why people die when they do. And when it's little children who die, reciting this verse can be utterly cruel—as though, for example, God "gave" a father and mother their precious child for two years and then decided to "take" their child by striking her with a terrible disease or sending a drunk driver or whatever.

Though it initially sounded pious, the "Lord-gives-and-Lord-takes" philosophy implies that Job was *right* when he accused God of capricious cruelty. It also means we must see the hand of God behind every child as well as every adult who has been slain by a disease, an accident, or a murderer throughout history. At least as I read this work, one of the reasons it was written was to *refute* this view—which is precisely why God *rebukes* Job for expressing it (38:1–2) and why Job repents and confesses that he spoke ignorantly.

The "Straightness" of Job

This brings us to the point that reveals the Israelite nature of Job's faith. Even though Job says some remarkably harsh things to God and about God, and even though Job's "friends" sound completely pious throughout this drama, it is the *friends* whom God rebukes. "I am angry with you," God says. And then he adds, "because you have not spoken of me what is right, as my servant Job has" (42:7).

Now, in affirming that Job spoke rightly, God can't possibly mean that Job had spoken *accurately*, because as we've just seen, Job has accused God of "wrongdoing" throughout this book in no uncertain terms, God rebukes Job for expressing this view in no uncertain terms, and Job repents of this view in no uncertain terms. So what did God mean by saying Job spoke "what is right"?

The answer, I believe, becomes clear when we look more deeply into the original Hebrew. The word for "right" (*kûwn*) has the connotation of something that is "straight." Depending on the context, the word can have the connotation of "true" or "accurate," or it can have a connotation of "straightforward" or "honest." For all the reasons I just shared, I'm convinced this latter meaning is what is intended in this passage.

As I interpret this verse, therefore, God is pointing out that, while both Job and his friends spoke ignorantly, Job at least spoke *straight*.

At least part of what motivated his friends' indicting speech, we've seen, was their need to feel secure. They were trying to convince themselves, against all evidence, that Job was less righteous than they were because they wanted to feel assured that what happened to Job could not possibly happen to them. As we saw was the case with certainty-seeking faith, these friends were trying to get *life* by convincing themselves that their self-serving theology was true.

So, for example, Eliphaz at one point says,

> Who, being innocent, has ever perished?
>   Where were the upright ever destroyed?
> As I have observed, those who plow evil
>   and those who sow trouble reap it. (4:7–8)

Of course, no one with his or her eyes even half open has ever actually seen *this*. We all live in the same unjust universe in which the wicked often prosper and the righteous often suffer, as we noted earlier. Eliphaz is affirming this not because he's actually seen it, but because this is something he *wants* to be true and that he is *trying to convince himself* is true.

Job's Vindication of God

It's evident that Job's friends were exercising a fear-motivated "Jacob"-like faith, which annoyed God, while Job was exercising an "Israelite" faith that pleased God. Job wasn't a physical descendent of Jacob, but he certainly was related to him spiritually. And so, while God had to confront his mistaken blame-God theology, he applauded Job's raw *honesty*. He applauded the fact that Job wasn't afraid to "argue [his] case with God" (13:3). God affirmed his audacity to go to the mat with him and struggle with him in a straightforward, no-holds-barred, ruthlessly authentic fashion.

Consequently, whereas Job's friends unwittingly sided with Satan, the "Accuser" (Rev. 12:10), Job unwittingly sided with God. Indeed, he didn't just side with God: he *vindicated* God! Job was the hero who saved God's reputation before the heavenly council (and thus to we who are his audience). And how did this hero accomplish this?

It obviously wasn't by embracing all the right beliefs about God, still less by trying to become free of doubt that his beliefs were right. This is what Job's friends did. This is what the religious leaders whom Jesus confronted did. And this, we have unfortunately seen, is what many Christians today do. But it's certainly not what Job did.

Nor did this hero serve and vindicate God by retaining a pious attitude and appearance while using pious-sounding language. This too is what Job's friends, Jesus's opponents, and many Christians today do. But it's certainly not what Job did.

Job refuted Satan's allegation that God was a Machiavellian deity simply by *talking straight*. Misguided as his theology was and angry as his words were, Job continued to serve God by honoring him with an open heart, allowing all the despair that was in it to be aired. And he served God by giving God the opportunity to put on display his very non-Machiavellian character as he patiently allowed Job to vent his anger.

Were God anything like the God that Satan accused him of being, both in the garden and in the heavenly council, God would have zapped Job as well as Satan for insubordination. The true God did not, however, which is proof to the heavenly council and to the audience of this book that the Accuser is, and always has been, a liar.

It wouldn't yet be revealed until a long time after Job was written, but we later learn in Christ that the true God not only does not zap ignorant humans who sincerely rail against God, as Job did; he loves them to the point of giving his life for them.

The Lessons of Job

This inspired epic poem doesn't explain why some people suffer and others do not, but it offers a singularly profound insight into why we ultimately can't know the reason why fortune and misfortune take place so randomly. It's not that God acts arbitrarily, as Job thought. Nor is it that people get what they deserve, as Job's friends thought. Rather, as God's grand speech out of the storm (Job 38–41) suggests, good and evil and everything else unfold with apparent randomness because the causes that factor into what comes to pass flow out of a cosmos that is unfathomably vast and complex: a cosmos that includes a heavenly realm that sometimes influences events, as it did Job, but that we are not privy to, and a cosmos that is perpetually under siege by powerful hostile cosmic forces, represented by Leviathan and Behemoth.

More importantly, for our purposes, this inspired poetic drama also provides us with a poignant illustration of what it means to have an "Israelite" faith that honors God. It's not a faith centered on right beliefs and pious language. And it's certainly not a faith that focuses on feeling secure and worthwhile by convincing ourselves that we're right. It's rather a faith *grounded in authenticity* that is therefore unwilling to sweep questions, doubts, and complaints under a pious rug to avoid the pain of cognitive dissonance. It's a faith that is not afraid of going to the mat with God.

In the next chapter we'll discuss the most important biblical illustration of Israelite faith and discuss the huge difference this can have on how we understand and practice Christian community.

5

Screaming at the Sky

You can't get to any of these truths by sitting in a field
smiling beatifically, avoiding your anger and damage and
grief. Your anger and damage and grief are the way to
the truth.

—Anne Lamott

I'm not keeping one bit of this quiet,
   I'm laying it all out on the table;
   my complaining to high heaven is bitter, but honest.

—Job 7:11 (Message)

In the previous chapter we saw that, despite his angry and confused
rant against God, Job, like so many other heroes of faith in the
Old Testament, is honored for espousing a faith that was grounded
in authenticity. We have not yet explored the most important illustration of this sort of faith, however. In chapter 9, I'll demonstrate from
Scripture that *everything* we think about God and about what it means
to follow God should be grounded in Jesus Christ. So in this chapter
I'd like to explore how Jesus exemplified the authenticity of biblical

faith. Following this, I will share the life-changing experience that first taught me the value of becoming ruthlessly honest with God.

The Faith of the Questioning Savior

The Israelite Faith of the Church

Some people claim that, because the New Testament gives us a much fuller revelation than the Old Testament, our concept of faith is quite different from theirs. "Of course people in the Old Testament struggled," one student said to me in response to a lecture I'd just given. "They didn't have the full picture we have. But," she continued, "now that we have the whole picture in Christ, God blesses us with unwavering faith." I suggested to her that perhaps she was reading the modern doubt-shunning model of faith into her interpretation of the New Testament.

Aside from the handful of verses that are misinterpreted to support the certainty-seeking model of faith, which I'll address in chapter 10, there is no reason to think the nature of faith changed with the coming of Christ. It's true that we who know God as he's revealed in Jesus, and especially as he's revealed in the crucifixion of Jesus, have a much more accurate and fuller revelation of who God is, as we'll discuss in chapter 9. In this sense it's true that the *content* of our faith has changed. But there is no reason to think that *what it means* to have faith has changed.

To the contrary, Paul declares that all who believe in Jesus are spiritual descendants of Abraham, precisely because we relate to God on the basis of faith the same way he did. This is why Abraham is called "the father of all who believe" (Rom. 4:11; cf. v. 16) and why all who place their trust in Christ are called "the Israel of God" (Gal. 6:16). Doesn't this suggest that we're to embrace the same sort of Israelite faith that Abraham and other biblical heroes embraced?

It's true that Abraham is praised by Paul for his undoubting resolve to believe God could give him and his wife, Sarah, a son, though they were well beyond childbearing age (Rom. 4:19). Yet, as we'll discuss in the next two chapters, the resolve attributed to Abraham and other biblical heroes has nothing to do with psychological certainty, but

everything to do with *trusting another's character* in the face of uncertainty. And we'll see in yet another chapter (chap. 10) that there is a
place in the life of faith where entertaining doubt serves no purpose—
though there is never any place for artificially suppressing doubt.
Abraham certainly trusted God's character, and it was precisely this
trust that allowed him to be authentic in his relationship with God.

This is exactly the kind of faith Jesus demonstrated.

Can We Reconsider the Plan?

It may strike some readers as odd to look to Jesus as an example
of a faith that is willing to struggle. He was the sinless Son of God
who obeyed God perfectly and exercised perfect faith. What possible
struggle could he have?

I agree that, while Jesus was genuinely tempted, as we all are, he
never struggled *with sin* (Heb. 4:15). But this doesn't mean Jesus
never struggled, for not all struggling *is sinful*. Many of our struggles
are simply the result of our being *human*. So, for example, as a full
human, Jesus had to "[learn] obedience from what he suffered," just
like the rest of us (Heb. 5:8). Moreover, as we're about to see, Jesus
even struggled on issues related to faith—which, I submit, simply goes
to show that perfect faith, which I assume Jesus had, is not a faith
that is free of struggles. It's rather a faith that is *willing* to honestly
struggle.

One such struggle took place in the Garden of Gethsemane, just
prior to his crucifixion. Though the sinless Son of God had perfect
faith, we find him asking God the Father to alter the plan to redeem
the world through his sacrifice—if it is "possible" (Matt. 26:42). As the
nightmare of experiencing the sin and God-forsakenness of the world
was encroaching upon him, Jesus was obviously, and understandably,
struggling. So, even though this plan had been predestined for ages
by the Trinity, Jesus desperately asked for an alternative.

Of course, there was no other alternative in this instance. Jesus had
to suffer. And though it caused him to sweat drops of blood, Jesus
willingly submitted to the Father's will. Yet the very fact that Jesus
tried to influence the Father to change the plan (and sweat blood in
the process) demonstrates that his perfect faith and obedience didn't

mean he never struggled and never tried to push back on God's plan, just as Moses and so many other heroes of faith had done before.

So, whether your struggle is with doubt, confusion, the challenge of accepting God's will, or any other matter, the fact that you have this struggle does not indicate that you lack faith. To the contrary, your faith is strong to the degree that you're willing to honestly embrace your struggle.

Why Have You Forsaken Me?

Yet the example of Jesus struggling in Gethsemane pales in significance compared to the way he struggled, and the way he displayed the "Israelite" quality of faith, on the cross. In the moment when the Son of God, for the first time in eternity, experienced separation from the Father as he bore the sin of the world, Jesus cried out, "My God, my God, why have you forsaken me?" (Matt. 27:46). Though the plan that involved this sacrifice had been settled within the Trinity for ages, it seems that in this singularly hellish moment Jesus had become foggy about it. And so the Son of God *questioned the Father*: "*Why?*"[1]

If one believes that a person's faith is as strong as they are certain and free of doubt, they have no choice but to accept that Jesus's faith faltered at this crucial moment, which would imply that Jesus sinned at this crucial moment. This is impossible, however, for it conflicts with both Scripture and the uniform conviction of the historic orthodox church. If we accept the "Israelite" conception of faith we've been defending, however, then there is no problem whatsoever. Since faith and doubt are not antithetical, a perfect faith need not be one that is free of doubt. What a perfect faith *needs* to be is first and foremost authentic, which is precisely what Jesus demonstrated when he cried out.

A Unity in Separation

The authenticity of Jesus's perfect faith that was expressed in his cry of abandonment is related to, and in fact parallels, the most profound dimension of Jesus's love, which also is expressed in this cry. To grasp this point, readers first need to be made aware of a thorny dilemma that Jesus's cry of abandonment has posed for theologians throughout history. This is an exceedingly complex issue, but, at the risk of overgeneralizing, I am going to briefly paint an outline of this issue with the broadest possible strokes.

The issue revolves around whether Jesus's cry reflects something that actually happened between the Father and the Son or not. On the one hand, if we *affirm* that this cry indicates that the Son of God was actually separated from the Father on the cross, then this seems to imply that God's tri-unity was temporarily disrupted, which is tantamount to saying God temporarily ceased to exist! For good reason, the historic orthodox church has always viewed this as impossible. On the other hand, however, if we *deny* that this cry indicates that the Son was actually separated from the Father on the cross, this would seem to suggest that Jesus's cry was inauthentic. In fact, it arguably makes the biblical teaching that Jesus *became* our sin (2 Cor. 5:21) as well as our curse (Gal. 3:13) look like a charade.

The most common way orthodox theologians have resolved this issue is by distinguishing between the humanity and the divinity of Jesus. The human Jesus experienced separation from the Father, many have argued, but the divine Jesus did not. Related to this, many have held that the human Jesus suffered on the cross—including the suffering of his separation from the Father—but the divine Jesus did not.

There are a host of problems with this proposed solution, in my opinion, not least of which is that, if the *divine* Jesus didn't experience everything that the *human* Jesus experienced, we have to wonder how Jesus is *one indivisible person*, as the church has always held. Related to this, by driving a wedge between the divine and the human Jesus, this solution arguably undermines the authenticity of the revelation of God in the crucified Christ. How does Jesus's love-motivated suffering reveal God's self-sacrificial character if we aren't seeing the suffering *of God* when Jesus suffers?

I'd like to propose that this dilemma can be resolved if we simply hold fast to John's magnificent teaching that "God is love" (1 John 4:8). God *is* love, which means love isn't simply a verb that God *does*; it's the noun that *God eternally is*. Love is the very essence of God, as Father, Son, and Holy Spirit.

This is a beautiful revelation, but it becomes even more beautiful when we find John removing any confusion about the nature of the love that eternally unites the Trinity by saying, "This is how we know what love is: Jesus Christ laid down his life for us" (1 John 3:16). John is teaching us that the love that unites the Trinity is one and the same as the humble, other-oriented, self-sacrificial love that was displayed when Jesus laid down his life for us.

We might say that when God displays his true eternal nature to a fallen world, *it looks like Calvary*. This is why the cross is presented in the New Testament as the quintessential expression of God's love (John 3:16; Rom 5:8) and why the Son is put forth as "the exact representation" of God's "being" or "essence" (*hypostasis*, Heb.1:3). When we behold the crucified Christ, we are beholding the eternal essence of the Triune God.

How does this resolve the dilemma we're wrestling with? It resolves it because it means that we can *affirm* that the Son of God experienced separation from the Father and that his cry of abandonment was authentic. But far from *disrupting* the unity of the Trinity, this horrendous separation, along with Jesus's cry, *perfectly reveals* this unity, for all three persons entered into this separation *out of perfect love*.

Consider that when God bore our sin and experienced the God-forsakenness that is sin's consequence, he was going to the furthest extreme possible out of love for us. He was, in fact, in some sense experiencing his own antithesis, for nothing could be more antithetical to the all-holy God than to experience sin, and nothing could be more antithetical to the perfectly united God than to experience separation from himself. We cannot begin to imagine the nightmare the Son must have endured in this moment. But this is precisely why this nightmare, expressed in Jesus's cry of abandonment, perfectly reveals the unsurpassable nature of the love that God eternally is. The unthinkable extremity to which God was willing to go for a race of rebels who could not have deserved it less reveals the unfathomable intensity of the other-oriented love that unites the Triune God.

The Revelation of a Perfect Struggling Faith

Not only is God's love perfectly revealed as the Son experiences separation from the Father, but Jesus's perfect faith is revealed in his cry of abandonment by the Father. And just as God's perfect love is paradoxically manifested in the experience of separation, so too

Jesus's perfect faith is paradoxically manifested in his cry of abandonment. For Jesus's faith in his Father was an Israelite faith that is anchored in an authentic, honest relationship with the Father. And this is precisely what Jesus's cry of bewilderment illustrates.

We might say that just as Jesus's perfect unity with the Father was deeper than his experience of separation, so too Jesus's faith in the Father was deeper than his experience of abandonment. Indeed, these are, in my view, two sides of the same coin.

Had Jesus instead managed to suppress his sincere bewilderment to preserve a more pious appearance, *then* he would have demonstrated a defective faith. For while an unquestioning crucified Messiah would certainly have appeared more pious and would have more closely conformed to what we might have expected a sinless Messiah to look like, it would have demonstrated a less-honest relationship with the Father for Jesus to refrain from expressing the full horror of what he was experiencing.

And so, in the same nightmarish moment that Jesus perfectly revealed the true God to us, he perfectly revealed the true nature of faith to us. His cry demonstrates that cultivating a faith-relationship with God has nothing to do with how appropriately religious things appear, but everything to do with the honesty and authenticity of the relationship.

When the Volcano Erupts

Since it illustrates several important aspects of the nature of biblical faith, I'd like to spend the remainder of this chapter sharing the experience that taught me the value of being ruthlessly honest with God.

My Return to Christ

I mentioned earlier that one year after coming to Christ in a theologically aberrant Pentecostal church, I completely lost my faith. Overwhelmed by innumerable intellectual objections that I could find no adequate response for, I felt I had no choice but to abandon faith in the Bible, in Jesus, and even in God. For about nine or ten miserable months, I futilely tried to accept that reality is absurd, amoral, and pointless—which I continue to believe it is if not created and sustained by a rational, moral, purposing God. But the sheer pain of living in such a universe began to make me suspect there must be something wrong with this nihilistic worldview. How, I wondered, could nature evolve a being such as me who was so thoroughly out of sync with it?

This may surprise some readers—it still sort of baffles me—but as I began to find my way back into the faith, I decided to return to the peculiar fundamentalist Pentecostal church I had left. There were a number of reasons for this, not least of which is that I had an ex-girlfriend in the church whom I hoped to get back together with (which fortunately never happened, because I soon met Shelley!). But the most important reason was that, even though I had to hide my many questions about the Bible from my friends, the aberrant theology of this church was the only one I really knew and that I continued to identify as "true Christianity."

My Ongoing Struggle

My return to the faith and to this church in particular alleviated the misery of my sense of meaninglessness, but it also meant I had to once again adopt the strict lifestyle that this church believed in. I had no trouble walking away from most of the sin I'd returned to during my exile, for the truth is that I was so miserable during this exile, I had difficulty enjoying any sin the way I did before I first became a Christian. But as I mentioned in the introduction, there was a vice I had never been able to shake, even when I first surrendered to Christ. It was my bondage to pornography.

My atheistic father had strong moral convictions on matters of social justice and racism, but he had none when it came to sex. Once he divorced my stepmother when I was thirteen, he made no attempt to hide his stash of pornography from me. To his way of thinking, it was perfectly normal for young men to view pornography. As a result, in the four years between my parent's divorce and my conversion at the age of seventeen, I'd developed a powerful addiction to this vice. And so, while I was able to "clean up my act" in every other respect when I returned to church, I was once again not able to kick this.

What made matters worse is that this holiness church taught that every single sin caused you to lose your salvation until you repented of it. Some churches believe in eternal security; this one believed in eternal *insecurity*. As a result, in both my first and second attempts at "living the life," as we called it, I found myself getting "saved" and "unsaved" almost every week, and sometimes several times a week! I'd typically repent of my sin and get "resaved" in our Sunday night service, but I'd again lose it by Tuesday or Wednesday as I caved in to the temptation of porn.

A Parking Lot Confession

My cycle of getting "saved," "unsaved," and "resaved" went on for over a year after I returned to church. Eventually, my constant guilt and frustration began to morph into a sense of hopelessness. I sincerely wanted to be free, and I continually asked God to deliver me from my bondage, but it seemed he was telling me I had to swim or sink on my own. In time, my desperate attempts at swimming completely exhausted me. I eventually arrived at the point where I felt I had no choice but to accept the inevitable: I was going to drown.

It happened after one of the Sunday night services. On this night, I found myself unable to respond to the altar call. I simply had no motivation to get "resaved" and to promise God I'd never again look at porn. In fact, on this night, this promise, which I'd made so many times before, struck me as a joke. I admitted to myself that I knew perfectly well that by Wednesday I'd fall again. Who was I kidding? I figured God was getting as tired of this silly merry-go-round as I was. I concluded I was simply hopeless and destined for hell.

The misery I felt during my exile, when I thought life was pointless, had been terrible. But the hopelessness I felt as I walked out of the church on this night was far worse. The sense of doom produced when you sincerely believe in an eternal hell while also feeling certain there is absolutely nothing you can do to avoid it is simply indescribable.

I walked out of church with my friend Brett, the only person I'd dared to share my struggles with. (In this church, no one dared to talk about these kinds of things.) Though less severe than mine, Brett also struggled with a pornography addiction. Standing by his truck parked under a light in the church parking lot, I bluntly told Brett that I was never coming back to church. Brett wasn't altogether surprised, for I had been sharing my self-loathing and disappointment over my failure quite a bit over the last two months. I had even expressed thoughts of quitting several times, though I don't think Brett seriously worried that I'd ever follow through on this.

For several hours Brett and I talked under a lamppost in the church's empty lot. He made a number of sincere and valiant attempts at giving me hope, but there was nothing he could say that I hadn't already told myself a hundred times before. I wanted a lifeline I could believe in, but Brett's words rang completely hollow. Indeed, the more we talked, the more strongly I felt the *absence* of hope, like the intensifying stench of a decomposing corpse. And as this stench intensified, the sorrowful dimension of my despair was largely replaced by anger. The tone of my voice, which had been somber, if not morbid, became increasing loud, abrasive, and, frankly, vile.

I recall feeling a bitter rage swelling up like lava rushing to the surface of a volcano. As I've reflected on this moment over the years, it's become obvious to me that this seething rage wasn't just about my inability to stay "saved" by avoiding porn. I now understand that it was, in fact, a rage that had been accruing over a lifetime of my disappointing those in authority.

Never Good at Being Good

As a child with ADHD and possibly a mild case of Asperger's Syndrome (long before these were diagnosed as such), I had always *wanted* to be good and to please the adults in my life. Despite my sincerity, however, I consistently found myself doing things that irritated, and often enraged, authority figures. As is quite common for children with these disorders, it often seemed to me as if I had engaged in my impulsive misbehavior while asleep and that I would only wake up to what I'd done when an angry authority pointed it out to me.

When the severity of my crime warranted it, I'd be sent to the office of "Mother Superior"—the dreaded "boss" of the strict Catholic school I attended. This was a woman who was built like a tank and could swing the "ugly stick" (her disciplining tool) like a professional baseball player swings a bat. Before telling me to bend over to receive my punishment, she would ask me: "Mr. Boyd, *why* did you throw that spit wad?" or "put that tack on Sister Margaret's chair?" or "pull Amy's hair?" or whatever. For two years straight she'd get enraged when I would answer, as I almost always did, "*I don't know.*" But I was *telling the truth*! I rarely knew why I acted the way I did. I *discovered* what I did after the fact. My misdeeds often surprised me, and I was always sincerely sorry for them. But by then it was too late.

My childhood perception probably distorted reality, but it seemed to me that moments when one authority or another wasn't mad at me were rare. When I reflect on my rigid grandmother who cared for my three siblings and me after our mom died when I was two, or when I remember the physically abusive stepmother we acquired when my dad remarried, as well as the disciplinary nuns who taught at my school, I can only remember them being *angry*. With the exception of my father and grandfather, I honestly cannot recall *any* authority who spoke a single tender word to me while I was growing up. And, unfortunately, my father's work kept him away from home the vast majority of the time, while visits to my dear grandpa's house were infrequent.

Given my experience, it's hardly surprising that I grew up assuming that God too was angry with me. The "God" that the nuns (and occasional priests) conveyed in classroom teachings was frightful. And it didn't help that when I attended Mass before school each morning, all the pictures, statues, and stained glass windows representing God, Jesus, and the saints depicted them with somber and intimidating expressions. No one seemed nice!

The only exception was a statue of Mary tenderly holding the baby Jesus in her arms. She had a slight, kind smile and a beautifully serene demeanor as she lovingly gazed down at her baby. It was located on the left side of the front altar, and I would often spend the duration of the morning Mass staring at her compassionate face. I'd sometimes daydream about what it would be like to have Mary as a mother. And I'd sometimes struggle with feelings of guilt because I envied Jesus for having a mother who was so different from my constantly angry and physically abusive stepmother.

It is no wonder that, from the first grade on, I constantly prayed to Mary. If I had any hope of getting into heaven, I thought, it was *through her*. The nuns taught us that a good son always listens to his mother, so if we wanted to get Jesus's attention, we should, naturally, talk to his mother. Well, *I talked Mary's ear off*! I would sometimes kneel in prayer throughout the entire morning Mass. While the other kids thought I was trying to show off and the nuns thought I was just plain weird, I was actually pleading with Mary to put in a good word for me. "I know I'm not a good boy," I'd confess, "but I'm really trying! Oh Mother of God, *please* tell that to Jesus," I'd pray.

After I learned about hell in second grade, I sometimes would add to my pleas: "Mary, I *really* don't want to go to the devil! Please don't let Jesus send me to the devil." The lurid teaching we received on hell had terrified me. Over the next two years I had a vivid reoccurring nightmare about being pushed by the devil off a ledge into a sea of boiling lava at the base of a smoldering volcano.

It frankly breaks my heart when I now imagine my grandchildren or any child at this tender and impressionable age praying the sort of desperate prayers I prayed out of fear of hell. And yet, as much as I wanted to avoid it, I strongly suspected this was where I was destined to end up.

My voyages into unbelief as a teenager and then as a freshman in college had temporarily relieved this sense of doom, and it had almost disappeared when I first became a Christian and, very briefly, when I had returned to my faith. But here I was on this chilly October night in 1977, once again confronting this terrible fate. It seemed inevitable.

I simply was never very good at being good.

The Eruption and the Revelation

Unleashing My Anger on God

At some point in my increasingly angry conversation with Brett, the volcano erupted. Brett was saying something when I felt this hot rage rising to the surface. Brett ended abruptly when he noticed me becoming highly agitated. I began to walk in a circle and groan, as if I'd just stubbed my toe or something. I grabbed my head, pulled my hair, straightened my arms, clenched my fists, pulled my hair again, and continued this erratic behavior for a minute or so as my groaning grew louder. "What? *What?*" I recall Brett asking.

I suddenly stood still, looked up to the sky and let out an angry scream. I then proceeded, in a very Job-like manner, to vomit a several-minute-long diatribe against God that was utterly vile, if not blasphemous.

For reasons that will become clear below, I think it is important for readers to get as vivid a sense as possible of the nature of my outburst against God. I of course can't exactly recall everything I said, and, in any case, recounting all of this is unnecessary. But I'd like to share, as accurately as I can recall, the essence of what I screamed and cried that night, though I'll alter my vile language to render it appropriate for a general reading audience.

I should warn you ahead of time: *this isn't pretty.*

I began by screaming, "F***!" several times. I recall noticing Brett taking several steps back, as if he expected lightning to strike me at any moment.

As I continued, I sometimes faced the sky and other times faced the ground. My voice occasionally cracked from the intensity of anger, pain, and sorrow as I railed at God while fighting back tears.

> You say you love me, but it's a f***ing lie—and you know it! *You know it!!*
>
> You don't love *me!* You don't really love *anyone!* What you love is your G** d*** rules! Well guess what? I've never been able to keep your f***ing rules!
>
> *You* stacked the deck against me! *You* gave me a personality *you knew* wouldn't be able to meet your stupid standards. Then *you* took my mom and gave me that abusive b**** instead! A little wiggle of your little finger and my mom lives, and I get raised by someone who actually gives a s*** about me instead of someone who beats the s*** out of me! But you had something else in mind with your wonderful cosmic plan.
>
> You were laughing every time she took a two-by-four after me, weren't you? God of love, my a**!
>
> I never had a chance! I'm not the one who packed my body so full of hormones I can't handle it. That's *you!* And I didn't choose to be born in a home with a dad who thinks porn is as normal as breathing! That's *you!* You rigged the whole f***ing thing against me!
>
> But now I'm the guilty one and you're supposedly without blame. So I'm going to go to hell while you enjoy the bliss of heaven. This

f***ing game you play with eternal lives is a mile-high mountain of pure, undiluted, steaming bulls***!! Total bulls***!!

But you're the Supreme Being, so you get to give and take whatever mom you d***-well please and get to save and damn whoever you d***-well please. It's *your* demented game, so you, of course, get to win.

And I, of course, get to lose . . . and that's no f***ing surprise to anyone. I've always been a loser at your game.

I paused for several moments, as if to catch my breath. I could feel my heart pounding. I cast a brief glance at Brett. He had a confused and frightened look on his face. My rage then suddenly turned to sorrow, and tears began to flow down my face as I brought my anti-God tirade to a close.

I tried. I *really* f***ing tried! You know I f***ing tried!! But now I'm just f***ed.

I told you it wasn't pretty.

I didn't make the connection at the time, but as I've reflected on this night, I've noticed the close parallel between this awful rant of a nineteen-year-old and the desperate pleas to Mary by the scared seven-year-old. "I'm trying. . . . I don't want to go to the devil." The difference, however, is that, unlike the seven-year-old, the teenager had arrived at the dark place Job was at; he had lost hope in the possibility of a Mary-like figure in heaven to have compassion on him and to plead his case before the Almighty.

The Revelation

What happened next is indescribable. It was the most important moment of my life.

Brett and I just stood in silence for several moments, gazing at the ground. He was in a state of shock. I recall feeling very tired, but also oddly relaxed, like I'd just completed an unpleasant but necessary task.

At some point Brett broke the silence, and we began to quietly converse again. I remember nothing of this conversation except that at some point he said, "We must be missing something, Greg. We *must* be! Why are *other* people able to 'live the life' but we can't?" Disgusted by his hope, I angrily tossed my King James Bible on the hood of his truck. "Well, what might *that* be?" I said sarcastically. "I've read that d*** book from cover to cover, and I sure as h*** don't see it!"

I stepped over to the truck and started to mockingly read from the page the Bible had flopped open to. Under the parking lot light, and with the intention of ridiculing Brett's hope, I began reading the first verse my eyes landed on, putting it in the form of a sarcastic question.

"'There is therefore now no condemnation to them which are in Christ Jesus?' Is *that* the precious gem you think we're missing?" I then began to read it a second time in the same mocking way. "'There is therefore now . . . ,'" but something made me stop. After a bewildered moment of silence I read the verse again, but this time more slowly and as a serious question.

"'There is therefore now no condemnation to them which are in Christ Jesus?' What does that *even mean?*" I asked Brett. He shrugged his shoulders and said, "Not sure."

The verse I happened to land on was, of course, Romans 8:1 (quoted above in the KJV). Now, I'm honestly about as disinclined to try to discern the hand of providence in chance coincidences as anybody on the planet. And for all I know, God could have perhaps worked the miracle in my life that he was beginning to work using *any* verse I might have happened upon. But I honestly have a hard time denying God's influence in the way my Bible flopped open on this night and the way my eyes landed on this particular passage. This verse was about to turn my world upside down.

I slowly read the verse again, and then again a dozen or more times. In between several of the readings I turned to Brett to discuss parts of it. "No condemnation?" I asked, for example. "That means we aren't condemned, right?" "Not condemned *by God*," Brett added. And then after another couple of readings I turned and asked, "In Christ? What does it mean to be 'in Christ'?" Brett said something like, "Paul says this about everyone who simply believes." "So if we believe," I replied, "then we're 'in Christ'?" "And *that*," Brett added, with excitement in his voice, "means there's no condemnation for us!"

Brett and I undoubtedly would have learned the things we were discovering in Romans 8 had we converted to most other Bible-believing

Protestant churches, but you need to understand that, in the holiness Pentecostal church we had been attending, *nothing* like this was *ever* taught! This was all radically new to both of us. And as I began to slowly read the rest of the chapter and the teaching began to sink in, I could feel the weight of damnation lifting. I can't begin to convey the radical shift in emotions I was undergoing. A person finding a pool of cool water after having gone days in a hot desert without a drop would not experience greater relief than I was experiencing at this moment.

In between some of the verses, I would make comments or ask questions of Brett, who also was beginning to understand this material for the first time, though he wasn't getting nearly as carried away by it as I. By the time I'd reached verse 31, my excitement had turned to joy that was approaching the intensity of my earlier volcanic rage. With a loud voice I read,

> What shall we then say to these things? If God be for us, who can be against us? . . . Who shall lay anything to the charge of God's elect? It is God that justifieth. Who is he that condemneth? It is Christ that died, yea rather, that is risen again. (8:31–34 KJV)

"Unbelievable!" I exclaimed. "Brett, do you get that? *Do you get that?*" I began to laugh as I continued. "If the almighty God declares us to be righteous and free of condemnation, no one can argue with him!" "He's God!" Brett replied. "And it's only because he placed us in Christ because of our faith!" I added. "It's free and incontestable!"

Brett smiled as I roared with joyful laugher. After a moment I continued—and now I was preaching.

> Who can charge us with *anything*? It can't be *God*, because he's the one who justified us! And it can't be *Christ*, because he's the one who died so we could be justified in the first place and who intercedes for us. And if neither of *them* can be argued with, then no one—*no one*—can ever—*ever*—charge us with *anything*!
>
> Why have I never seen this before? Why have I never heard this before? It's beautiful! It's unbelievably fantastic! It's the best news imaginable!

I startled Brett with a bear hug as I laughed and cried and began repeating, "I'm not going to hell! Brett, I'm not going to hell!"

What Just Happened?

Faith That Is "Straight"

It would take me years to fully work through the revelation I received on this remarkable night. In fact, the understanding of this remarkable chapter that I have today is quite different from aspects of the way I understood it that night. But I believe that what happened on this life-transforming night was that, when I finally got real with God, *God could finally get real with me.* So long as my mind and heart were obsessed with trying to be good enough to "get saved" by a sub-Christlike picture of a God who loves and saves people based on their performance, the truth of God could not get through. Only when I finally crashed and burned on this salvation-by-goodness program could God finally get through to me.

Many might assume that God was offended if not outraged by my terrible tirade against him. Like my friend Brett, they might have been inclined to expect me to be struck dead by lightning. But as blasphemous as my outburst was, and while I certainly needed to repent of it, I believe God *applauded* it, for the same reason he applauded Job's tirade. My tirade was *straight.* It came from my gut. It was honest.

Ironically, while I obviously had *believed* in God before, I'm convinced that the first time I ever exercised authentic biblical *faith* in God was when I *proclaimed my angry disdain toward him*! I'm not saying I wasn't "saved" before this moment, because I know my heart was sincerely oriented toward God even though I had a jaded image of him and a misguided idea of what it meant to relate to God. But only when the pain, frustration, questions, and sin that had been stuffed in my innermost being could be expressed toward God could I be said to have an *Israelite faith* in God.

As I've said, biblical faith is not concerned with how religious and holy people appear. To the contrary, it is sometimes evidenced most when things appear *Godless*! As we've seen, the most profound display of Jesus's *faith in* the Father as well as the most profound revelation of his *loving unity with* the Father was when he expressed his sorrowful sense of *abandonment by* the Father. So too, it was only when I got honest with myself and God about my sense of hopeless alienation from God and the rage I had within me—that is, it was only when

I began to exercise *authentic faith*—that I could begin to receive a revelation of God's true loving nature and begin to experience loving union with him.

Biblical faith, we see, runs much deeper than the way people appear and even much deeper than what people consciously experience or think. The faith of an Israelite rather begins with a commitment to get honest, face truth, regardless of how ugly the truth is, and speak straight from the gut.

Honesty to Honesty

Though it was saturated in sin, there's a sense in which my outburst on that October night when I was nineteen years old was a holy prayer. And it was this honesty that finally put me in a position where God could finally break through my false pictures of him and reveal his true nature.

It was as if, in response to my vile diatribe, God said,

Finally! Thank you, Greg! That was *real*! And now that you've given me the *real you*, with all that is ugly in you, you're finally in a place where you can receive the *real me*, with all that is beautiful about me. And my beauty can now begin to make something beautiful out of all that is ugly in you.

Authenticity is at the foundation of biblical faith, because a genuine relationship can only be as real as the parties involved are real. And until our relationship with God is real, it can never be truly transforming. It will only remain a pseudo-relationship that produces a religious facade. Our inner ugliness can never be transformed by such a relationship. It can only be hidden.

Seeing for the First Time

When I finally poured the real me out before God, I began to get a picture of God that I could not only *say* I loved, as I'd always done before, but that I *actually* loved. For the first time I was beginning to see a God whose love for me was greater than sin—the God whose love and compassion I was so desperately trying to find as a child in the face of Mary! Indeed, for the first time I was encountering a God who loved *me*, not my behaviors or anything else *about* me.

This is the God who embraces me, places me "in Christ," and proclaims me to be his child whom he will not condemn *before* I get my act cleaned up. In fact, this is the God who by grace gets my act cleaned up precisely by loving me *exactly as I am*.

With this revelation of the beautiful God came an entirely different motivation for living that I had never known before. For the first time I was beginning to discern a God whom I actually *wanted* to live for. I was beginning to discover the motivation of Paul when he proclaimed, "Christ's love compels us" (2 Cor. 5:14). All my life I'd tried to be good to avoid hell, or the ugly-stick flogging, or my stepmother's beatings with a two-by-four. But while most people would undoubtedly be better at behaving well with these frightful motivations than I ever was, no one could ever be *transformed* by these sorts of motivations.

Threatening motivations address *behavior*, but they can never transform our *identity*. They motivate people to change as a means of *protecting themselves*, but for this reason they can never move us *beyond ourselves* to become someone fundamentally different from who we currently are. And threatening motivations can certainly never transform us into people with an other-oriented, self-sacrificial, loving character. Only a motivation that is anchored in love can do this.

All this is to say that, for the first time in my life, I was finding my true source of *life*. I had tried to get *life* by being good. When I proved incapable of that, I had for a time tried to get *life* by being bad. (Peers applaud the jokester who specializes in annoying authorities.) Then, when I converted, I tried to find *life* by believing all the right doctrines our church taught and by engaging in all the right holy behaviors while futilely trying to avoid all the behaviors that our church taught were sinful. Obviously, none of these strategies worked.

But when on this glorious October night I abandoned all hope of getting *life* from my beliefs and behavior, and when I therefore could finally get honest about my disgust toward my false view of God and the false ways of getting *life*, I found myself in a position in which I could finally find true *life*. God responded to my outburst by revealing to me, through my reading of Romans 8, that I am unconditionally loved, that I have absolute worth, and that I am absolutely secure in his love. *This* is what I, like everyone else, had been desperately hungry for all my life. *This* is what I yearned for as a seven-year-old gazing upon the Blessed Virgin, longing for the mother's love that seemed to glow from her eyes as she looked at the baby Jesus.

Breaking Free!

The implications this revelation had, not only for my pornography struggles, but also for every area of my life, were absolutely revolutionary, as they are for all who receive it. This too is part of the reason why embracing an Israelite faith rooted in a commitment to raw honesty is so important.

What the fear of hell could not do, my discovery of the love of God could do: it began to permanently break the stronghold of pornography over my life. It's not that I had a 100 percent victory over this sin from this night on. But this experience broke the chains, making it possible for me to move in the direction of total freedom. I think it will prove beneficial to some to close this chapter with a brief reflection on how the love of God does this.

For one thing, as I said in chapter 3, pornography addiction, like all other forms of sin, is most fundamentally fueled by the hunger for *life*. Yes, there was a simple biological pleasure involved in my addiction, but the pull of this and every other sin runs much deeper than that. In viewing pornography, I was feeding hungry parts and medicating hurting parts of my soul. When I found the true source of life, this false feeding and constant medicating were no longer needed.

Another dimension of God's liberating power is the above-mentioned fact that the love of God is a far more persuasive motivator than fear. I no longer would try to abstain from porn just to avoid God's wrath, for I now *wanted* to live for God because I was compelled by his unfathomable love. This in turn gave me wisdom about my struggle that I'd never had before. Operating out of love rather than fear gives us clarity we otherwise lack.

Until this night, for example, it had honestly never occurred to me to simply give my father an ultimatum: either the porn goes or I go. Though it would annoy him to have this choice forced upon him, I knew my father would choose to get rid of the porn because he liked having me living at home with him. So why hadn't this ultimatum occurred to me earlier? Looking back on it, I'm absolutely certain it was because, as is true of all our sin bondages, as much as I hated my bondage, a part of me also *enjoyed* it. A part of me *expected* to sooner or later break my commitment to abstain from it, and a part of me wanted that easy access to porn once I decided to go back to it.

Until I encountered the true God, I wanted to avoid the consequences of my sin, but I didn't *really* want to be free of it. Until I encountered the God whose love filled my inner hunger, I couldn't afford to be honest enough with myself, or with him, to admit this. To get *life* from holy behavior, people *need* to convince themselves that they're sincerely trying their best. A dishonest relationship with a false image of God always requires a dishonest relationship with oneself to be sustained.

Conversely, a real relationship with the real God always requires that we begin with a commitment to be honest with God and honest with ourselves.

Some of us have had the good fortune of failing miserably at being good and have, as a result, found ourselves in a position where we had no choice but to be honest. As happened to me on that October night thirty-six years ago, such people arrive at a point where we have absolutely nothing to lose. But others who are naturally better at being good, whether defined as engaging in holy behavior or convincing ourselves we believe the right things, will need to make a deliberate choice to get honest.

The question comes down to this: Will you trust that God is as beautiful as he's revealed himself to be in the crucified Christ and thus dare to peel away all facades, face whatever ugliness you find in your soul, and offer it up to him? The very act of baring our souls to him in this way allows God to reveal greater depths of his love, as he continually proves that our sin is no obstacle to his love. And this is precisely how God frees us from our sin.

If the Son of God could cry out in bewilderment in the garden and ask the most honest question in his heart while he hung on the cross, we are in good company when we do the same.

6

From Legal Deals to Binding Love

The relationship between commitment and doubt is by no means an antagonistic one. Commitment is healthiest when it is not without doubt but in spite of doubt.

—Rollo May

Let us rejoice and be glad
    and give him glory!
For the wedding of the Lamb has come,
    and his bride has made herself ready.

—Revelation 19:7

In sharp contrast to the common view that a struggling faith is necessarily "weak" and an unquestioning faith is necessarily "strong," we've seen that the heroic faith of Jesus and other biblical heroes was strong precisely because it did not try to suppress questions. Conversely, Job's friends were chastised precisely because they tried to remain certain about their beliefs in the face of evidence against them. It's apparent that the first step of faith in Scripture is not to engage in some sort of psychological self-manipulation but rather to commit to cultivating an open and honest relationship with God.

Having established this foundation, we are now ready to move on to what scholars generally consider to be the most defining characteristic of biblical faith. As we'll see, this also contrasts strongly with the certainty-seeking model of faith. In fact, the material I'll be sharing in this and the next chapter has helped multitudes of certainty-seeking people radically reframe what it means to have faith, and to do so in a way that has often had significant positive implications for their lives.

Covenants and Contracts

Faith and Belief

Let's start by talking about the difference between "faith" and "belief." While the Bible often uses the terms interchangeably, its core concept of faith goes far beyond the way we generally speak of "belief" today. For us, a belief is simply a mental conviction that something is true. By contrast, the biblical concept of faith involves a commitment to *trust* and to *be trustworthy* in a relationship with another person.[1]

To illustrate, like most other sane people in the twenty-first century, I *believe* the earth is round. But it would sound rather odd for me to say I exercise *faith* in the earth's roundness. The reason is that my belief in the earth's roundness requires nothing of me. I don't need to make a commitment to trust or to be trustworthy to the earth or to anything else in order to hold this belief. It's just a mental conviction that something is true.

On the other hand, the reason I'm married to Shelley is because I don't merely *believe* Shelley exists; I have *faith* in her. True, it would be rather hard for me to be married to Shelley if I didn't first believe she existed as well as believe some other relevant facts that were important to my idea about the kind of woman I wanted to marry. In this sense, faith *presupposes* belief. But faith goes far beyond belief in that its focus is not on a mental conviction but on willingness to act on that mental conviction.

Shelley and I are married because thirty-four years ago we promised to *trust* each other, and to be *trustworthy toward* each other, in terms of living up to our wedding vows "for better or for worse." *This* is the essence of the biblical concept of faith.

Let's Not Make a Deal

The marriage analogy of biblical faith is particularly appropriate because marriage is a covenant, and as is true of a host of other concepts in Scripture, faith in the Bible is a *covenantal* concept. One of the reasons so many Christians today have mistaken ideas about faith is that the concept of covenant is increasingly foreign to us in the postmodern West. We tend to think of relationships in *contractual* rather than *covenantal* terms.

The only official covenant that remains in our culture is marriage, and even this is increasingly being treated like a contract instead of a covenant. This is extremely unfortunate, for, as we're about to see, there is a world of difference between the two. The most basic difference is that a contract is a legal arrangement made *between* people, while a covenant is a pledge of *trust* that *involves the people themselves.*

To illustrate, if you purchase a car from a car dealer, you sign a contract that guarantees the dealer that you will give a certain amount of money in exchange for the car you're purchasing. The transaction is between you and the dealer, and the thing that guarantees that he or she will be paid is not the trustworthiness of your character but the legally binding force of the contract. If you fail to make the payments called for in the contract, law enforcers will simply come and repossess your car. In a contractual arrangement, we see, people place their trust in the binding force of the contract *rather than in each other.*

By contrast, when two people exchange wedding vows, they are (at least in the traditional understanding of marriage) entering into a covenant in which they pledge their very lives to each other. They are entrusting the overall quality of their lives to each other. Their futures become inextricably woven together. In biblical terms, they become "one flesh."

The trust of two people entering into marriage is clearly *in each other*, not in a legal document. And if one of them turns out to be untrustworthy, the harm done to their spouse, their family, their friends and children, and ultimately to society as a whole, is something that no legal enforcer could ever recover.

I hope it's becoming clear that, though covenants and contracts may look similar on the surface, they're actually worlds apart. In fact, covenants are not only different from contracts; in some respects they're *opposites*. People enter into covenants because they trust one another; people enter into legally binding contracts precisely because *they don't*. And while covenants are based on people pledging themselves *to* one another and are by nature *other*-oriented, contracts are based on people feeling the need to protect themselves *from* one another and are by nature *self*-oriented.

In this light, it's not at all surprising that when people today read Scripture with a contractual rather than a covenantal mind-set, it distorts everything, including the Bible's teaching on faith. And when you add to that the modern mistaken tendency to identify faith with belief and to assume that a person's faith is as strong as they are certain, the potential for significant misunderstandings is even greater, as we're about to see.

The Covenantal God

While people today relate to one another almost exclusively through contracts, people in biblical times related mostly through covenants. This is why we find that, throughout the biblical narrative, God enters into covenants, not contracts, with people. While the specific terms of each covenant vary, each involves God pledging himself to people while calling on them to trust him and to demonstrate a trustworthy character in living up to the terms of the covenant.

Some of the covenants God enters into are formally announced while others are simply assumed, but they all involve faith—which means, they all involve a pledge of trust and trustworthiness. The first formal covenant between God and humans was made immediately after the flood. God spelled out to Noah the behaviors he expected of humans while promising to never again flood the earth (Gen. 9:1–16). Following this, God entered into a covenant with Abraham and his descendants (Gen. 15; 17); then with Moses and the Israelites on

Mount Sinai (Exod. 20–31); and then with King David, given through the prophet Nathan (2 Sam. 7:4–16). Finally, and most beautifully, God entered into a covenant with everyone who is willing to accept it through Jesus's sacrificial death on the cross. I'll say more about that covenant in a moment.

The Court-of-Law Framework of Theology

It's not going too far to say that the entire biblical narrative is woven together around the concept of covenant. Yet, because we live in a contractual rather than a covenantal culture, we tend to read this narrative as though it were woven together by contracts.

Actually, we can't place the blame for this entirely on our modern culture. The truth is that there's been, almost from the start, a strand within the Western theological tradition that has tended to conceive of our relationship with God in legal terms, where contractual concepts are more at home than covenantal concepts. To the best of my knowledge, this tradition began in the second century with Tertullian, who, not coincidentally, was trained in Roman law before he became a theologian.

Within this legal strand of the Western theological tradition, God is viewed primarily as a judge, humans are thought of as guilty defendants, and Jesus is conceived of as a sort of defense attorney. Within this court-of-law framework, the atonement (that is, what Jesus accomplished on the cross) is construed as a sort of legal loophole that our defense lawyer worked out with the judge that somehow gets us off the hook by allowing the Father to punish him instead of us. And our salvation, purchased by Jesus's substitutionary death, is envisioned as an acquittal that allows us to avoid being sentenced by the Judge and consigned to prison (hell) forever.

"What's wrong with *that*?" some readers are undoubtedly wondering? "That's the very view I was taught!" Well, it's not entirely wrong. The New Testament does use some legal metaphors in describing God and our relationship with him. For example, God is depicted as a judge. Jesus is once referred to as our advocate before God (1 John 2:1). And the atonement is several times expressed in quasi-legal terms (e.g., Rom. 3:25; Heb. 9:15). At the same time, these legal metaphors are conceived of within a broader and more dominant covenantal context, which I'll flesh out in a moment.[2]

What began happening after Tertullian within the legal strand of the Christian tradition is that these metaphors began to be interpreted literally and became increasingly important, while the broader covenantal context was increasingly lost. The result was that our relationship with God came to be thought of more and more in terms of a legal contract rather than primarily as a marriage-like covenant.

Still, the court-of-law model of theology continued to play a subsidiary role in the thinking of most theologians within the Christian tradition until certain influential Protestant Reformers like Martin Luther and John Calvin made it a centerpiece of their theology in the sixteenth century. It's again no coincidence that, like Tertullian before them, both Luther and Calvin studied law before becoming theologians. Under their influence, the legal way of framing theological topics became much more prominent, especially among Protestants. And when this court-of-law framework was fused with the contractual mind-set of modern Western culture, as well as with the mistaken identification of faith with belief, it created what I consider to be a perfect storm of legal theologizing. And one of the storm's most damaging effects had to do with our understanding of faith.

A Litany of Legalities

You can see the pervasiveness of the court-of-law paradigm for theology in the sorts of questions Christians tend to ask. For example, I can't tell you how many times people have asked me to specify exactly what they need to believe in order to be "saved." Some have seriously wondered if a person who denies biblical inerrancy or who denies the earth was created in six literal days can be "saved." A religious television personality recently suggested on his show that I was going to hell because I disagreed with his interpretation of hell, and I've several times heard people suggest that I and anyone else who denied the "penal substitution" interpretation of the atonement were at least likely not saved.[3] And, most disconcerting of all, as our country has become increasingly politically polarized over the last several decades, I've encountered more and more people who seriously question the salvation of sisters and brothers in Christ who espouse different political opinions![4]

I'm not suggesting there is no legitimate place for reflecting on who is and is not encompassed by the salvation offered us in Christ—though I think it's worth noting that no one in the New Testament ever claimed to know that another human was damned.[5] My purpose is rather to call attention to the court-of-law framework these questions presuppose. God is a judge, we are defendants, salvation is about staying out of prison, and what is at issue in each question or accusation are *the specific terms* of a contract *between* God and us that allow us to remain acquitted and thereby stay out of prison. The focus of these questions has nothing to do with the trustworthy *character* of God or of us. And this is precisely why each question assumes that faith (which in Scripture is all about character) is the same as our Western view of belief (which is a mere mental conviction).

Other questions and concerns Christians commonly raise today reflect the same framework. If I had a quarter for every time I've been asked about "eternal security," for example, I'd be a fairly wealthy man. Can a person lose their salvation? If so, what are the specific conditions for this disqualification? What specific sins can cause one to become unsaved? And, as I mentioned in chapter 2, many have wondered how much doubt is permissible before their acquittal is revoked. Exactly how close to the certainty bell must one be able to hit the faith puck to stay saved? All these questions presuppose that our relationship with God is determined by our adherence to the specific terms of a legal contract.

The same holds true of the multitude of legal-type questions that I and other pastors regularly get about what exactly constitutes a particular sin. To no one's surprise, at the top of the list are questions about what technically constitutes "fornication." How far can a couple go before they've "crossed the line"? I've met a significant number of unmarried people who have convinced themselves that, so long as a couple stops short of vaginal penetration, they have not technically had "sex." It took me quite a while to accept that certain unmarried couples were not joking when they would tell me some of the sexually intimate things they do while allegedly avoiding "sex"—some of which would make many married couples blush! But they're serious! This is what happens when people frame their relationship with God in terms of a legal contract. Reasoning like clever lawyers, they assume that if the acquittal-contract doesn't explicitly close a loophole they've uncovered, they have the "right" to take it with impunity.

When Paul warned the Corinthians to "flee from sexual immorality" (1 Cor. 6:18), I kind of doubt he meant, "see how close you can get without crossing the line."

Treating the Bible like a Legal Textbook

One more thing I'd like us to notice is that when Christians try to answer these sorts of legally framed questions, they typically do so by appealing to particular Bible verses. It is, of course, appropriate and necessary to respond to questions by appealing to Scripture. But when we pose our questions in a legal way, we inevitably end up using the Bible in a legal manner—that is, like a legal textbook. But since biblical authors wrote in covenantal rather than contractual terms, their writings don't serve our legal purposes very well.

Not surprisingly, people often find that for every list of verses they've compiled to answer a question one way, someone else has compiled a different list to answer the same question a different way. A classic example is the earlier-mentioned issue of eternal security. There are about an equal number of verses that people appeal to in order to prove that people can or cannot lose their salvation.[6]

This is why debates that are framed within the legal paradigm of theology are often exercises in futility. Each person cites the list of verses that each thinks supports their side of the debate. Then, like two lawyers sparring in a courtroom over legal precedents that support or refute their respective cases, each offers alternative interpretations of the other's verses, followed by a refutation of their opponent's alternative interpretations, followed by a refutation of each other's refutation, and so on.

Done in the right spirit, debates like this can be educational and fun. Unfortunately, the spirit with which they are often conducted is closer to the atmosphere of a courtroom. And far from being fun, in conservative circles this is the standard method used to differentiate orthodoxy from heresy and, on "doctrines necessary for salvation," to differentiate the saved from the lost. Moreover, because these debaters typically get *life* from the rightness of their beliefs, as we've said (chap. 2), these debates generally are more hostile than they are educational. It's impossible for people to sustain a calm and rational discussion when their idolatrous source of *life* hangs in the balance.

One almost gets the impression from this line of questioning and arguing that God's primary concern was to form a kingdom of the world's most competent lawyers. So he inspired the Bible to serve as a textbook of legal conundrums to separate the sharpest legal wits from the incompetent, with the latter group becoming fuel for hell's fires.

The Real "Good News"

My point is that when our relationship with God gets framed in terms of a legal contract, people are inclined to treat the Bible like a confusing litigation manual, the purpose of which is to resolve technical theological disputes and clarify ambiguities surrounding the terms of our contractual acquittal before God. All of this presupposes a picture of God as a judge who leverages people's eternal destinies on how well they can litigate theological disputes or at least on how lucky they were to align themselves with a competent expert (a pastor/teacher) who correctly interprets this legal manual.

Is *this* the "good news" Jesus and his earliest followers were so excited about proclaiming?

Not by a million light years! As we've been saying, God isn't interested in entering into a legal contract with us; he wants a profoundly interpersonal, covenantal relationship with us that is characterized by honesty, trust, and faithfulness. Along the same lines, salvation isn't primarily about receiving an acquittal so we can avoid prison when we die. As we said in chapter 3, it's about participating in the abundant life and ecstatic love of the Triune God, and doing so now, *in this life*.

In keeping with this, if we understand it in biblical terms, faith isn't primarily about our beliefs—as if God were an academic who was obsessive about whether you arrive at the right intellectual conclusions. Even less is faith about engaging in psychological gimmickry as you try to suppress doubt to convince yourself your beliefs are the right ones so that you can feel accepted, worthwhile, and secure before God. Rather, as we're going to see, faith is about trusting in the beautiful character of Christ as our heavenly husband, about being transformed from the inside out by the power of his unending love, and about learning how to live in the power of the Spirit as a trustworthy spouse who increasingly reflects his love and his will "on earth as it is in heaven."

This, friends, is the *real* "good news." Let's dig a little deeper to flesh out just how good it actually is.

Betrothed to the Beloved

The Bride of Christ

As I mentioned earlier, the final covenant God enters into in the Bible is the one he makes with us through Jesus Christ. It's called the "new covenant" (Luke 22:20; Heb. 9:15), and it's extremely significant that one of the main ways the New Testament expresses this covenant is in terms of a marriage.

Tapping into the imagery of Yahweh as Israel's husband that runs throughout the Old Testament (e.g., Isa. 54:4; Jer. 3:14; 31:32; Ezek. 16:32; Hosea 2:7, 16), the New Testament depicts Jesus as the heavenly bridegroom who came to earth in search of a bride (e.g., Matt. 9:15; 25:1–13; John 3:29). In keeping with this theme, Paul depicts all who belong to the church as being betrothed to Christ (Eph. 5:25–33; cf. Rom. 7:4; 1 Cor. 6:16–17; 2 Cor. 11:2–4), and the book of Revelation depicts the church—that is, the collective body of all who say "yes" to the bridegroom's proposal—as the "bride" of Christ who will feast at a wedding festival when the Lord returns (19:7, 9; 21:2, 9; 22:17). The marriage-like nature of the new covenant is reflected in a number of ways throughout the New Testament, though we need to understand a little about ancient Jewish marriages to pick up on them. Because this is so central to the New Testament's concept of faith, it will be well worth our time to flesh this out a bit.

The Betrothal Period

In ancient Jewish marriages a couple was *legally* married for a year or two before they had a wedding and became *fully* married, at which point they consummated their marriage through sexual intercourse and by beginning their life together. Only at this time did they enter the "one flesh" relationship that lies at the heart of the biblical concept of marriage (Gen. 2:24). The period leading up to a couple's wedding and consummation was known as the "betrothal" period.

The betrothal period was a time in which the husband and wife worked on acquiring the skills and character they would need in their future life together. Other women typically mentored the betrothed wife, while the betrothed husband would often go away to secure an income and build a home for his wife and future family, if this was necessary.

This is the state Mary and Joseph were in when Mary supernaturally conceived Jesus, which explains why she was still a virgin even though she was legally Joseph's wife (Matt. 1:18) and why he would have needed to divorce her to terminate their relationship, which he planned on doing until the angel informed him of how she got pregnant (Matt. 1:19).

It's clear in the New Testament that the church—the "bride of Christ"—is currently in this betrothal period, waiting for our heavenly bridegroom to return. This is reflected in Jesus's statement to his disciples that he needed to "[go] and prepare a place for you," promising that he would "come back and take you to be with me that you also may be where I am" (John 14:2–3). While he is gone, we who are his corporate bride are to be making ourselves ready so that when Jesus returns he will find a "radiant" bride who is "without stain or wrinkle or any other blemish, but holy and blameless" (Eph. 5:27). We are to be clothing ourselves with a radiant wedding gown that is woven together by the "righteous acts of God's holy people" (Rev. 19:7–8; cf. 21:2).

These are simply different ways of saying that we are to be demonstrating our trustworthiness as Christ's bride as we prepare for our future, eternal, co-ruling life with Christ in the kingdom (2 Tim. 2:12; Rev. 5:10; 20:6; 22:5). Jesus's parables of the wise and foolish virgins are intended as warnings to those who would be part of his betrothed bride about the need to be prepared for his return (Matt. 25:1–13).

Baptism and Communion

The betrothal period of ancient Jewish marriages began with a ceremony and feast that officially inaugurated and celebrated the new betrothal covenant and that served as a foretaste of the future, more elaborate wedding ceremony and feast. It's my conviction that our betrothal ceremony is baptism, in which a person signifies their personal identification with the death and resurrection of Jesus and by this means is incorporated into his collective bride (Rom. 6:1–10; 1 Cor.1:13; 12:13; Gal. 3:26–29). And it's my conviction that our betrothal feast is communion, by which we celebrate our betrothal to Christ and anticipate our wedding ceremony that includes the much more grand "wedding supper of the Lamb" (Rev. 19:9).

Not only this, but whenever God established a new covenant with people, he gave them a "sign" to help them remember it. The rainbow became the sign of God's covenant with Noah, for example, while circumcision became the sign of God's covenant with Abraham. Our betrothal meal also serves as our covenantal sign, which is why we are instructed to remember him and the price he was willing to pay to acquire us as his bride whenever we share communion together (1 Cor. 11:24–25). By this means we are reminded of Christ's pledge of covenantal love and fidelity toward us, expressed in his broken body and shed blood. And by this means we renew our covenantal pledge to Christ, which is to demonstrate our fidelity to him by following his example and loving others with the same self-sacrificial love he has extended to us (e.g., Eph. 5:1–2).

The Gift of the Spirit

A final example of the way the marriage-like covenant with Christ is reflected in the New Testament concerns the way it talks about the Holy Spirit. Newly betrothed husbands in the ancient Jewish world would typically give their betrothed brides a gift before "going away to prepare a place" for them. This gift served as a promissory pledge that they would return as soon as all preparations were in place.

The promissory betrothal gift that Jesus and his Father give us is the Holy Spirit. In the covenantal framework of the New Testament, the very fact that the Spirit is repeatedly referred to as our "gift" suggests this (e.g., Acts 2:38; 10:45; Eph. 1:13–14). It is even more strongly reflected in Paul's declaration that the gift of the Spirit is our "deposit guaranteeing our inheritance until the redemption of those who are God's possession" (Eph. 1:13–14; cf. 2 Cor. 1:22; 5:5).

Jesus also speaks of the Holy Spirit in ways that indicate that the Spirit is our betrothal gift. For example, soon after he told his disciples that he was going to prepare a place for them, Jesus said: "If you love me, keep my commands" (John 14:15). He was, in essence, instructing them to demonstrate their love as a faithful bride while he was away. But he immediately assured them that they would not have to do this on their own, for once he left, he said he would "ask the Father, and he will give you another advocate to help you and be with you forever—the Spirit of truth" (vv. 16–17). While other married women typically mentored betrothed Jewish girls, as I said above, it's evident that Jesus intended our "helper" to be the betrothal gift he was giving us, for he told his disciples the Spirit "will teach you all things and will remind you of everything I have said to you" (v. 26).

What's particularly beautiful about this betrothal gift is that the Holy Spirit is none other than the *Spirit of Jesus* (Acts 16:7; Rom. 8:9; Phil. 1:19). In fact, immediately after promising his disciples that "another advocate" would come (John 14:16), Jesus added, "*I* will not leave you as orphans; *I* will come to you" (John 14:18, emphasis added). We see a reflection of the mystery of the Trinity in these teachings inasmuch as Jesus personally identifies with the Spirit while also referring to him as distinct from himself. This unity-in-distinction between the Spirit and Jesus is something we find elsewhere in the New Testament (e.g., Rom. 8:9–10). But the bottom line is that, even though our betrothed husband has *physically* departed to prepare a place for us, he has, nevertheless, in some beautifully mysterious sense, given us *himself* as a betrothal gift.

Not only this, but the Greek word that is translated as "orphans" (*orphanos*) in John 14:18 doesn't refer only to parentless children. It can refer to anyone who is discomforted, which is why many translations have "comfortless" or "desolate" instead of "orphans" (e.g., KJV, RSV, ASV). In this light, it's apparent that our heavenly groom has given us himself not only as a betrothal gift but also as a way to comfort, mentor, and empower us to live as a faithful betrothed spouse while we wait for his return.

Married Salvation

This, folks, is what it means to be "saved." When we place our trust in Christ and pledge our life to him, we are saying, "I do!" to his marriage proposal, offered to us on the cross. We are made members of his corporate bride who is destined to share in the love of the Triune God throughout eternity and to co-rule with her husband in the age to come. We won't consummate this marriage until Jesus returns to establish God's kingdom on earth in its fullness, but until this time we aren't to merely be waiting around for this to happen. No, in this betrothal period, we're to be learning how to be the faithful, radiant bride Jesus came to redeem.

Among other things, we are to individually and corporately use this betrothal period to work with the Spirit and encourage one another to be increasingly freed from the "pattern of this world" and conformed to Christ's likeness (Rom. 12:2). As a bride who is destined to co-rule with her husband, we're to be exercising the authority we've been given in order to grow the mustard seed of the kingdom that Jesus planted with his life, death, and resurrection (Matt. 13:31–32). This involves us working with the Spirit to live lives of love that battle the fallen principalities and powers (Eph. 6:12), just as Jesus did, and that gradually take back for our groom every aspect of the world that humans were originally commissioned to have "dominion" over but that was surrendered in the fall (Gen. 1:26–28).[7]

We start by working with the Spirit to take our thoughts captive to Christ (2 Cor. 10:5). By this means we are to then bring our behaviors under God's loving reign, which in turn allows us to influence our relationships, society, and even nature in a kingdom direction. And we are to be practicing for our future reign with Christ by exercising the spiritual authority he's given us to impact all these areas through prayer.[8]

All this is part of what it means to be "saved," and how impoverished the acquittal concept of salvation looks by comparison! This is why the way that the New Testament talks about salvation is so different from the way contemporary Christians tend to talk. Christians today typically talk about salvation in the past tense. "When *were you* saved?" I often hear people ask. But the New Testament talks about it in three tenses: we *were* saved (e.g., Rom. 8:24; Eph. 2:5), we're *being* saved (1 Cor. 1:18; 2 Cor. 2:15), and we *shall be* saved when the Lord brings this age to a close and sets up the full reign of God (Rom. 5:10; 1 Cor. 3:15).

This makes no sense if you think of salvation as a contract, but it makes perfect sense once you realize that salvation is about our marriage to Christ. We *were* saved when we initially responded to Christ's proposal, made on the cross, by saying, "I do," as we pledged our life to him. We *are being* saved as we learn how to yield to the abundant life of God abiding within us and as we are being transformed into the radiant bride Jesus is coming back for. And we *shall be* saved, in the fullest sense of the word, when he returns and we appear with him "in glory" (Col. 3:4). At this time, John declares, we will finally "see him as he is," for "we will be like him" (1 John 3:1–3).

A Commitment to Live Faithfully

My hope is that this chapter has helped us see how radically different the Bible's covenantal model of faith is from the certainty-seeking, contractual faith that is so prevalent today. Both involve believing certain things to be true, but the focus of the two models is entirely different. Certainty-seeking faith is a *psychological model* focused on what is going on *inside a person's head*. The issue addressed by this model is, how certain do you feel about this or that belief? By contrast, the New Testament's covenantal model is focused on what a person *does with their life* and on the condition of their *relationship with God*.

As we'll discuss in the following chapter, psychological certainty is inconsequential to the covenantal understanding of faith. The only thing that matters is that a person is *confident enough* of their beliefs *to act* on them. And whereas certainty-seeking faith motivates people to strive for certainty, thereby creating all the problems we've discussed, the covenantal model motivates people to commit to a course of action *in the face of uncertainty*.

Our heavenly bridegroom has proposed to us by giving his life for us on the cross. We say, "I do," to this proposal and enter salvation by placing our faith in him. This faith presupposes that we believe that the one who was crucified some two thousand years ago was God's Son, but this belief is not itself faith. We exercise saving faith when we *act on* this belief by committing to live as a trusting and trustworthy bride. And while there was a moment when we first made this pledge (when we *were* saved), this past pledge is significant only insofar as we're faithfully living it out in the present (we're *being* saved). The important question, therefore, is not, Did you once pledge your life to Christ? The important question is rather, Are you honoring the pledge you made to Christ by living as a trustworthy spouse *in the present*?

Embodied Faith

You only truly believe that which moves you to action.
—Douglas Cheney

Faith without deeds is dead.
—James 2:26

I'm hoping that this chapter helps us see how the psychologically focused understanding of faith, combined with the legal way of framing theology, is at the root of most of the struggles that serious Christians have with faith while at the same time ensuring that most professing Christians won't take their faith very seriously. In fact, for reasons that will become clear in a bit, I believe this misguided view of faith is one of the greatest challenges facing the church in America today. We'll see that the covenantal understanding of faith addresses this problem while also providing us with a new and helpful way of reframing doubt. Faith is not just something located in our heads. It is an active and vital thing that can be identified by the way we live our lives. And this is better news than you can probably imagine.

The Visibility of Faith

Don't Listen; Watch

One of my favorite philosophers is the nineteenth-century "father of pragmatism," Charles Peirce. Peirce was a bit of an eccentric, and he had a rather messed up life, but he was absolutely brilliant. Though it doesn't seem Peirce took the Christian faith very seriously until the later part of his life, he offers some remarkable insights into the nature of belief, and they happen to intersect very well with what we've been learning about the biblical concept of faith.

People often think of beliefs as if they were mental objects floating around in our head, existing independently from our embodied life in the physical world. If this were the case, you could presumably have a belief that could have no possible implications for how you live. Peirce saw this notion as mistaken. He argued that each and every belief is actually a "rule of action."[1] *What it means* to believe something, in other words, is that a person would respond to a certain circumstance in a certain way if it were to arise. Hence, if a person isn't willing to act in a way that reflects their belief, they don't *really* believe it, even if they claim they do.

Suppose you're on a bus and a lady sitting next to you informs you she's a physician. As you chat, this doctor casually shares with you that she's been studying a flu virus that could hit at any moment and that will likely prove fatal for about 40 percent of those who contract it. Even worse, she tells you that she has learned that this flu is terribly contagious and will probably infect upward of 70 percent of the population.

Trying to contain your panic, you ask if there is a vaccination for this flu strain, and she says that yes, there is, and there's plenty to go around. You feel a flood of relief and make a mental note to schedule an appointment with your doctor to be vaccinated as soon as possible. Then, out of curiosity, you ask the doctor if she has already received the vaccination, to which she nonchalantly responds, "Nah."

What conclusions would you draw from this response? Assuming you were confident that this lady was not suicidal, you'd have no choice but to conclude that this doctor doesn't *really* believe the things she just told you. For if she believed what she told you, she'd obviously do everything she could to protect herself. As Peirce said, a belief that is truly believed is a belief that a person is willing to act on when circumstances call for it.

Living Faith and Dead Faith

The idea that our beliefs are revealed in our choices and behaviors is related to James's teaching that "faith without deeds is dead" (James 2:26). What James is *not* saying is, "Your faith is not enough. You also need to add on a bunch of good works!" Rather, he's making the observation that if you say you have faith, yet do not make choices and engage in behaviors that reflect this faith, there's simply no *life* in your professed faith. The truth is, faith is functionally indistinguishable from the choices and behaviors that naturally flow out of it.

Claiming to have faith while living a life that does not bear witness to this faith is like claiming a corpse is alive despite the fact that it has no pulse and no brain activity. Living humans have pulses and brain waves just as people with faith in Christ's lordship are motivated to follow his teachings and his example. Jesus once asked people, "Why do you call me, 'Lord, Lord,' and do not do what I say" (Luke 6:46)? He was simply pointing out that these people were contradicting themselves. *What it means* to relate to someone as "Lord" is that you submit to that person. A confession of faith in Christ's lordship that doesn't result in a pulse that beats obedience is a "dead" confession of faith.

Another way of making this point is to say that a covenantal faith is *by definition* a faith that involves action, for a covenant is by definition something a person *commits to* and *lives out*.

Observing Faith in Action

Another indication that living faith always involves action is that Scripture sometimes speaks of faith as a visible thing. So, for example, the Gospel of Mark tells the story of a group of guys who brought a paralyzed friend to Jesus with the hope that Jesus would heal him (Mark 2:1–5). Unfortunately, the home Jesus was preaching in was already full. So these clever fellows climbed up on the roof, carrying their paralyzed friend with them. Then they ripped a hole in the roof so they could lower their friend down on a mat.

When "Jesus saw their faith," Mark says, he responded by announcing that this man's sins were forgiven and then by healing his body (Mark 2:1–12). What Jesus "saw" was not an internal thing, as though he were looking into the psyche of the man's friends to see how far up the "faith pole" these guys were slamming their "faith puck." Rather, what he saw was the great lengths these men were willing to go to see their friend healed.

Observing a Faith That Persists

Something similar can be observed in Jesus's parable about how we "should always pray and not give up." This parable is about a widow who persistently knocked on the door of the unjust judge until he finally agreed to grant her justice just so she would leave him alone (Luke 18:1–5). Obviously, Jesus wasn't suggesting that God is like the unjust judge; he is rather saying that our prayers should be like this persistent widow.

And then, most importantly, and somewhat ominously, Jesus concluded his teaching by asking, "When the Son of Man comes, will he find faith on the earth?" (Luke 18:8). Coming on the heels of this parable, it's clear that Jesus was wondering if he'd find people manifesting their faith by engaging in prayer that was as persistent as this woman was in getting her case heard. This again demonstrates that the kind of faith that constitutes a relationship with God is a faith that, by definition, involves action and that can therefore be seen.

Getting Real with Faith

Honestly Examining Faith

It's evident that, according to the New Testament, a faith that is alive is always a faith that is *visible*. As Peirce understood, this is a principle that applies far beyond our relationship to Christ. And sometimes light can be shed on our relationship to Christ by exploring how this principle works outside this relationship. So let's return for a moment to the topic of marriage.

Suppose I want to honestly evaluate how I've been doing as a husband. I want to know if I've been faithfully helping Shelley to feel loved, cherished, and honored, and if I've been caring for her in sickness and in health and providing for her needs, as I vowed on our wedding day. To determine this, should I look within myself to explore what I believe about Shelley and how certain I feel about these beliefs? Not if I'm truly wanting to know how I'm doing, for we all know how easy it is for us to fool ourselves about things. If I *really* want to know how I'm doing, the best way would be to look at *my behavior* and ask, have I been *doing* what I promised I'd *do*? In fact, an even more reliable indicator would be to ask *Shelley* and perhaps *others* who observe our relationship to give me their honest perspective.

Of course, if I'm only really concerned with *feeling* like I'm *already* a good husband, I should avoid this kind of honest feedback. It might mess up my "I'm a great husband" idol. If this is all I'm interested in, then I'm better off looking within myself at what I believe and how certain I feel about these beliefs. But to know the truth of how well I'm keeping my covenantal vows, my focus must be on what is visible. For whether we're talking about our relationship with God, our marriages, or our friendships, covenantal faith is always *visible*. It's *living*. It *acts*.

Faithfulness and Community

Giving honest feedback is one of the roles fellow disciples are supposed to play within the body of Christ, according to the New Testament. This is how the bride is supposed to be making herself ready as she waits for her bridegroom to return.

If we are serious about growing as people who faithfully manifest the reign of God in our lives, it's absolutely essential that we be in relationship with people whom we love and trust enough to "[speak] the truth in love" (Eph. 4:15) and who love and trust us enough to invite us to do the same. There are, in fact, a multitude of "one another" commands in the New Testament, and each one reflects the sort of loving, committed, and honest relationships that disciples need to have with one another. These verses also reflect an assumption found throughout the New Testament, namely, that the quality of our relationship with Christ is closely associated with the quality of our relationships with others within his body.

Unfortunately, the rampant individualism of Western culture has made this essential, communal aspect of the kingdom lifestyle prescribed in the New Testament all but nonexistent in the modern Western church. To the degree that people conform to the Western version of "the pattern of his world" (Rom. 12:2), they assume they have "the right" to spend their time and money however they want and to reflect whatever attitudes and engage in whatever behavior they want, and no one has "the right" to tell them otherwise. Indeed, because of this demonically self-centered individualism, most Western people live in ways that block others from even knowing about, let alone speaking into, the details of their lives.

Western people today may have *acquaintances*, but few have relationships that even remotely approximate the honest, vulnerable, committed, covenantal relationships that weave the body of Christ together in the New Testament. Related to this, while the New Testament views the church as a community of people who unite around a mission, who spend significant amounts of time together in study, worship, and ministry, and who help one another become "fully mature in Christ" (Col. 1:28; cf. Eph. 4:13; James 1:4), most Westerners assume church is a place they go to once a week to sit alongside strangers, sing a few songs, and listen to a message before returning to their insulated lives.

So too, whereas the New Testament envisions the bride of Christ as a community of people who convince the world that Jesus is for real by the way our unity reflects and participates in the loving unity of the Trinity (John 17:20–23), the Western church today has been reduced to little more than a brief gathering of consumers who are otherwise unconnected and who attend the weekend event with hopes of getting something that will benefit their lives. From a kingdom perspective, this individualistic and impoverished consumer-driven view of the church is nothing short of tragic, as is the perpetual immaturity of the believers who are trapped in it.

If we are serious about our covenant with Christ, we have no choice but to get serious about cultivating covenant relationships with other disciples. There are no individual *brides* of Christ. Jesus is not a polygamist! There is only one corporate bride, and what it means to be betrothed to Christ is that we are each joined to this one bride.

Moreover, this "joining" is not an ethereal reality, as though we could be "joined" by virtue of the fact that we merely share some beliefs and sentiments with others. Rather, just as covenantal faith is inherently visible, so too our connection to the covenantal community is inherently visible. Indeed, the visible way we engage in the "one another" covenantal commitments of the New Testament is one of the key ways our individual and corporate faith is made visible.

When Marriage Vows Become Dead Idols

Throughout the remainder of this chapter I'll be using the marriage covenant as a way to help us appreciate the stark difference between covenantal faith and what passes for faith today. In the end I'll also use the marriage analogy to highlight the unique way covenantal faith frames doubt as something that can benefit faith rather than something that is an enemy of faith.

I should warn you ahead of time that some readers may find some of this material a bit confrontational, while others may be alarmed by the implications of what I'm saying, if in fact my observations about what passes for faith today are correct. I assure you that my intention is not to shame anyone or to be yet another Chicken Little running around shouting, "The sky is falling!" My goal is to simply describe the radical difference between covenantal faith and the dead, contract type of faith many hold today, despite the fact that they may look the same on the surface. And I'll simply let the alarming implications of what I'm saying speak for themselves.

However you react to this material, I encourage you to press on. For if my description is in fact accurate, and if you find that I am describing your faith as I describe what often passes for faith today, it means you are currently missing out on a treasure God offers all who join themselves to his corporate bride. It's the treasure of participating in God's abundant life, and it is accessed only by entering into, and growing in, a marriage-like covenantal relationship with Christ.

I'll first flesh out some insights surrounding what passes for faith today by sharing a story of a husband and wife in a deeply troubled marriage that I encountered a number of years ago. Following this,

I'll share some of the struggles I've encountered in my own marriage and talk about what those struggles have taught me about faith and doubt.

Meet Carol

In a healthy marriage, the husband and wife feel secure in their relationship because the relationship is actually healthy. Both parties in healthy marriages arc faithfully living out in the present the pledges they made on their wedding day. But I've encountered husbands and wives in bad marriages who felt secure in their marriages simply because their partner made a *legally binding pledge* to them in the past, with no regard for how they themselves are fulfilling their own pledge to their spouse in their day-to-day lives.

One of the most memorable examples of this attitude was someone I'll call Carol. Carol was an attractive, middle-aged woman who was quite frankly one of the most angry, miserable, hate-filled people I've ever met. Carol and her husband (whom I'll call Harry) were married in a strict fundamentalist Baptist church fourteen years earlier. About a year before the encounter I'm describing, Harry had, for a number of reasons, decided to leave this church and had started attending the church I pastor. Carol attended with him a few times but soon returned to her home church.

The first time I met Carol was on her final visit to my church. We were chatting by ourselves in the gathering area after the service when Carol suddenly pointed a finger at me and in a bitter, self-righteous tone, told me that, unlike her church—"the church Harry *should* attend"—Woodland Hills "doesn't preach the whole counsel of God." I didn't bother to inquire what she meant by that.

What I rather wanted to discuss was the possibility of sitting down with her and Harry to talk about their marriage. Carol didn't know this, but as a last-ditch attempt to save their marriage, Harry had asked for this, not so much to counsel them, for I'm not a marriage counselor, but to try to encourage Carol to agree to counseling—something she'd refused to do for years. As a way to stress the importance of meeting together, I gently broke it to Carol that Harry was contemplating leaving her.

I was surprised at Carol's response. She actually laughed! "Don't you care?" I asked. "Oh I care," she said, nodding her head while continuing to chuckle. Then the bitter tone returned when she said, "God *hates* divorce and there's no way this could ever happen to us!"

"But Carol," I replied, "it takes two to be married, and I'm telling you Harry is at his breaking point." "Look," she said, "you're supposed to be a pastor, right? So I'm thinking you should probably know this." I had to start praying mental blessings over Carol at this point to keep my anger in check. "My husband made a solemn promise before God to be married until death, and that was for better or for worse!" She sarcastically offered to send me a copy of their marriage certificate as proof.

I began to respond, but Carol immediately cut me off. "My Harry would never seriously consider divorcing me," she said. I remember being struck by the insinuation that she owned this poor man. "Harry is too committed to God's Word and, frankly, *way* too much of a coward to ever break a vow he's made to God! The man can't stand up to a fly," she said with a chuckle. And just in case she hadn't been rude enough to me, Carol continued on to inform me, in a loud enough voice for others standing nearby to hear, "If you're half the man of God you claim to be, you ought to be putting Harry in his place if he so much as utters the d-word!"

I spent the last few minutes of our unpleasant conversation trying first to persuade Carol to allow me to sit down with her and Harry, and then, when she refused this, simply encouraging her to go to a counselor with Harry. She dismissed my suggestion, calling counseling a "humanistic replacement of the Word of God." Harry ended up leaving Carol within a week and divorcing her within the year. He told me Carol and her church had pronounced God's judgment on him for breaking his solemn vow and had pronounced judgment on me for not demanding that Harry return to his wife.

Replacing Marriage with a Pledge of Marriage

It was clear to me that Carol was finding security in the fact that she and Harry had pledged their lives to each other fourteen years earlier rather than in the marriage they pledged to have. The covenantal pledge that binds people in marriage is a pledge *to live a certain way*, and life is always lived *in the present*. But rather than treating her pledge like a covenantal promise and giving it meaning by faithfully living it out in the present, Carol was treating her pledge like a legal contract and finding its significance in the sheer fact that it is legally binding.

Carol was, in fact, replacing the marriage she pledged to have with the legal fact that she and Harry had made this pledge. And this is precisely why Carol anchored her security in her marriage in a past pledge rather than in the actual relationship she pledged to have.

Insofar as Carol's past pledge didn't point beyond itself to the relationship it was supposed to create, Carol's pledge was *dead*. But insofar as the pledge actually replaced the relationship it was supposed to create, her pledge was *worse than dead*: it had become an idol. Carol was, in effect, having a legal relationship with their pledge rather than a covenantal relationship with Harry, to whom she had made her pledge.

The truth is, the only faithful way of feeling secure in our marriages is to invest in the *actual relationship* that we pledged to pursue when we entered into our marriage covenants. And the very fact that a person, such as Carol, would find security or any other significance in the *mere fact* that they entered into a legally binding pledge (she had a copy of the marriage certificate as proof!) is evidence that they are being *unfaithful* to their pledge.

The Tragedy of Carol-Like Faith

One of the most unfortunate consequences of the legal theological paradigm that is so prevalent today is that it inclines people to think about their faith in contractual rather than covenantal terms, just as Carol thought about her marriage. Like Carol, people are inclined to think that the most significant thing about their past pledge to Christ is that it is *legally binding*, as if they had entered into a *deal* with Jesus when they prayed the sinners' prayer or some such thing. And so, like Carol, they are inclined to feel secure in their "salvation" because of the sheer fact that they made this pledge, and entered into this "deal," at some point in the past rather than in the fact that they are actually living out their pledge by surrendering their life to Christ *in the present*.

Whenever this happens, a life-transforming covenantal relationship has been replaced by an illusory cheap deal. The fullness of *life* that is salvation in the New Testament has been exchanged for a shallow postmortem acquittal. And the living covenantal faith of the New Testament has been replaced by James's "dead" faith. As Carol did in her marriage, people imprisoned in this version of Christianity end up exchanging a genuine relationship *with God* for a relationship *with the idol of a legally binding pledge.*

Who Are We Kidding?

Yet another unfortunate consequence of the legal theological paradigm is that, because it locates the significance of our pledges in the past rather than the present, it makes it easy for people to deceive themselves about what they *really* believe. As I noted earlier, this is something we are all inclined to do. We convince ourselves we believe one thing while our actions, if we pay attention to them (or even better, invite *others* to pay attention to them), might reveal that we actually believe something quite different.

I can't count the number of times I've seen this played out between couples that come to me for marriage advice. These couples *say* they love each other and that they desperately want their marriage to work, but their treatment of each other sometimes tells a very different tale. I've seen a man talk about the "holiness" of his "vows before God Almighty" in one breath while he demeaned and belittled his wife in front of me in the very next breath. I've seen men who physically intimidate and harm their wives to get them to "submit" to their "God-given authority" while insisting that their motivation is love. Carol is another case in point. She did not display even the tiniest bit of love or respect toward Harry, but she waved around the dead idol of her marriage certificate as proof of the legitimacy of their godly status as husband and wife.

It was in the self-interest of these individuals to convince themselves they were loving, faithful, and righteous, though their behaviors betrayed a very different reality. And the primary reason for this self-delusion, I submit, was that they were viewing their marriage within a legal paradigm—as a contract, rather than as a covenant. For as

I noted in the previous chapter, contractual thinking always orients people toward their own self-interest and tends to pit people against one another as they fight for their "rights."

By contrast, covenants are, by their very nature, always other-oriented. And when a couple lives out their covenant pledge to love and serve each other, it allows them to experience a rich depth in their relationship that contracts can never produce. It also considerably lessens the opportunity for conflict precisely because the two are free of the contractual obsession with protecting their self-interests and their "rights."

I'm not suggesting that couples should always be examining their behaviors to determine how well they're living out their covenant vows. I'm merely describing the disastrous consequences and delusional thinking that legal paradigm thinking can produce. A marriage that is held together only by a legal document is a corpse disguised as a living being. But a marriage that is held together by other-oriented love and covenantal bonds will shine in comparison. A marriage based on covenantal trust will not always be easy, but it will be living and growing. We'll get to that in a bit.

A Crisis of Immunized Faith

A Faithless Christianity?

My concern is that the legal paradigm of theology that dominates the thinking of Christians in the West, and especially in America, has led many to embrace a dead, contractual "faith." The clearest proof of this is that research reveals that most Americans' profession of faith has almost no impact on their lives.[2] Most who profess faith in Christ spend their time and money almost exactly the same way non-Christians do, and most reflect the same materialistic and individualistic values and priorities as non-Christians. Which is to say, it seems the faith of most professing American Christians is, quite literally, invisible.

I'm concerned that we have, to a frightful degree, traded our marriage covenant for a legal contract that we think acquits us. And because this contract-type acquittal is granted to us "by grace"—and "grace," within a legal paradigm, is interpreted to mean, "no cost"—people generally assume that their acquittal contract has no necessary impact on their lifestyle. This is why, when someone (like myself) comes along and points out that the New Testament teaches that a disciple's life is supposed to be transformed as they are incorporated into the bride of Christ, they are often accused of preaching "salvation by works."

It is, of course, very true that salvation is given completely by grace. No one can or needs to earn or merit one iota of love or acceptance by God. But God's grace is not a mere acquittal; it also empowers us to live a Christlike life. So too, salvation is not avoiding the destructive consequences of our sin: it's rather about participating in the full *life* of God and therefore growing out of the sin that leads to destructive consequences.

Moreover, faith is not mere belief, as we've seen, but a willingness to act on our beliefs by trusting our Lord and committing our life to him. And our relationship with God is not an individual, private affair. It is a covenantal relationship that includes truth-speaking, covenantal relationships with others within the corporate bride of Christ.

The transformation that salvation by grace brings about is a process, of course. We are part of a bride who is *learning* how to yield to God's transforming grace and who is *making herself* ready. We all have ongoing sin struggles of one sort or another. We are all "works in progress." And so we all stand only by the mercy and grace of God. This is why the New Testament speaks of salvation in present and future tenses instead of simply in the past tense, as we noted in the previous chapter.

Even so, if the abundant life of God is truly flowing into us, there will be *some* signs of this life, however faint. What is of concern, however, is that this is what is largely missing in American Christianity, according to the above-mentioned research. While only God knows whether any *individual* is alive or dead, this research into how professing Christians actually live makes it hard to deny that the church *as a whole* looks rather dead.

Just Enough Truth to Pass

I have thus far argued that the contemporary contractual understanding of faith and of Christianity as a whole is radically different from the New Testament's covenantal understanding of faith and its vision of the kingdom of God. I would now like to take this a step further and suggest that not only is contractual Christianity radically different from the kingdom of God, it is, I believe, the kingdom's *greatest obstacle*.

Why does being "Christian" in America make so little difference in so many people's lives, when the kingdom movement revealed in the New Testament revolutionized people's lives? This drastic difference is hardly surprising when you consider that the gospel that people are often given today is little more than a contract of acquittal that is signed by praying the sinner's prayer or some such thing. Nor is it surprising that this powerless version of the gospel *absorbs* rather than *confronts* the culture of the people who sign this contract. Within this gospel, people give their mental assent to certain beliefs and are thereby ushered into a "kingdom" that looks almost identical to the earthly kingdom they were supposed to be called *out of*. They can keep all their cultural assumptions, and, apart from avoiding certain behaviors that are singled out as the deal-breaker sins, their lives can continue on just as before.

All who are invested in the kingdom Jesus inaugurated in this world must find all of this deeply disturbing. What is even *more* disturbing, however, is that this contract Christianity seems to function for many like an immunization shot. When a person is immunized against the flu, they receive just enough of the flu virus to trick their body into acting as if they had the real thing so that they build up a *resistance* to the real thing. So too, there is just enough truth in this certainty-seeking, contractual, belief-oriented, individualistic version of Christianity to trick people into thinking they have the real thing. They thus aren't open to, or hungry for, *true faith* because they assume they already have it when they simply *believe*.

Like Carol, whose security was in her marital pledge rather than in the quality of the relationship she pledged to have, many people today resist the need to cultivate an actual *marriage-like relationship* with Christ because, as I noted earlier, they find their security in their past *pledge*. They prayed "the sinners prayer," got baptized, affirmed the "doctrines essential to salvation," or did whatever their church requires. So long as they retain a sufficiently strong faith—that is, a faith that is sufficiently free of doubt—they believe these things permanently guarantee they're okay with God. When they did these things, they were told, the Judge accepted the sacrifice of his Son as the payment for their crimes, they were acquitted, and that is the end of the matter.

The transition from the covenantal paradigm to the legal paradigm and from covenantal faith to mere beliefs preserves just enough of a kingdom exterior to pass for the real thing. But what is easily missed when matters are construed this way is that the kingdom is all about cultivating an actual *life*-giving relationship with God, and this can only be done moment by moment, for life can only be lived, and relationships can only be cultivated, in the present. Surface resemblances notwithstanding, the legal paradigm easily misses the *life* flowing out of the covenant relationship with the King that defines the kingdom of God.

Am I Saying Most Americans Are Lost?

At this time, a little caveat may be called for. I imagine some readers may be wondering: "Is Boyd actually suggesting that the majority of American Christians are not saved?" If you were wondering this, I'd like you to reflect for a moment on the framework that is presupposed by your question. I strongly suspect your question is premised on the very legal paradigm I'm arguing against. For, so far as I can see, it is this legal paradigm alone that forces questions about the legal prerequisites for being "saved" or for staying "saved."

If you think of God as a judge and salvation as acquittal, then when I point out that masses of professing Christians are immunized against the real kingdom because they confuse covenants with contracts and faith with beliefs, it will sound as if I have just altered the legal conditions of our acquittal and that I'm thereby claiming that a large mass of people fail to meet these conditions and are therefore going to hell.

I am, in fact, making no such claim, for I'm not talking about the legal conditions of an acquittal. Indeed, while people who participate in the abundant life of God need never worry about their destiny, any more than a person in a good marriage needs to worry about divorce, I don't believe it is anyone's right or responsibility to entertain any opinion about the destiny of those who show little to no signs of God's life within them, whether they profess faith in Christ or not.

To be clear, as I said above, there is an important place for disciples to "speak the truth in love" with fellow disciples *with whom they have entered into a covenant relationship*. Outside of these sorts of covenantal relationships, however, I believe we are to have no opinions other than the one Paul expressed when he said he "resolved to know nothing except . . . Jesus Christ and him crucified" (1 Cor. 2:2). This is why Paul elsewhere said that, as a leader of kingdom communities, he must, when necessary, confront antikingdom behaviors in the lives of those he was responsible for. But he immediately added, "What business is it of mine to judge those outside the church" (1 Cor. 5:12)?

Regarding all people who have not invited us to speak into their lives, therefore, I encourage followers of Jesus to collapse all judgments and to instead simply remind ourselves that we have one mandate, which is to agree with God that the person we're viewing has unsurpassable worth as evidenced by the fact that Jesus died for them. And, in fact, the loving feedback we give one another in our covenant relationships should be free of judgment as well. For there's a world of difference between loving *discernment* exchanged in the context of a covenant relationship and *judgments* that can only be destructive to both parties.[3]

I therefore trust it's clear that I have no interest in spending one moment speculating about who will ultimately end up where. Yet, as a leader and teacher in the kingdom, I have a great deal of interest in distinguishing *what is* and *what is not* the kingdom. And this is what I have been doing as I've contrasted, as clearly as I know how, the covenantal faith that characterizes the kingdom with the contractual belief that characterizes so much of American Christianity today.

Covenantal Faith and Doubt

Covenantal and Contractual Struggles

Using Carol as our example, we've seen what happens in marriages when vows that are treated as legally binding contracts fail to keep the spouses together. I'd now like to bring this chapter to a close by contrasting this with what can and should happen when a couple faces conflict while regarding their marital vows to be the covenantal promises that they actually are. We'll see that this highlights the way a covenantal understanding of faith frames doubt very differently from the way it's framed when people embrace a contractual view of faith. And the marriage I'll use as an example is my own.

Like most marriages, ours hasn't always been easy. The truth is, Shelley and I have gone through some profoundly difficult stretches of conflict and alienation. But our struggles were always covenantal, not contractual, in nature. That is, we didn't ever argue over the precise wording of our wedding vows or engage in lawyer-like searches for legal precedents to prove whose interpretation of our vows was right, the way some Christians, operating within a legal paradigm, use the Bible. Nor did we ever wonder how much we could get away with before the other would petition for a divorce, the way we've seen some Christians, working within this same paradigm, wonder about "eternal security," as we saw in the previous chapter.

Along the same lines, Shelley and I have never tried to anchor our security in our marriage on the fact that many years ago we made a promise to stay married, the way Carol did, as we saw above. And never did Shelley or I explore ways we could feel justified cheating on each other, the way we've seen some Christian couples, thinking like good lawyers, gerrymander to find loopholes around the precise meaning of "fornication" or some other sin. This is the way legal *contracts* are disputed, but any couple that treats their marriage this way, and any Christian who treats their relationship with God this way, is in a precarious, unhealthy, unwise, and unbiblical place.

When I say our struggles were covenantal, what I mean is that we engaged in them with the same *commitment to act* that we entered into when we first said, "I do."

Giving Our Marriage the Benefit of the Doubt

Everyone who knows us well knows that Shelley and I are wired *very* differently. They say that "opposites attract," and if ever this was true of a couple, it is true of us. For example, Shelley is an extrovert who would prefer to be around people every waking moment. I, on the other hand, have a nearly compulsive need to be alone for long stretches at a time. So too, I am a compulsive reader, while Shelley hardly ever enjoys a book. In fact, on just about every aspect of a personality profile, Shelley and I are at opposite ends of the spectrum. Our differences are so vast that there have been times when it seemed that about the only thing we had in common was our children and our faith.

Not surprisingly, there have been many times when one or both of us have felt misunderstood, unappreciated, unloved, and even betrayed. And on top of all this, to be perfectly honest, there have been periods in our marriage in which Shelley and I simply didn't do a very good job of demonstrating covenantal love and trust toward each other. In all honesty, this is much truer of me than it is of Shelley (and no, I didn't just write that because Shelley will probably read this book!).

The main way I failed to demonstrate covenantal love and trust was that, as our vast differences surfaced in the first year of our marriage, I resigned myself to the conclusion that Shelley could never possibly understand, let alone appreciate, my inner world. While I felt lonely, as did Shelley, this actually wasn't as hard for me to accept as you might think—and certainly not nearly as hard as it was for Shelley. For while I wouldn't learn this about myself until fifteen years later as Shelley and I finally faced the void together, I had as a young child concluded that my inner world was too strange for *anyone* to ever understand. It turned out that the innermost self of the guy Shelley married had long before retreated to a fortified castle on a tiny island in the middle of a vast ocean.

As I just intimated, our marriage took a radical turn as we headed into our sixteenth year of marriage. We had done the best we could holding things together while dancing around the elephant in the room of our marriage, but as our children were growing up and becoming more independent, the elephant became undeniable. Shelley and I decided to face what had previously been too scary to face. We mustered up the courage to get brutally honest with each other, to look into the void, and to confess how hopelessly alien we seemed to each other.

What followed was, frankly, several months of hell. Honestly, the only thing that kept us together was the promise we made to each other and to God that we would never quit our marriage. It's not that we appealed to our vows as a legally binding contract, the way

Carol did. We simply took our covenantal pledge to hang in there "for better or for worse, until death parts us" seriously. And because of this, we decided that, as followers of Jesus, we had no choice but to try to find a way to make our marriage work.

Two aliens *had* to find a way to get on the inside of each other's strange worlds. We found that the very fact that we shared the pain of this alienation, as well as the difficult challenge of finding a way out of it, bonded us together. And it was in the process of trying to help Shelley navigate the maze of my inner world that I discovered that I'd been living in an island castle since childhood. The beauty of relationships forged in covenantal love, whether they're with our spouse or simply with deep friends, is that we learn more about our own souls as we learn how to touch the soul of another.

Our commitment to find a way of bridging the void between us turned this lowest point of our marriage into a marvelous opportunity to discover a depth of love we'd never dreamed possible. And because of this, I can now testify from my own experience that, regardless of how different two people may be and how far apart they may feel, if both parties are willing to work on it—that is, willing to *act* in ways that express their commitment—they *can* learn to get inside each other's foreign worlds and *can* discover a profound and deeply rewarding love for each other.

This isn't a flippant "Jesus-saves-marriages" pep talk. This is a truth Shelley and I have learned through a lot of blood, sweat, and tears. And I'm not saying this will be easy. When people are as different as Shelley and I, I promise you, it is *not*. It may require outside help from friends and/or a professional counselor. Shelley and I relied on both. And I'm also not saying it is *ever* easy sailing. Shelley and I continue to have to work at understanding each other and communicating with each other. But I am telling you it *can* be done so long as both people are willing to keep striving to fulfill their covenantal pledge to each other.

Wrestling "from the Inside" of the Covenant

I share this not just to give encouragement to struggling marriages, though that's never a bad idea. I rather do so because it illustrates the true nature of covenantal faith and faithfulness. They're not about how much certainty or doubt you have in any given moment. They're not about what you may or may not be feeling at any given moment. And they're certainly not about leaning on a legally binding contract in the past. Covenantal faith and faithfulness are rather about your commitment to honor a covenantal pledge by how you live in the present. And they apply to our covenantal relationship with God through Christ as much as they do to our covenantal relationship with our spouse and/or with our close friends.

We enter the new covenant with God and are betrothed to Christ when we pledge to trust him to be our Savior and promise to live a life that is surrendered to him as Lord. Perhaps you feel 100 percent certain Jesus is Lord, or perhaps you're at present only slightly more convinced he is Lord than that he is not. This is of no consequence so long as you remain *confident enough* of this belief to commit to living *as if* it is true. As is true of our earthly marriages, it is the commitment to *faithfully act* on our beliefs for the rest of our lives that forges the covenant, regardless of how certain or doubtful we are of the beliefs we are committed to acting on.

So long as both spouses remain committed to their covenantal vows, whatever issues they wrestle with from this point on are wrestled with *from the inside* of the covenant rather than as a *precondition* to entering the covenant. And so it is in our relationship with Christ. I'll discuss this at length in chapters 8 and 9, but for right now I'll simply note that, so long as we remain confident enough that Jesus is Lord to commit to living *as if* he were Lord, then whatever doubts and questions we have about other theological, spiritual, or personal issues can and should be wrestled with *from the inside* of this covenantal commitment rather than as a *precondition* for entering into, or staying within, it.[4] Never should our doubt or confusion about any other issue be allowed to jeopardize or qualify in any way this all-important commitment that constitutes the heart of the kingdom.

This is not to minimize the importance of these other issues. They can be important for any number of reasons. As we've seen, for example, our theological understanding of God, of faith, and of salvation can positively or negatively affect our walk with God. Moreover, as we'll discuss in chapter 11, our theology of providence, of suffering and evil, and of what we are to trust God for can help or hinder our relationship with God, as well as our ability to help others who are in crisis. Such matters are clearly important, but they should be struggled with from the inside of our covenant with God and never allowed to jeopardize it.

The Freedom to Be Concerned with Truth

Not only does getting honest with our questions and doubts not jeopardize our covenantal relationship with God, when we struggle with them from the inside of our covenant relationship, they can actually *help it*. For example, when Shelley and I finally quit trying to dance around our alienation out of fear that confronting it might dissolve our marriage, we were finally able to face the truth, explore the reasons for our alienation, and begin to do something about it. We found that, as is true of all relationships, the quality of our relationship was dependent on our ability to know and affirm *the truth* about each other.

So too, when our sense of security before God is anchored entirely in our commitment to live as the betrothed bride of Christ, and when we are therefore no longer trying to get *life* by convincing ourselves our beliefs are true, we are freed to honestly explore whether our beliefs are *in fact* true. As we saw in chapter 2, when too much hangs on being right, we can't entertain the possibility that we're wrong, which means we can't be genuinely concerned that we're right. The freedom to doubt our beliefs within the context of our covenant with God positions us to not only be more truthful about ourselves before God, but to also be more open-minded and objective in our reflections about our beliefs and our understanding of God's Word.

The Map Is Not the Territory

Moreover, when our confidence before God is derived completely from our trust that God is revealed in the crucified Christ and our commitment to live as if this is true, regardless of our level of certainty, we are better able to remember that "the map is not the territory." This is a popular psychological maxim that simply expresses the fact that our interpretation of a thing—our "map"—is not identical to the thing we interpret—the "territory." We are inclined to forget this and to instead assume that our maps *are* the territory. And to the extent that we do so, we are not able to effectively communicate with and learn from other people's maps. If we assume our map *is* the territory, then people who see things differently than we do are simply *wrong*.

When Shelley and I finally got honest about the reality of our relationship, we found that our maps were so different, it seemed as if they were of *completely different* territories! To learn how to get on the inside of each other's maps, which is what all effective communication is about, we had to constantly bear in mind that our maps were *not* the territory. And the process of learning how to get inside each other's maps—which, as I've already acknowledged, is a process that continues to this day—has stretched our own ideas about the world and about each other. It has also proved to be incredibly rewarding, not only for our relationship together, but also for each of us individually. It was by this means, for example, that I learned I had from early childhood moved my inner self to an inaccessible island castle. In coming to know another profoundly, we come to know ourselves more profoundly.

Hindering Communication with Others

One of the most unfortunate consequences of certainty-seeking faith is that, because it rewards people for feeling certain they're right and discourages people from questioning their perspectives, it conditions people to insist that their maps *are* the territory. People who embrace this kind of faith will be more inclined to assume that their *interpretation* of a biblical verse is the *meaning* of the verse itself. So to disagree with their interpretation is to disagree with *the verse itself*. In fact, the mind-set that this model of faith produces inclines people to forget they're interpreting at all. As an angry man told me in a theological dispute some years ago, "I don't *interpret* the Bible. I just *read* it!"

Certainty-seeking faith thus discourages people from cultivating the ability to remain aware of the important distinction between their map and the territory. But unfortunately, as Shelley and I learned, remaining aware of this distinction is the only way to effectively communicate with people who see things differently from the way you do. It's not surprising, therefore, that Christians and other religious people who embrace certainty-seeking faith typically have trouble effectively communicating with people whose views significantly conflict with their own. Nor is it surprising that they tend to view the world in black-and-white, right-and-wrong, and us-and-them categories. When you can't acknowledge the significant gulf that exists between your map and the actual territory, things tend to appear perfectly obvious. The world is neatly divided up into those who see it *rightly* and those who see it *wrongly*. And the ones who see it rightly are the ones who agree with me, and the ones who see it wrongly are the ones who see it otherwise.

Moreover, since the truth is obvious to people who forget that their map is not the territory, when you disagree with them, the suspicion will be that you're either blinded by sin or motivated by something other than a desire to know truth. This is why conservative Christians tend to have a reputation for becoming accusatory, resorting to ad hominem arguments, and being intolerant. In our increasingly pluralistic world, the inability to accept that no one's map is identical to the territory and that any number of people can sincerely espouse conflicting maps is a great liability. Indeed, as I discussed in chapter 2, it has throughout history proved to be positively dangerous.

Hindering a Relationship with God

For all the same reasons certainty-seeking faith disables people from relating well to people who have different perspectives from their own, it unfortunately also disables them from relating well to God, whose perspective is always very different from our own. People who share a deep, healthy relationship with another, whether it be with their spouses or close friends, discover that there is always more to learn about the one they love, and they discover there is a profound joy in engaging in this unending process. But to remain open to further insights into another person requires us to always remain open to modifying our maps.

If this is true of our relationships with other people, how much more true must it be of our relationship with our Creator? Through Isaiah the Lord tells us his ways and thoughts are further above our own than the stars in the heavens are above us on the ground (Isa. 55:8–9). Yet, if a person has habitually clung to their map as if it were the territory itself—and especially if they have done so as a means of feeling worthwhile, significant, and secure—they will not be open to, let alone seeking, what God may want to share with them regarding his mind, his ways, or his Word.

What could be more tragic? For if there's anything we know about the God who revealed his glory by bearing our shame and his holiness by bearing our sin on the cross, it's that the one true God is the God of the *unexpected*. While the self-sacrificial, loving character that God revealed on the cross is always the same, he is nevertheless a God who remains beautifully mysterious even after he's made himself known. Yet we can only be genuinely open to always going deeper in our relationship with God and to receiving unexpected insights if we hold our maps in a flexible way, always remembering that our map of God is never the territory. If our security is in our map *about* God rather than in *God himself*, as revealed on the cross, we simply cannot leave the safety of our own shore to embrace the untamed beauty of a God for whom no map is ever fully adequate.

The Benefit of Doubt within the Safety of Covenant

A true and living faith is never a destination; *it's a journey*. And to move forward on this journey we need the benefit of doubt. There's a kind of doubt that is appropriate as we're making our way toward a covenantal relationship with Christ, for we need to rationally decide what and who we're going to base our faith on (see chap. 8). Otherwise our faith commitment is determined by nothing more than chance. But the kind of doubt I'm presently talking about is doubt that struggles *on the inside* of our covenantal relationship with Christ.

Exploring doubts in this covenantal context allows us to be honest, open, and as objective as possible as we work through issues without fear that the covenant itself hangs in the balance of how we resolve them. And the freedom to explore these kinds of doubts makes us adept at remaining humble as we remember that our maps are always limited and tentative, whether we're talking about our relationship with God or with other people.

With our confidence in the loving, self-sacrificial character God displays on the cross, exploring doubts can free us to honestly explore our map of *ourselves*. Knowing how easy it is to be self-deceived, this kind of doubt creates a space that allows us to examine—or to ask others to examine—the extent to which our faith is visible. It thereby allows us to explore whether we really believe what we say we believe. So too, by freeing us to question our own perspectives, getting honest about our doubts makes us more adept at communicating with others whose perspectives differ significantly from our own.

Finally, and most importantly for our purposes, this kind of doubt empowers us to better relate to God, whose perspective is always further beyond our own than the stars are beyond us. As Shelley and I learned as we embraced the scary truth of the gulf that separated us while committing to work together to bridge it, doubts that we explored within a covenant commitment allowed us to wrestle toward an ever-deepening, increasingly intimate relationship with another. Doubt isn't an enemy of covenantal faith. It's a much-needed companion.

If you're among those who have felt the need to try to avoid doubt and strive for certainty, if you are among those whose security has been wrapped up in a commitment you made at some point in the past that you thought "sealed the deal" between you and God, or if you are one of those many who embraced the idea that faith is an invisible thing that has no necessary connection to how you live, day in and day out, maybe it's time you consider a reframe. Maybe it's time to let go of the legal deal and embrace the covenantal relationship. Maybe it's time to get married.

This commitment requires your all, and it requires it every day. But it offers you everything, and you will enjoy it throughout eternity.

Part 3

EXERCISING FAITH

8

A Solid Center

It is your work to clear away the mass of encumbering material of thoughts, so that you may bring into plain view the precious thing at the center of the mass.

—ROBERT COLLIER

For no one can lay any foundation other than the one already laid, which is Jesus Christ.

—1 CORINTHIANS 3:11

In part 1 we looked at a mistaken, though widespread, view of faith. In part 2 we explored the biblical, covenantal concept of faith. In the final section of this book I'd like to offer some suggestions I hope will help us effectively, and biblically, practice faith—*and doubt.*

A Tumbling Edifice

A Walk down Memory Lane

A friend of mine funds a halfway house for Christian men in recovery by selling used books online. The halfway house's financial situation was looking grim, so I decided it was time to thin out the library I've accumulated over the last forty years. I combed through my library and got rid of every book I felt I'd likely never again need, giving away a total of more than 2,800 books. (Talk about a nice tax write-off!)

Sifting through my collection was a walk down memory lane. I was amazed at the power older books had to evoke memories. Like all of us, I often find that certain sights, sounds, and odors evoke particular memories. But I've never had such a wealth of long-forgotten memories so vividly conjured up, and in such detail! When I came to an older book in my library, I paused for a few moments to peruse it and read some of the comments I wrote in its margins. (Then, as now, I passionately interact with my books by writing on almost every page.) This is why it took me two and a half days to complete a task that would otherwise have taken a couple of hours. And as I read each comment, I could often recall the exact moment I penned it: where I was sitting, what I was drinking or eating, what I was thinking, and even what I was feeling.

Reviewing the books I'd read during my foray into fundamentalism was also quite amusing. I giggled, and was almost embarrassed, when I read various passionately scribbled notes I'd written in response to various authors' views on an assortment of topics I now find irrelevant, if not silly. My young mind saw eternal significance in issues surrounding evolution; the rapture; the tribulation period; "liberal" translations of the Bible; the historicity of Job, Samson, and other biblical characters; the contradictions between the Gospels; and a host of other topics. It was a fascinating reminder of how much my faith has evolved over the years.

The Need for a Different Paradigm

This is how it should be. Any faith that is alive must evolve. As my dearly departed friend Clark Pinnock used to say, theological reflection is a pilgrimage in which change should be celebrated, not feared.[1] I feel sorry for those who feel the need to cling to and protect an inflexible theology on the fear-based and arrogant assumption that, in contrast to all who disagree with them, they just happened to have received "the whole truth and nothing but the truth."

When I reflect back on the version of the Christian faith I was given in the early years of my walk, I'm almost surprised that my faith survived. I deeply appreciate the sincerity and passionate commitment of the friends I made when I first became a Christian. And, as I've shared, I had some amazing experiences with God in this Pentecostal church. But the faith I was given was an inflexible and fragile teetering tower of assumptions that was bound to come tumbling down as my knowledge of the complex world expanded.

As I've shared, it wasn't long before it did come tumbling down. In fact, it came down again a number of times in the years that followed. I doubt I'd be a follower of Jesus today were it not for the fortunate fact that, through this painful cycle of theological breakdowns, I eventually found an alternative way of practicing faith—a way that allowed me to simultaneously be grounded in my relationship with Christ while being creatively adaptive with my theology.

I was fortunate, but the majority of young people who encounter intellectual challenges to their faith or who simply encounter a world that is more complex and ambiguous than their faith can handle are not. As I pointed out in the introduction, four out of five college-bound young people end up leaving the church by the age of twenty-two.

It's tragic because it is *entirely unnecessary*. The problem is not that the Christian faith cannot stand up to critical scrutiny. The problem, I believe, is with the way Christians are typically taught to intellectually ground their faith and with the inflexible way most are taught to embrace their theology. Neither is any longer sustainable in the challenging, pluralistic, and highly ambiguous postmodern world in which we live.

In this chapter I'd like to discuss an alternative way of intellectually grounding our faith, as well as a flexible way of structuring our theology.

A "House-of-Cards" Faith

Have you ever seen a really intricate house of cards? They are structures that are erected by leaning playing cards against one another. Some are amazingly elaborate and can reach impressive heights.[2] They're never very sturdy, however. The house as a whole depends on each and every card staying in place. If any card is removed, the whole thing collapses.

This is quite a bit like the way my early faith was held together, and I've found that it's more or less the way most evangelicals embrace faith. While the fundamentalist church I came to Christ in acknowledged that there were certain beliefs that were "nonessential to salvation" and were thus okay to disagree over, we had a host of beliefs that we insisted were absolutely crucial. If any of these were removed, the whole edifice of our theology flattened out like a pancake.

The same thing can be applied to Scripture. As you may recall, I was taught that if the earth was not created in six literal days and if Adam and Eve were not literal, historical people, then the whole Bible may as well be a book of lies. Flick this one card out, and the whole structure of faith collapses. When I began to question how old the earth was and how humans came into being, I may as well have been calling into question the historical existence of Jesus!

And the same thing applied to every single passage of Scripture. Since we were taught that it had to be absolutely "inerrant" to be God's Word, our faith in it could be destroyed by one verse being proved to contain a mistake. The Bible was itself a house of cards.

One of the reasons I was able to eventually find my way back into the faith after my first house of cards crumbled was that I found a way to embrace the essence of Christianity while also embracing a degree of ambiguity about creation and evolution, as well as about the discrepancies and archeological problems I was beginning to discover in the Bible. Still, though my restored faith was less vulnerable than my previous house-of-cards faith, it was *still a house of cards*. I simply knew of no other way of structuring my theology. From my crumbled old house I simply built a smaller, somewhat less vulnerable structure.

Not surprisingly, as I continued to study and my worldview continued to expand, it was just a matter of time before a card in my rebuilt house got knocked out, bringing my house to the ground once again. Because I had been through this once before, this collapse wasn't nearly as devastating as my first crash, but it was nevertheless painful. I soon managed to reassemble my remaining theological cards and rebuild a still smaller, and therefore less vulnerable, house. But as I continued to study and grow, it was just a matter of time before the same thing happened again . . . and again.

I would venture to guess that this cycle repeated itself about a dozen times throughout graduate school and the early part of my teaching career. It's not that I lost my faith each time this happened. But in each instance I confronted a problem in my belief system that forced me to rethink my whole theology from the ground up. I eventually began to think that this unpleasant cycle would perhaps never end. Perhaps, I thought, this is simply the fate of any Christian who refuses to stop critically exploring issues.

It wasn't any catastrophe or divine revelation that changed this. I don't even recall a distinct moment when I consciously adopted the approach I'm about to share. But at some point I began to see that the problem was not merely that I hadn't yet found the "right" structure with the "right" set of "unflickable" cards, as it were. The problem, I began to discern, was that there was something fundamentally amiss with this fragile way of doing theology.

It was this insight that eventually led me to embrace a completely different way of grounding and framing my theology.

The Foundation of Christ

The Case for Christ

The all-important center of the Christian faith is not anything we believe; it's the person of Jesus Christ, with whom we are invited to have a *life*-giving relationship. It will likely surprise some readers to hear this, but please hang with me while I explain myself. Everything began to change for me several decades ago when I began to realize that I didn't need to rely on the Bible as the inspired Word of God in order to enter into this relationship with Christ. Rather than believing in Jesus *because I believe the Bible to be the inspired Word of God*, as evangelicals typically do, I came to believe the Bible was the inspired Word of God *because I first believe in Jesus*. This is how I now encourage people to structure their faith, for I have found it to be a much surer intellectual foundation for my faith than the conviction that Scripture is the Word of God.

Here's how I arrived at this perspective. From years of researching and wrestling with this material, I discovered I have compelling reasons for believing that Jesus is the incarnation of God that *have nothing to do with the belief in the inspiration of Scripture*. Some of my reasons are *philosophical* in nature. For example, I find the biblical worldview that is centered on a Creator who has the loving character that Jesus reveals makes better sense of my total experience of the world than any competing story or theory. Some of my reasons are *existential* in nature. For example, the story of the God of unsurpassable love who went to the furthest extreme possible to save a race of hopeless rebels "rings true" in the deepest part of my being. It is, in the words of C. S. Lewis, the greatest myth ever told, though unlike all other myths, this one gives us reason to believe it actually happened![3] And some of my reasons are more *spiritual* in nature. For example, I have on occasion experienced Christ in ways that would make it extremely hard for me to deny his reality.

Yet the most compelling and most objective reasons I have for believing in Christ are *historical* in nature. To illustrate one example in its simplest and most succinct form, no one disputes that a movement of people who came to be called "Christians" exploded in the third and fourth decades of the first century. It says a lot that by AD 64 this movement had become so widespread throughout the Roman Empire that Nero could make a scapegoat out of Christians by blaming a citywide fire in Rome on them.

From the earliest documents, we know that these early Christians proclaimed that Jesus lived a scandalously loving life, even befriending prostitutes and other "sinners." They proclaimed that he made divine claims about himself and performed a multitude of miracles. And they proclaimed that Jesus died a cursed death on the cross, rose from the dead, and was, in some spiritual sense, still with them. The disciples proclaimed this in a largely hostile environment, at great cost to themselves (most of them were martyred or exiled), about a man who lived in the recent past (indeed, his mother and brother were in their company), and, at least initially, in the same region where he ministered. And, most surprisingly, we know that something motivated these earliest disciples to overturn one of the most fundamental aspects of their Jewish, monotheistic faith by ascribing divine attributes and activities to this man and by worshiping and praying to him!

The all-important historical question is, *What can explain all of this?*

There is no difficulty explaining this if we accept that these disciples were simply telling the truth. For the purpose of explaining what needs to be explained, we don't need to insist that their presentation is historically accurate on every point or that it is entirely devoid of legendary accretion. We need only accept that their testimony is *generally* reliable. If, generally speaking, Jesus lived the way they said he lived, made the claims and performed the miracles they said he performed, and died on a cross and then appeared to them, as they claimed, we can understand why they would have said these things about him, why they would have put their lives are risk by proclaiming their message about him, and why they would have allowed their Jewish faith to be overturned by treating this man as God. If we do not accept that their proclamation is generally true, however, we must provide an alternative explanation for this proclamation and this behavior.

One possibility is that these disciples were simply lying. This is a difficult thesis to defend, however, for there is absolutely no motive for them to do this. Nor is there any evidence that they had the sort of character that would make them capable of this. It's also hard to see how they could have pulled off this hoax even if they had the motive and character to do so. They were proclaiming a message that was heretical in the eyes of Jewish authorities and who would have had little trouble exposing it as a fraud, if, in fact, this is what it was. For good reason, few serious New Testament scholars opt for this possibility.

The only remaining possibility, however, is that these disciples sincerely believed they were preaching the truth, but they were mistaken. The Jesus they proclaimed was largely, if not entirely, a legend. My friend Paul Eddy and I have carefully examined every scholarly version of this hypothesis, and our conclusion is that every one of these legendary theories is highly problematic.[4] Among a multitude of other considerations, it's very hard to see how a legend about a person who was God and human could have gotten off the ground in such a short period of time, when this man's mother, brother, and friends were yet alive and were in the company of those who worshiped him.

Not only this, but as with the lying hypothesis, it's hard to see how such a heretical legend could not have been exposed as such, given that there were multitudes of Jewish authorities who would have been motivated to do so. On top of this, the story these disciples tell is antithetical to what we'd expect of a legend in this social setting. And finally, the story these disciples tell in the Gospels lacks virtually all the telltale signs of legends (unless, of course, one assumes that any report of a miracle is by definition legendary).

While a great deal more could be said in support of this argument, I trust this suffices to demonstrate that the case for accepting that the historical Jesus roughly corresponds to the portrait these disciples give in the Gospels is extremely compelling. And notice, I have not appealed to Scripture *as the inspired Word of God* to make this case. We, of course, must rely largely on the Gospels and the Epistles to know what these earliest Christians believed, but the case I've just made doesn't require us to assume these documents are inspired. It only requires us to critically assess them the way critical historians would assess any other ancient documents.

When I combine these historical considerations with the above-mentioned philosophical, existential, and spiritual reasons for believing in Christ, I feel I am on as solid ground as anyone could hope to make a rational decision about what they are going to base their worldview on and what they will pledge their ultimate allegiance to. I have over the years thoroughly explored and taught college courses on all the various religions and philosophies humans have espoused throughout history, and I have to confess that, while one might always wish for more evidence and stronger arguments, I find the case for embracing a worldview centered on Christ to be much stronger than any case that can be made for embracing any competing worldview that could conceivably make a claim to my ultimate allegiance.

Am I *certain* of this? Of course not. It requires faith to accept that the historical Jesus roughly corresponds to the portrait painted by the earliest Christians. But it also requires faith to believe that their portrait is either fraudulent or substantially legendary. And as I assess the matter, I have more reasons to embrace the former faith than the latter. So while I cannot be certain, I am *confident enough* to commit to living my life on the basis of my belief that Jesus Christ is the definitive revelation of God. And, most importantly for our purposes, I'm absolutely convinced that the case I've just made for believing in Christ provides a much stronger intellectual foundation for our faith than does the belief that the Bible is the inspired Word of God.

A Foundation of a Person, Not a Book

It also seems to me that this way of grounding our faith is more appropriate to the faith we hold. For in this approach, the foundation of our faith is centered on a person, not a book. Whereas Islam has always presented itself as a "religion of the book," the kingdom of God has been from the start a movement that is centered *on a person.* The only foundation that can be laid, Paul says, for example, is "the one already laid, which is Jesus Christ" (1 Cor. 3:11). Jesus is, in the words of Peter, the "cornerstone" that "the builders rejected" (1 Pet. 2:6–7; cf. Eph. 2:20), which means that the entire edifice of the Christian faith is to be built *upon him.*

The earliest disciples certainly believed the Old Testament was inspired, but they never based their faith in Christ on this. They used it extensively, but only as a means of pointing people to Jesus, whom they *already* believed in *for other reasons.* This is the role that I believe the Bible, which now includes the New Testament, should play in our lives. For reasons I'm about to share, I agree that we should affirm Scripture's divine inspiration, and I believe we should use it to point people to Jesus. But for reasons that will also become clear in a little bit, I think it cannot bear the weight, nor was ever intended by God to bear the weight, of being the foundation for *why* we believe in Jesus.

Hence, I don't see beliefs rooted in Scripture as an end in and of themselves. They rather point us to Jesus and help bring us into, and strengthen us in, our relationship with Jesus. The moment we begin to think that Scripture or our beliefs are ends in and of themselves, we are in danger of making an idol of Scripture and our beliefs.

The Authority of Scripture

From Christ to the Bible

When the plausibility of our faith rests on Christ rather than Scripture, it changes our basis for believing in Scripture and alters the nature of our struggle with difficult aspects of Scripture. To begin, I'd like to return to and explain my earlier comment that, rather than basing our belief in Jesus on our belief in the inspiration of Scripture, we should instead base our belief in the inspiration of Scripture on our belief in Jesus. The logic behind this claim is straightforward enough.

On the basis of historical, philosophical, personal, and spiritual considerations, I believe that Jesus is the definitive revelation of God, as I've just argued. Yet the identity of the Jesus I now place my faith in is inextricably wrapped up in the narrative of God's dealings with Israel found throughout the Old Testament. He is, in fact, the center and culminating point of this narrative, and it's actually impossible to understand who Jesus is and what he is all about apart from this story. In fact, a number of New Testament scholars have shown that the way Jesus understood himself is saturated with Old Testament themes. For me, this alone is reason enough to regard this collection of books to be, at least in some sense, divinely influenced.

Perhaps an even more forceful consideration, however, is this. The Gospels, which Paul Eddy and I have elsewhere argued are generally reliable, consistently present Jesus as referring to the Old Testament as the inspired Word of God and even as equating what *it* says with what *God* says.[5] These same writings also give some indication that Jesus expected the Holy Spirit to inspire some of his followers to bear witness to him in a way that would allow the world to believe in him through their word (e.g., John 14:26; 15:26–27; 17:20). If Jesus is the incarnation of God, it seems to me rather unlikely that he would be mistaken about such a fundamentally important matter.

Some have argued that the references to Jesus pre-authenticating the writings of his disciples, all of which are found in John, are rather weak. I personally think they suffice, but even if we stick with Jesus's endorsement of the Old Testament, I have trouble believing that the God who consistently inspired a written witness of his interactions with people *leading up to* Christ would not continue this pattern *following* Christ. Why would the One who always taught his community to rely on a written witness of his interactions with them suddenly, after his most decisive interaction in history, leave his community with no written witness?

Not only this, but Jesus promised that he would be present in his corporate body by the power of the Spirit to continue to guide it (Matt. 28:20; John 14:18, 26). And under his spiritual guidance, the community he dwelled among quickly came to acknowledge that both the Old and the New Testaments were "God-breathed." As part of this community, therefore, I feel compelled to submit to this discernment. It strikes me as inconsistent, and not a little arrogant, for someone to profess Christ as Lord and yet set themselves in opposition to his promise and to such a fundamental decision of his corporate body.

My faith in Christ therefore compels me to embrace all of Scripture as the inspired Word of God. It seems unfaithful to Christ, as well as to his corporate body, to do otherwise.

This doesn't mean I do not have other reasons for accepting Scripture as God's Word as well. For example, the more I study this collection of works, the more I am impressed with the profound wisdom it displays, a wisdom that sometimes strikes me as impossible to explain on a strictly natural basis. So too, the more I study this collection, the more I'm amazed at a subtle but beautiful unity that weaves it together, especially as we read it through the lens of Christ, as we ought. And, finally, while I think this is massively overplayed in popular apologetic circles, there are *some* fulfilled prophecies that could be marshaled as evidence of Scripture's divine authorship.[6]

These considerations are helpful, yet they are, in my opinion, much less important than the endorsement of the Bible given by Christ. And so it is primarily on the authority of Jesus that I rest my conviction regarding the inspiration of Scripture, even when I confront material that is problematic, for one reason or another.

Reframing Biblical Struggles

I'll say a short word here about how the problematic aspects of Scripture are reframed when it is Jesus, and not Scripture, who serves as the ultimate foundation for our faith, though I'll deal with this topic much more extensively in the following chapter. In a word, I've found that anchoring the plausibility of my faith in Christ significantly lightens the burden I once felt over the "encyclopedia" of biblical "difficulties."

When Christ is our one sure foundation, our faith need never be threatened when we encounter discrepancies or archeological evidence that seems to indicate that a story lacks historical veracity. Nor do we need to feel compelled to go to extravagant and implausible lengths, as apologists sometimes do, to try to make everything consistent or to defend the historicity of a passage. If a plausible explanation is forthcoming, that is wonderful. But if not, it ought not to shake our faith or even cause our confidence in Scripture's divine authority to waver. Our faith in Christ and in Scripture is anchored in Christ, not in the absence of discrepancies or the absolute historical veracity of Scripture or in anything else.

Similarly, with the plausibility of our faith anchored in Christ, we need feel no consternation if we encounter vengeful prayers or exceedingly violent portraits of God or other material that we find hard to accept as divinely inspired. To be sure, because I feel compelled as an act of faithfulness to Christ to accept the entire canon as God's Word, I will certainly wrestle with these portraits. In fact, I suspect this is one of God's reasons for including this sort of material in his Word. He is aiming to raise up people who exercise an Israelite type of faith and who thus have the audacity to wrestle with him and his Word for whatever blessing that may come as a result.

Yet, because my faith is no longer leveraged on the perfection of this book, I can wrestle with this material in the secure context of a covenantal committed relationship with Christ. And precisely because my source of *life* is found in Christ, not my beliefs about the Bible, I am free to wrestle with difficult biblical material, as well as with any other theological conundrum, in an honest fashion that does not require me to force evidence or arguments in a preconceived direction.

And if, after a night of wrestling, I find I have only more ambiguity to show for it, my Christ-centered faith allows me to embrace this as well, for this too can be used to grow my character and deepen my walk with Christ.

A Collapsing House

The Need for Grounded Flexibility

When I anchored my faith exclusively in Christ, I found this not only freed me from my house-of-cards understanding of Scripture; it also freed me from the perpetually vulnerable house-of-cards way of holding together my theology. As I noted above, I, like most evangelicals, was led to believe that, if the Christian faith is true, then every aspect of it, or at least all of its most important beliefs, must be true.

Once upon a time it was possible for most people to maintain this sort of all-or-nothing view of the faith. Up until the last century, it was possible in most locations on the planet to go an entire lifetime without having any significant contact with people whose religious beliefs and worldview differed radically from one's own. And when you don't have your belief system challenged, it's not hard to believe that your views about everything are correct.

We live in a very different, quickly changing, increasingly pluralistic, complex, interconnected, and ambiguous world. It is simply no longer possible to sustain a house-of-cards model of faith in a healthy way. In fact, as people have acclimated to our increasingly ambiguous world, the *very suggestion* that beliefs could or should be held in this rigid way has become increasingly implausible. To many in our postmodern world, the idea of embracing *any* definitive belief is implausible. And this is why the majority of intelligent young people who are only given a house-of-cards model of faith to work with end up abandoning the faith, even when they desperately want to hang onto it, just as I did when I first abandoned the faith.

To accommodate the ever-expanding worldview of thoughtful people today, we need a model of faith that is flexible enough to accommodate people's expanding worlds while being sufficiently grounded to help them to confidently embrace definitive convictions that keep them from floating off into a sea of postmodern relativism.

As I struggled with theological issues over the years, I found that the number of beliefs I felt were foundationally important continually shrunk, as I mentioned earlier. And, as I also mentioned, I at some point began to suspect there was something fundamentally misguided with this house-of-cards way of structuring beliefs. When I finally acknowledged the futility of defending any set of beliefs that were held together in this way, I began to grow into a model that I believe provides a solid foundation for the core of my faith, while allowing me to be honest about whatever doubts I might have about any number of my beliefs, and to even discard any number of my beliefs if I felt the need to do so.

The More Important Matters

Most importantly, the model I'm about to share is not merely more advantageous for thinking people in our increasingly complex and ambiguous world; it is, I contend, a *more biblical* model that is anchored in a covenantal concept of faith. It is odd that, despite the common claim of conservative Christians to base everything on the Bible, the rigid, all-or-nothing way they typically hold onto their beliefs is actually *not biblical*.

For example, Jesus once accused the Pharisees of hypocrisy by saying, "You give a tenth of your spices—mint, dill and cumin. But you have neglected the *more important matters* of the law—justice, mercy and faithfulness" (Matt. 23:23, emphasis added). While Jesus clearly believed that all of Scripture is inspired by God, he just as clearly did not see everything as equally important. In his view, the command to practice "justice, mercy and faithfulness" outweighed the command to tithe.

This really goes to the heart of Jesus's problem with the religious leaders of his day. They lacked a sense of proportion. Their obsession with meticulous Sabbath laws caused them to overlook the more fundamental truth that "the Sabbath was made for people, not people for the Sabbath" (Mark 2:27 TNIV). It caused them to overlook the fact that they treated their animals better than they did people on this day of rest (Luke 13:15) and rendered them unable to celebrate the glorious way Jesus healed people on this day (e.g., John 5:1–18). Because they tried to get *life* from the meticulous way they kept the law, they completely missed the spirit of the law.

Conversely, Jesus taught that if we seek to keep the spirit of the law, we end up fulfilling the whole law. When he was asked about which commandment was the greatest, he replied that "all the Law and the Prophets hang on" the command to love God, which implies that we also love our neighbor as ourselves (Matt. 22:37–40). It is simply impossible to love God and not love our neighbor, which is why John claims that anyone who says they love God but who hates their neighbor is either self-deluded or lying (1 John 4:20). If we love God and our neighbor, as we should, Jesus was saying, we fulfill all other commands. But if we fail to love God and our neighbor as we should, then we fail to fulfill any command, *even if we meticulously obey it.* For the ultimate point of the law was not about regulating behavior but about cultivating a loving, covenantal relationship.

The same point echoes throughout the New Testament as various authors proclaim that loving God and our neighbor fulfills all that is required of us (e.g., Rom. 13:10; Gal. 5:14). If we lack love, however, then it doesn't matter what else we believe or do; it is worthless. Paul went so far as to argue that a person could have supernatural abilities, could have a faith that moved mountains, and could appear to do remarkably magnanimous deeds, but if they failed to love, their abilities, faith, and deeds were "a resounding gong or a clanging cymbal" (1 Cor. 13:1–3).[7] It's like dressing up a dead corpse, because just behaving a certain way without covenantal love motivating you is dead faith. This is why both Peter and Paul say that love must be placed "above all" other commands and virtues (1 Peter 4:8; Col. 3:14).

Clearly, not everything in Scripture carries equal weight. And clearly, the most important thing, and the thing that alone gives significance to everything else we believe in or do, is loving God and therefore loving our neighbor.

A Model of Concentric Circles

The One at the Center

In this light, I believe it is crucial for us to structure our faith in a way that reflects a sense of proportion and that is oriented around the loving, faithful, covenantal relationship God wants with us and that necessarily implies that we love our neighbor. As I've said, in the covenantal understanding of faith, beliefs are not an end unto themselves. Rather, they are intended to point beyond themselves by pointing us to, and sustaining us in, a relationship with God.

Hence, as I mentioned earlier, in place of the house-of-cards structure in which everything depends on everything else, I now envision my beliefs in the form of circles that are oriented around a single center. And this center is Jesus Christ, the one who perfectly reveals to us the love God eternally is, who perfectly embodies the love God has for us, who perfectly models the love we're to have toward others, and who is the means by which we enter into a loving, covenantal, faith-based relationship with God.

Participating in this love, centered on Christ, is the end to which all beliefs point. This relationship is what gives significance to everything we believe. And, as I've repeatedly said, this center is the one and only source of the *life* that is the heartbeat of the kingdom to which we belong.

The Concentric Circles of Belief

With this center always in view, I assess my beliefs in terms of their relative importance. I thus envision three concentric circles surrounding the center. The proximity of each circle to the center reflects its relative importance.

Because all followers of Jesus are called to belong to his body, the church, I believe we must carry out our assessment of our beliefs in dialogue with the historic-orthodox church tradition. For this reason, I place in the innermost ring those beliefs that have traditionally been understood to constitute orthodox Christianity. These are sometimes referred to as the "dogma" of the church and they are reflected in our foundational ecumenical creeds (e.g., the Nicene and the Apostles' Creed).[8] The belief that God is a Trinity, that Christ is fully God and fully human, and that the world is created and governed by God are examples of the dogmas that compose this innermost ring.

In the next ring I place beliefs that orthodox Christians have always espoused, but over which there has been some disagreement. These are the different doctrines that distinguish various denominations, and most derive from different ways of interpreting the dogmas found in

Figure 8.1 Concentric Circles

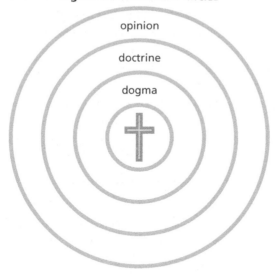

the ring just outside the core circle. For example, orthodox Christians have always believed that God governs the world, as I noted above, but at least from the fourth century on, there has been no uniform agreement as to *how* God does this. Some have held that God governs by controlling every event in history, while others have held that God has given a degree of free will to humans and angels. To distinguish this circle from the innermost circle, I would label the beliefs that compose this circle "doctrine."

Finally, in the outermost ring I place beliefs that individual Christians have occasionally espoused but that have never gained widespread support and that have rarely been adopted by a recognized church body. While the circle of "doctrine" comprises the different ways Christians have interpreted "dogma," this third circle usually comprises different ways of interpreting particular doctrines. Two examples of the innumerable beliefs that could be placed in this circle would be the "gap theory" that posits a long interval between Genesis 1:1 and 1:2 as a way of reconciling this creation account with evolution, and the "open view of the future" that holds that the future is not fully settled. To distinguish this circle from the circle of "doctrine," I would label it "opinion."

There is of course plenty of room for disagreement over the details of this paradigm of three concentric circles surrounding the center, Jesus Christ. While the church uniformly agrees on what constitutes dogma, one person may regard a belief to be "opinion" that another regards as a "doctrine." But the most important aspect of this paradigm is that it clearly articulates the fact that not all beliefs are equally important while making it clear that everything revolves around, and is oriented toward, the all-important, *life*-giving, covenantal relationship with God through Jesus Christ.

Advantages of the Concentric Circles Model

Beyond the fact that it is more biblical, this model of faith has a number of distinct advantages. Among other things, it allows people to adjust their beliefs to accommodate their ongoing intellectual and spiritual development, while at the same time grounding them in a *life*-giving relationship with Christ. Its flexibility allows people, and even encourages them, to fearlessly and honestly wrestle with whatever issues come their way and, so long as their *life* remains anchored in Christ, to do so in a non-defensive and objective way. For the same reason, this model empowers Christians to discuss and debate issues with other Christians or with nonbelievers in loving, non-defensive, and rational ways. This model thus avoids all the unhealthy pitfalls that we saw accompany certainty-seeking faith, especially when combined, as it usually is, with the house-of-cards structure of beliefs.

It's also been my experience that this model is profoundly helpful in sharing the gospel with others. Far too often people who are genuinely hungry for the *life* that Christ alone can bring, and people who would otherwise have surrendered their life to Christ, are barred from doing so because they are presented with a package-deal gospel. They are led to believe that to accept Jesus as Lord, they have to (for example) accept the "inerrancy" of the Bible, reject evolution, interpret every biblical story literally, accept that every biblical narrative is historically accurate, and/or accept every doctrine a particular church teaches. Just as tragic but even more ungodly, in our increasingly polarized political context, people are often given the impression that accepting

Jesus as Lord means they must become Republican (or Democrat) and/or take particular stands on politically divisive issues!

By identifying the center as the intellectual foundation of the faith and the sole source of *life*, and by distinguishing it from all other beliefs, this model allows hungry people to enter into a relationship with Christ and participate in the *life* he gives without requiring them to first resolve a single other issue. This model creates space for people to think on their own, to discover truths for themselves, to grow at their own pace, and to embrace whatever level of ambiguity they feel they need to embrace, Yet, it creates this space without in any way watering down the traditional definition of historic-orthodox Christianity.

Moreover, this model not only gives God a chance to immediately begin to work in the hearts and minds of new believers; it also gives the kingdom community a chance to begin to influence their lives, regardless of how far their lifestyle may be removed from the ideal of the kingdom or how far their worldview may be removed from the biblical worldview. All issues regarding beliefs and behavior can now be discussed from the "inside" of the faith, as they should, rather than as a precondition to coming to faith. And since all are getting their *life* from Christ rather than the presumed rightness of their opinions, these discussions can be carried out in a loving, non-defensive, and even fun way.

A church need not abandon or water down its doctrinal stance to welcome people in this radically open way. It simply needs to have an understanding that not everything is equally important, and the one and only thing that is absolutely essential is a relationship with Christ. It thus only needs to be encouraging all its people to get all their *life* from Jesus Christ and to therefore be gracious enough to allow space for people to disagree, to doubt, and to be in process.

9

The Center of Scripture

When I read Scripture, I know only Christ Crucified.
—Martin Luther

You study the Scriptures diligently because you think that
in them you have eternal life. These are the very Scriptures
that testify about me.
—John 5:39

As with most evangelicals, the house-of-cards theology I was
given when I first became a Christian was built on a way of
reading Scripture that was itself a house of cards. If the Bible is the
inspired Word of God, I was told, then every aspect of it must be
equally authoritative. If the authority or accuracy of any aspect of
Scripture is called into question, the whole thing is therefore called
into question.

Once the intellectual foundation of my faith shifted from Scripture to the historical Jesus and other nonbiblical considerations, as I
shared in the previous chapter, my problems with Scripture no longer undermined my faith in Christ as the Son of God. But they did

nevertheless continue to render my belief in the inspiration of Scripture vulnerable. And while this vulnerability no longer disrupted my core identity, which was now anchored in Christ alone, it nevertheless shook the foundation of my theology inasmuch as I have always affirmed Scripture to be the final authority in all matters of faith and practice.

Even more importantly, as I came to understand the cross as the key to understanding everything Jesus is about, as discussed in chapter 3, I've become increasingly aware that the God of other-oriented love that the cross reveals is in tension with portraits of God that depict him commanding or engaging in horrific violence. For example, I frankly found it increasingly hard to reconcile the portrait of Yahweh commanding his people to "destroy [the Canaanites] totally" and to "show them no mercy" as they slaughter men, women, children, infants, and even animals (Deut. 7:2) with the beautiful, merciful portrait of God that is unveiled on the cross.

At the same time, I became aware of the fact that my mental picture of God was only *partly* Christlike. And the reason was that I felt obliged to consider every portrait of God in Scripture to be equally authoritative. My amalgamated mental picture of God not only posed a serious theological problem for me; it was, even more importantly, compromising my capacity to get all my life from God alone in ways I hadn't before realized. For while God is infinitely more beautiful than we can ever imagine or conceive, the depth of *life* we experience from God can never outrun the beauty and trustworthiness of our mental conception of him.

You can see why I'm so passionate about the "Israelite" nature of the faith God invites us to embrace. I'm so grateful that, in his love and grace, God encourages us, as he did Jacob, to wrestle with him throughout the night for the "blessing" of a deeper understanding of him and his Word.

For reasons I'll share in this chapter, my struggling has led me to the understanding that confessing Scripture to be completely "God-breathed" does not entail that everything in Scripture is equally authoritative or that every portrait of God carries the same weight. In fact, as I'll show below, Scripture itself *refutes* this notion. I have come to understand that there is a center to Scripture, and it turns out to be the same center I found for my theology, the same center that constitutes the intellectual foundation of my faith, and the same center that is my source of *life*.

In a word, I have found that *everything* revolves around Jesus Christ, and Jesus Christ alone.

I previously argued that disciples today would enjoy a more intellectually defensible faith if they anchored it in the historical Jesus rather than in the inspiration of Scripture and would enjoy a sturdier yet more flexible theology if they adopted a concentric circles model of theology that is centered on Jesus. In the same way, I will now argue that disciples today would be able to embrace a more robust confidence in biblical inspiration and a more *life*-giving view of God if they adopted a Christ-centered understanding of Scripture.

The Revelation That Trumps All Others

A Story with a Surprising Twist

The assumption that everything in Scripture is equally authoritative inclines people to read it along the lines of a cookbook. Like a recipe, the meaning and authority of a passage aren't much affected by where the passage is located within the overall book. The truth, however, is that the Bible is not at all like a cookbook. It's a story, along the lines of a novel. And it's a story with a very surprising twist in it.

Have you seen *The Sixth Sense*, starring Bruce Willis, or *The Book of Eli*, starring Denzel Washington? *Spoiler Alert!* I won't give away the endings, but I'll just say that the last minutes of both shows completely reframe the movies. You have to rethink every single thing that took place in light of their last few moments. This is quite a bit like the kind of story the Bible tells.

The whole Old Testament leads up to, and is fulfilled in, Jesus the Messiah. But the *particular way* Jesus fulfills it reframes everything. Hardly anyone saw this coming! In fact, the way Jesus completes the story of God's dealings with Israel was so unexpected, most who were looking for the Messiah couldn't accept him once he came.

For example, most Jews were looking for a Messiah who would reinforce Israel's status as God's favored nation by leading a revolt against its oppressors (the Romans) and reinstating it as a sovereign nation. Jesus instead turned Jewish religious nationalism on its head by proclaiming a kingdom in which many "outsiders" (gentiles and sinners) would become "insiders," while many who assumed they were "insiders" (the religious elite) would find themselves on the outside.[1] And far from leading a revolt, Jesus commanded people to love their enemies (e.g., the Romans) and to therefore refrain from all violence, choosing instead to do good to their enemies, bless their enemies, serve their enemies, and turn the other cheek when struck (Matt. 5:39–45).

In fact, not only does Jesus not lead people in a military conquest over their enemies; he allows himself to be executed on a cross to reveal God's profound love for enemies! And in this scandalous and unexpected action, his followers discerned the ultimate revelation of God's true nature. With his life, ministry, teaching, and especially his sacrificial death, Jesus provided a picture of God and his kingdom that forces us to reframe everything that led up to him.

What this means, I believe, is that we shouldn't place the revelation of God in Jesus *alongside* the portraits of God in the Old Testament. Rather, we'll only begin to see how Jesus reframes the story line of God's dealings with Israel if we place his revelation *over* all previous revelations, and if we then interpret all previous revelations *through the lens* of this one.

As I will now show, this is precisely what Jesus and the authors of the New Testament instruct us to do. As much as they affirm the inspiration of the Old Testament, they are even more emphatic in proclaiming that the revelation of God in Christ completes, and in this sense trumps, everything that preceded him. For reasons of space, I must restrict myself to five brief illustrations of this all-important motif.[2]

The Revelation That Carries More Weight

First, at one point in his ministry Jesus says, "I have testimony weightier than that of John" (John 5:36). Jesus elsewhere claims that "among those born of women there has not risen anyone greater than John the Baptist" (Matt. 11:11). Jesus places the words and ministry of John above any of the Old Testament prophets, and yet he tells us that his testimony is "weightier" than John's!

It's clear that, while Jesus affirms the inspiration of the Old Testament, he believes that John's ministry and teaching carry more weight than any Old Testament writer and that his own testimony carries more weight *than both*. This alone demonstrates that, while everything in Scripture is inspired, not everything in Scripture carries equal weight. We must consider all that we learn from Jesus about God and his kingdom to have more authority than everything that preceded him.

The Revelation That Supersedes All Others

Second, the author of Hebrews makes this point in an emphatic way when he writes:

> In the past, God spoke to our ancestors through the prophets at many times and in various ways, but in these last days he has spoken to us by his Son. . . . The Son is the radiance of God's glory and the exact representation of his being. (Heb. 1:1–3)

This author acknowledges that God spoke in a variety of ways in the past. But he at the same time emphasizes that the revelation of God in Jesus *supersedes* all these past revelations. Unlike past revelations that were mediated through prophets, Jesus is *God's own Son*. The author is essentially saying that the revelation of God in his Son contrasts with the "various ways" God was revealed in the past, because in the Son we finally have God *in person*.

So too, while Old Testament writings may reflect aspects of God's glory, this author says that the Son alone reflects the "radiance of God's glory." To grasp his point, we could say that "radiance" (*apaugasma*) is to "glory" (*doxa*) what *light* is to *the sun*. When God's glory is manifested, the author is saying, *it looks like Jesus*. Every previous reflection of God's glory, by contrast, was a mere approximation.

John reflects essentially the same perspective when he proclaims Jesus to be "the Word (*logos*)" of God who is himself "God" (John 1:1). When God speaks or presents himself to us, John is saying, *it looks like Jesus*. And notice the definite article. Jesus isn't *one of* God's words, as though his revelation of God could be placed alongside others. No, Jesus is *the* Word. Hence John continues by noting that when "the Word became flesh," we beheld "the glory of the one and only Son" (v. 14). And while "no one has ever seen God," he adds, "the one and only Son, who is himself God . . . , has made him known" (v. 18). The remarkable emphasis on the *one and only* status of Jesus distinguishes him from, and sets him over, all previous revelations.

Closely related to this, while Old Testament writings may capture glimpses of what God is like, the author of Hebrews proclaims that the Son alone is God's *exact representation*. The Greek word translated "representation" (*charaktēr*) refers to a stamp, carving, or image. The author is thus saying that in the Son alone we discover *exactly* what God is like. Paul's teaching that Jesus is the one true image of God says the same thing (2 Cor. 4:4; Col. 1:15).

And, most importantly, this "representation" reveals exactly what God is like in his very "being." The Greek word translated "being" (*hypostasis*) refers to the essence or substance of something. This author is thus teaching us that, while previous revelations may reflect approximations of God's attributes or of what God is like in his activity, the Son alone reveals exactly what God is like in his *very essence*, in his *innermost heart*, or in his *eternal nature*. The Son thus sums up, and supersedes, all that was true about previous revelations.

The Only One Who Truly Knows God

Jesus himself makes a similar point in a remarkable passage that will serve as my third illustration. At one point Jesus says to his disciples, "All things have been committed to me by my Father" (Matt. 11:27). He then proceeds to claim that one of the things included in the "all things" that have been given to him is the authority to reveal the Father. So, Jesus says, "No one knows the Father except the Son and those to whom the Son chooses to reveal him" (Matt. 11:27).

This is arguably the single most outrageous thing Jesus ever said—and he said quite a few outrageous things! Jesus is actually claiming that *no one* knows God *except him*! If we take this literally, it would include every Old Testament author! This is an outlandishly arrogant claim for anyone to make, at any time. But for a first-century Jew to say this to other Bible-believing Jews is beyond mind-boggling!

This is one of the reasons I contend that if a person doesn't regard Jesus to be the embodiment of Yahweh on earth, they ought to dismiss him as a complete megalomaniac! Many people today claim that, while his disciples went too far when they claimed he was God, Jesus was nevertheless a great moral or spiritual teacher. This view is simply untenable. Great moral and spiritual teachers don't go around making the sort of claims Jesus made—such as, *no one knows God except me*! No, the choice is between accepting Jesus as the embodiment of God or dismissing him as a complete lunatic.[3]

In any event, the teaching is remarkable, to say the least. Now, as is true of the ancient Near East in general, ancient Jewish culture made much use of hyperbole (exaggerated language). In this light, combined with the fact that Jesus himself quotes the Old Testament as the Word of God, I don't believe we should take Jesus's statement too literally and conclude that Jesus didn't believe Old Testament authors knew *anything* about God. But, at the very least, this hyperbolic statement indicates that Jesus sees his knowledge of the Father, and the knowledge he reveals to others about the Father, as dwarfing in significance all who came before him. And this suggests, at the very least, that the revelation of God we are given in Jesus massively outshines the revelation of God through all who preceded him.

The One Who Surpasses the Law and Prophets

A fourth illustration took place on the famous Mount of Transfiguration. While in prayer, Peter, John, and James behold Jesus's "glory" and then witness Moses and Elijah talking to him about "his departure, which he was about to bring to fulfillment at Jerusalem" (Luke 9:31). As Moses and Elijah are about to leave, Peter asks if he, John, and James can build three shelters for the three of them. But a cloud suddenly envelopes them, and they hear a voice from heaven saying: "This is my Son, whom I have chosen; listen to him." Following this, when they look around, "they found that Jesus was alone" (vv. 33–36).

While scholars debate a number of things about this fascinating passage, there is widespread agreement that Moses represents the law while Elijah represents the prophets, and that the point of this passage is to demonstrate the superiority of Jesus over the Law and the

Prophets.[4] This is reflected in the fact that Moses and Elijah speak *to Jesus* about the completion of *his* mission in Jerusalem, suggesting that the Law and the Prophets find their ultimate significance in him.

Moreover, the voice tells the disciples to listen *to Jesus*, suggesting that they are to submit to Jesus's teachings and revelation *alone*. And the superiority of Christ is reflected in the fact that the radiance of Jesus outshines that of Moses and Elijah as well as in the fact that the disciples are not allowed to hang on to Moses and Elijah by building them shelters so they can stay. After the voice from the cloud has spoken, only the Son remains.

A Revelation That Renders Others Obsolete

Finally, the superiority of Christ over the Old Testament is revealed in the fact that Jesus felt free to at times replace its teachings with his own. For example, while the Old Testament commands people to make oaths in God's name (Deut. 6:13), Jesus forbids it (Matt. 5:33–37). And while the Old Testament commands an "eye for eye and tooth for tooth," Jesus commands people to "not resist an evil person," adding that "if anyone slaps you on the right cheek, turn to them the other cheek also" (Matt. 5:38–39).

Some scholars have tried to argue that Jesus was not revising Old Testament commands but merely altering traditional *interpretations* of its commands.[5] This view is possible concerning other passages in which Jesus contrasts "you've heard it said" with "but I say to you," but it's simply not possible regarding the "eye for eye" command, for this command is found several times in the Old Testament (e.g., Exod. 21:24; Lev. 24:19–20; Deut. 19:21).[6] In fact, in the version of this command in Deuteronomy, the command is not merely a restriction on how much punishment is *allowed*; it's about how much *is required*. "Show no pity," the text states, "life for life, eye for eye, tooth for tooth, hand for hand, foot for foot" (Deut. 19:21).[7]

Though it is difficult for some to accept, I see no way of avoiding the conclusion that Jesus is in this passage explicitly repudiating this command and replacing it with his command to never retaliate and to love and bless our enemies.[8] What makes this repudiation even more significant is that this law of just retribution (called the *lex talionis*) is reflected in various ways throughout the Old Testament. It therefore seems to me that Jesus's replacement of the violence of this law with his command to instead love our offenders implies that we should replace *every* Old Testament law that requires offenders to be violently punished with his command to love.

An episode from Jesus's ministry similarly reflects the radical way Jesus repudiates the violence of the Old Testament, even when it appears to come from God. After being rejected by some Samaritan towns, James and John asked Jesus if they could "call fire down from heaven to destroy them." Jesus "rebuked" them and, according to many early manuscripts, added: "You do not know what spirit you are of" (Luke 9: 54–55). What's most interesting is that the disciples were simply asking to follow the precedent set by Elijah in the Old Testament when, in this same location, he twice called fire down from the sky to incinerate foes (2 Kings 1:10, 12, 14). While it raises many questions we cannot address in this context, I see no way of avoiding the conclusion that Jesus would have rebuked a person who is held up as a hero in the Old Testament for participating in a violent supernatural feat that Jesus clearly would have considered to be ungodly, if not demonic.[9]

As I said, Jesus radically reframes *everything*. In a first-century Jewish setting, it's hard to imagine anything that would be more shocking than for someone to place his own teaching above Scripture—except perhaps someone adding that they should never retaliate but should instead love and bless their enemies, and someone who rebuked his own disciples for wanting to follow the precedent of an Old Testament hero! And it's important to remember that to talk about "enemies" among Jews in first-century Palestine was first and foremost to talk about the Romans, who occupied their sacred land and who oppressed them, sometimes in terribly violent ways. Most Jews felt righteous hating these godless oppressors, which is why so many longed for a Messiah who would lead them in a divinely assisted violent conquest over them. How it must have grieved many when Jesus instead commanded followers to reject violence and to love and do good to their enemies, even going so far as to make this a precondition for being considered a child of God (Matt. 5:44–45; Luke 6:35)! It's little wonder that some of these people helped get him executed.

In any case, this remarkably bold teaching demonstrates that Jesus placed his own teaching and his own revelation of God above that of the Old Testament. Though it is inspired and reveals some truth about God, if we follow the lead of Jesus and the authors of the New Testament, we simply cannot place it on a par with the revelation of God in Christ.

The Fortified Belief in Scripture

Reading Scripture in the Light of Christ

The five illustrations I've just reviewed indicate that we cannot read the Bible as we would a cookbook, giving equal weight to everything it teaches. We should rather read it like a novel in which the final chapter forces us to rethink everything that preceded it. More specifically, they suggest that we should read the Old Testament *through the lens* of the revelation of God in Christ, and especially through the lens of the cross, which sums up everything Jesus was about.

This is how Jesus himself suggested we should read the Scripture when he taught that all Scripture is *about him* (Luke 24:25–27; John 5:39–47). This way of reading Scripture is implied as well in Paul's teaching that the Spirit has removed the "veil" over our "hearts" and "minds" (2 Cor. 3:14–16) so that we can now see "the glory of God shining in the face of Jesus Christ" as we read Scripture (2 Cor. 4:6; cf. 3:17–4:5). And it's reflected in the way various authors of the New Testament read the Old Testament. In sharp contrast to the common teaching of modern evangelicals that Bible interpreters should always stick to "the original intended meaning" of a passage, the way the New Testament authors use the Old Testament reflects little concern with this.[10] Their primary concern was rather to see how it points to Jesus.

To give just one example, after telling us that Mary and Joseph have been warned by God in a dream to flee to Egypt to escape Herod's vicious slaughter, Matthew adds that this "fulfilled what the Lord had said through the prophet: 'Out of Egypt I called my son'" (Matt. 2:15). Matthew is quoting Hosea 11:1, but if you go back and check, you'll find that the "son" the Lord was referring to was the nation of

Israel, and he's referring to the time he delivered it from its bondage in Egypt.

As is true of almost all the passages that Gospel authors claim Jesus "fulfilled," Matthew is not saying the Hosea passage *predicted* an event in Jesus's life. He is rather simply highlighting a parallel between what Yahweh did with his national "son" and what he did with his incarnate Son. In this way, Matthew is showing how Jesus filled to the full ("fulfilled") the significance of Yahweh's deliverance of his people in the Old Testament. And he is doing this as a way of depicting Jesus as the fulfillment of Yahweh's plan for Israel.

A Less Vulnerable Confidence

There are two reasons I think it's crucial for us to appreciate the way the New Testament places Jesus over the Old Testament and looks for Jesus in the Old Testament. First, our confidence in Scripture as the inspired Word of God can be strengthened once we abandon the misguided notion that everything in Scripture is equally important. Among other things, it means there is no need for our confidence in Scripture's inspiration to be shaken whenever parts of it get called into question. If God's ultimate purpose in "breathing" (*theopneustos*, 2 Tim. 3:16) Scripture is to point us to Christ and to help us cultivate a relationship with Christ, then so long as we remain confident that Scripture doesn't *fail to do this*—in this sense, it is "infallible"—whatever problems we might encounter in matters surrounding this book are irrelevant to the question of whether it's divinely inspired.

The reason conservative evangelicals have tended to assume that the Bible must be free of things like human limitations, imperfections, and faults is because they have tended to assume that, since God is perfect, his written Word must be perfect. This is why many have gone to such extreme lengths to try to explain away all these things. I'm deeply sympathetic to this way of thinking, for I once thought this way myself. But it frankly now strikes me as curious that we should feel the need to explain away such things in God's revelation in Scripture when the ultimate purpose of Scripture is to bear witness to the One who most perfectly revealed God *by bearing the sin and the God-forsaken curse* of humanity.

That is, since God "breathed" his fullest self-revelation by identifying with all our sin and the God-forsakenness it deserved, why should anyone find it unusual or disturbing if the revelation in Scripture that is ultimately intended to point us to this fullest revelation on the cross shares, to one degree or another, in our limitations and imperfections? To the contrary, it seems to me we should have been dismayed if his written word was completely devoid of human limitations, imperfections, and faults, for this would have strongly conflicted with the way he reveals himself on the cross when he bore the sin of the world.

I confess, primarily on the authority of Christ, that Scripture is inspired and perfect *for what God intends it to do*. In this sense I can affirm that it is "infallible" and even, if one prefers the word, "inerrant." But the thing that God most wants Scripture to do—point to the cross—leads me to *expect it* to reflect some limitations, imperfections, and faults rather than to feel the need to defend it against these things.

So long as Scripture infallibly points us to Christ, therefore, I don't see that anything of consequence hangs in the balance on the multitude of issues that cause many evangelicals consternation. So long as it points us to, and helps us sustain a relationship with, the One who gave his life for us, what real difference does it make whether we are able to resolve certain discrepancies? What hangs in the balance in the debate over how literally or figuratively we should interpret the Genesis creation story or the stories of (say) Jonah, Job, or Samson? What does it matter whether one can defend (say) the Mosaic authorship of the Pentateuch or the absolute historical veracity of the conquest narrative?

The same holds true for a multitude of other issues that have typically preoccupied evangelical apologists, such as the question of whether the Genesis flood was a global or local flood. So long as we can trust that God uses these narratives to point us to Christ and to help us cultivate a relationship with Christ, it seems to me that how we resolve these issues, or even if we were to remain undecided about these issues, is completely inconsequential.

Motivations for Debating These Issues

Of course, we may have reasons *other than* protecting the doctrine of the inspiration of Scripture for debating issues surrounding the

Old or the New Testament one way or another. For example, in the previous chapter I mentioned that I think it is extremely important to defend the general historical reliability of the Gospels. If these were proved to be substantially *unreliable*, it would take away many of the historical reasons we have for believing that the historical Jesus was the definitive revelation of God. But this conviction is about the *apologetic significance* of the historical reliability of these works, *not* about their status as divinely inspired works.

Another reason one might feel the need to defend the historicity of certain characters and stories in Scripture is christological. That is, many conservative evangelicals have argued that if Jesus cites a figure or a story, such as Jonah (e.g., Luke 11:29–30), as historical, we must accept it as such, for to do otherwise would imply that Jesus was mistaken. I think this is an important consideration, but I would caution readers from leveraging too much on it. I've more than once seen it backfire. One student I knew, for example, temporarily lost his faith in Christ because he concluded that the genre of the story of Jonah trapped in the belly of a great fish was a folktale, which to him meant that Jesus had to be mistaken and thus could not be the Son of God.

In this light, I think it wise to advise those who currently feel the need to defend the historicity of biblical figures and events for this reason to at least be aware that other perspectives are possible. For example, it could be argued that at least some of Jesus's references were to figures and stories *as authoritative literature*, not *as historical persons* or *events*. Similarly, some have argued that Jesus may have been simply accommodating social conventions of the time. And still other scholars have argued that for the Son of God to become fully human, he had to surrender his omniscience and fully enter into the limited worldview of people of that time. It seems, for example, that Jesus's teaching that "the eye is the lamp of the body" reflects the mistaken ancient view that perception involves light *coming out of* our eyes (Matt. 6:22; Luke 11:34).

My intent here is not to weigh in on any of these issues one way or another. Indeed, I want to be clear that, when I state that issues surrounding the genre or historicity of biblical figures and narratives should be considered inconsequential to our confidence in biblical inspiration, I am not implicitly endorsing the less conservative way of resolving any of these debates. Not that it matters, but I'd like to go on record and say that, as I've studied all sides of these debates over the years, I have more often than not found myself persuaded by defenders of more conservative positions.

Still, I can't say that I've *always* been persuaded by conservative arguments, and most importantly, I don't feel I *need* to end up on the conservative side of these debates to remain confident that Scripture is divinely inspired, let alone for my faith in Christ to be secure. And *that* is my main point. My confidence in biblical inspiration is attached to my confidence that Jesus is the Son of God, which in turn is anchored in the reasons I've previously shared. And I recommend this posture for all readers, precisely because it means that your confidence in biblical inspiration, let alone your faith in Christ, isn't vulnerable to the "encyclopedia" of difficulties associated with Scripture.

Remaining True to the Crucified Christ

The Damage of Compromising Christ

The second and even more important reason why I believe it's crucial for us to appreciate the strong emphasis of the New Testament on the superiority of Jesus over previous revelations concerns our picture of God. When people regard all depictions of God in Scripture as carrying equal weight, it's simply impossible for them to embrace an uncompromisingly Christlike mental picture of God. When the picture of God revealed on the cross is placed alongside portraits of God commanding his people to engage in genocide (e.g., Deut. 7:2), and of God himself engaging in brutal violence (e.g., Gen. 6:7), along with portraits of God commanding people to stone a person who gathers wood on the Sabbath (Num. 32:36), as well as adulterers (Lev. 20:10; Deut. 22:22), fornicators (Lev. 21:9; Deut. 22:13–21), homosexuals (Lev. 20:13), and even children who are stubborn or who strike or curse their parents (Exod. 21:15, 17; Lev. 20:9; Deut. 21:18–21), the composite result is a self-contradictory mental portrait of God.

As I will argue in a forthcoming book, *The Crucifixion of the Warrior God*, this fusion of the Old Testament's violent portraits of God with the God revealed on Calvary is disastrous on a number of levels, not least of which is that it has throughout history justified and even inspired religious violence.[11] But for our present purposes, the most important negative effect of this fusion is that our amalgamated mental portraits of God compromise our capacity to rely exclusively on God to experience *life*. If the cross reveals only *part* of what God is like, then we cannot place our entire trust in the God revealed on the cross to get our innermost need for unconditional love, unsurpassable worth, and absolute security met. In fact, I strongly suspect that one of the primary reasons so many Christians are in bondage to the idolatry of rightness (chap. 3) is precisely because they have an amalgamated mental picture of God that they cannot get all their *life* from.

Jesus came into this world and died on the cross to blow apart all the deceptive mental pictures of God that we've been enslaved to since the original fall and that lie at the root of all idolatry and sin, as we discussed in that chapter. The revelation of God's true character on Calvary was the explosion of light that in principle expelled all darkness and the explosion of love that in principle destroyed all hate. It was the revelation that in principle defeated Satan and the fallen powers and thereby freed humans to be reconciled to God (Col. 2:14–15; cf. Heb. 2:14; 1 John 3:8). But we will only benefit from this revelation if we hold fast to the conviction that the perfect, self-sacrificial love manifested on the cross defines God to the core of his being (*hypostasis*, Heb. 1:3) and should never be qualified by being placed alongside competing portraits.

I thus encourage readers to recall not only what was said above regarding the superiority of Christ over all that preceded him, but also what was shared in chapter 4 regarding the identity of Christ. It comes down to whether we will trust Jesus when he tells us that if we see him, we see the Father (John 14:8–9). Will we trust that no one knows the Father except the Son and those to whom he reveals the Father (Matt. 11:27)? Will we trust the author of Hebrews when he tells us the Son alone is *exactly* what God's eternal essence looks like when it shines (Heb. 1:3)? Will we trust Paul when he proclaims that Jesus is the image of God and that in Christ, "the whole fullness (*plērōma*) of deity (*theotēs*)"—the fullness of everything that makes God *God*—"dwells bodily" (Col. 2:9 ESV)?

What about the Bible's Violent Portraits?

This obviously raises the difficult question of what should be done with portraits of God in the Old Testament that seem to conflict with Jesus's revelation of God.[12] If we believe the Old Testament is inspired, as I do, we obviously cannot simply dismiss them. Yet, if we believe the revelation of God in Christ supersedes these and should never be compromised, we also cannot simply accept them. What then is the alternative?

Many have argued that the answer is to understand the Bible as a record of God's *progressive revelation*. This view holds that, while God has always worked to reveal as much of his true self as his people could receive, he has also always been willing to acquiesce to the hard-heartedness of his people to whatever degree was necessary. It is for this reason that we find God sometimes taking on violent roles and giving violent commands in the Old Testament. Violence was unfortunately the only language most people of this time could understand, and so this is the language God was sometimes forced to speak.

In this view, however, these violent roles and commands don't reveal God's true nature. They rather reveal the hard-heartedness of the people God had to work with. But by patiently stooping to work with his hard-hearted people in this way, God was able to progressively reveal more and more of his true self and to acquiesce to their depravity less and less. And the culmination of this progressive revelation took place when God finally provided a full and unambiguous revelation of himself in Christ.

While I think this view is incomplete and faces several formidable challenges, it is, to a large degree, a compelling position. In the forthcoming book I mentioned above, however, I try to fill out the aspects that I think are incomplete and to do this in a way that avoids its challenges. My contention is that, if all Scripture is intended to point us to Christ, then the common apologetic strategy of providing reasons to justify God's violent behavior and/or to argue that these violent portraits are not as bad as they might initially appear doesn't accomplish all that much.[13]

In fact, it wouldn't be enough even if someone managed to find a way of arguing that portraits of God commanding genocide and engaging in other horrific behaviors were *compatible* with the revelation of God in Christ. The challenge we face is rather to show how these violent portraits actually *point to* Jesus. And since I maintain that the cross is the quintessential expression of everything Jesus was about (chap. 3), our challenge is nothing less than to show how portraits such as the one in which God commands the merciless slaughter of women and infants bear witness to the God who gave his life for enemies while praying for their forgiveness on Calvary.

If ever we need to embrace an honest "Israelite" faith that has the audacity to wrestle with God, it's here!

A Cross-Centered Approach

I do not claim to have the "right" answer to this question. The most I can do is go public with my wrestling and offer a few insights that I personally have found helpful. Whether others will find them so is yet to be determined. The book I'm currently writing will end up somewhere around six hundred pages, so what I'm about to share is nothing more than an indication of the direction my argument will take. Two points must suffice.

First, my approach is based on the precedent of the New Testament authors' Christ-centered way of interpreting the Old Testament, mentioned above, as well as the precedent of a Christ-centered, nonviolent way of interpreting divine violence that was employed by Origen and other early fathers. Reading Scripture through the lens of Christ, the New Testament authors and these early fathers found a meaning in Old Testament passages that the original authors themselves could not have imagined. And in the case of certain early fathers, such as Origen, this meaning provided them with a way of affirming the inspiration of the Old Testament's violent portraits while denying that God actually engaged in or sanctioned violence.

My approach, in other words, isn't an attempt to interpret what Old Testament authors said differently. I'm not engaging in clever exegesis. It's rather an attempt to show how we who read their writings through the lens of the cross can discern a deeper, nonviolent meaning.

Second, my approach is centered on the cross, by which God stooped to in some way *become* our sin (2 Cor. 5:21) and our curse (Gal. 3:13), thereby taking on the *appearance* of one who was guilty, though in fact *he was not*. When we read the Bible's violent portraits with the awareness that *the cross* reveals what God is *really* like, I contend that we can begin to discern what is going on behind the scenes when God is portrayed violently. He is, in a nutshell, stooping to in some sense *become* the sin and curse of the hard-hearted people he is working with. He is thereby taking on the *appearance* of one who engages in and commands violence, though in fact *he is not*.

Trusting Who You Know

However one explains the violent portrayals of God in the Old Testament, or even if one concludes we can't plausibly explain these portraits, the more important point is that we must simply trust that the way God is revealed in the crucified Christ is the way he *really* is.

I believe our situation is a bit like this. Suppose you have a dear friend whom you've known intimately and shared a loving, committed relationship with for a number of years. Though you are certain your friend is loving, compassionate, and deeply committed to nonviolence, you one day witness him mocking and hitting a disabled person on a public street corner before running off in a direction away from you. How should you think about this situation in the time before you can question him to his face?

You could allow your friend's disturbing behavior to call into question everything you thought you knew about him. But this response, I think, would be unfaithful to your friend and your committed friendship. A more faithful response, I submit, would be to continue to trust your friend and to assume that there must be *something else going on* that you don't know about.

Is it possible that the person you saw only *looked like* your friend? Perhaps this event was a public skit your friend was playing in. Maybe he and the disabled person were taking part in a reality television show that was documenting whether people would risk intervening on behalf of this disabled person, or perhaps it was instead a comic reality show capturing people's shocked expressions in response to this hideous event? In fact, it just might be that the event was intended to be a prank *on you*. Perhaps there was a hidden camera capturing your horrified expression as you witnessed your dear friend acting in such a hideous way.

However implausible these various scenarios might seem, they would each acquire more plausibility to the extent that you were convinced your friend was incapable of doing what he seemed to be doing when he abused this disabled person. And to this extent, the faithful way of responding to his apparently aberrant behavior would be to entertain one or more of these possible scenarios until you had a chance to question him in person.

This is something like the way I'm proposing we respond when we encounter biblical narratives that depict God doing things we can't imagine Christ doing. For example, I can't for a moment imagine Jesus—the one who made refusing violence and loving enemies a condition for being considered a child of God—commanding anyone to mercilessly slaughter *anyone*, let alone an entire population that included women and infants. And yet, Yahweh is depicted as doing this very thing in a book that Jesus himself considered inspired, and thus a book that I, out of obedience to him, feel compelled to regard as inspired.

I submit it would be unfaithful to Christ and the relationship he has forged with us on the cross to allow this or any other narrative to call into question the loving and nonviolent character of God that he reveals. So too, I believe it would be unfaithful for us to invest this or any similar narrative with the same authority we invest in Christ and to thereby conclude that Jesus only reveals part of God—as though there were a merciless, violent streak in God that remains hidden behind the cross.

A more faithful response, I believe, is to instead assume that there must have been things going on behind the scenes that we are not privy to. And until we can ask him face-to-face, the faithful thing to do is to try and imagine what this "something else" might have been.

As I'm wrestling with this, the "something else" I'm imagining is not about why God acted the way he is depicted as acting in certain narratives. Rather, the "something else" I'm looking for is about why God would stoop to *appear to act* in certain ways that reflect a character that is very different from his true character, revealed in Christ. And my proposal is that, if we read these narratives through the lens of the cross, we can see that what was going on back when these narratives were inspired was the same thing that was going on when on the cross God stooped to become our sin and our curse and to therefore appear not only far less beautiful than he actually is, but to appear guilty, though in reality he is beautiful and sinless.

Conclusion

Whether you find this brief outline of my proposed scenario of what else was going on when God is depicted in violent terms in the Old Testament plausible or not, I want to end this chapter by encouraging you to trust that when we see the self-sacrificial love of God manifested on Calvary, we are seeing *all* of God's *true* character. And trusting that this is the exact representation of what God looks like, down to his very essence (*hypostasis*, Heb. 1:3), I encourage you to find all your *life* in this one source. So too, I encourage you to embrace Scripture as God's infallible way of pointing you toward, and helping you cultivate a relationship with, Christ, who is this *life*.

I've found that by adopting this posture, I can wrestle with Scripture's problematic narratives, as well as with the myriad literary or historical issues that surround it, without having my confidence in Scripture's inspiration called into question and without it affecting my source of *life*. Indeed, while my mind certainly wants to find the plausible answer to these problematic narratives and a myriad of other biblical issues, I am at peace with ambiguity, with doubt, with questions, and with being proved wrong and changing my mind, *so long as* I remain anchored in the One who is the foundation of my faith, the center of Scripture, the center of my theology, and the center of my identity as my one and only source of *life*.

Substantial Hope

Imagination is everything. It is the preview of life's coming attractions.

—ALBERT EINSTEIN

Now faith is [the] substantiating of things hoped for, [the] conviction of things not seen.

—HEBREWS 11:1 DARBY TRANSLATION

In the last two chapters I've suggested a Christ-centered way of grounding our faith, structuring our theology, and framing our interpretation of Scripture that I have found to be biblical and rationally defensible. I have also found it to be profoundly helpful as an anchor to my faith in the sea of ambiguity and uncertainty that is our postmodern world. I'd like to now build on these insights by offering an insight from Scripture concerning the actual practice of faith. It's an insight that has been almost uniformly overlooked but that I, and many others, have found extremely helpful, not only in our relationship with Christ, but also in just about every area of our lives. For as we're about to see, whether people embrace "religious" faith or not, and whether people know it or not (most do not), faith permeates every area of our life.

In what follows I will first discuss two passages that are frequently misunderstood when applied to the issue of how to exercise faith. Not coincidentally, they are the verses most frequently appealed to in support of the kind of certainty-seeking faith discussed in part 1 of this book. I will then turn our attention to Hebrews 11:1, a passage that is commonly cited as a *definition* of faith, but rarely if ever mentioned as a passage that provides insight into *how to exercise* faith.

Must Faith Never Doubt?

A Classic "No-Doubt" Passage

I recently spoke at a Christian rock festival where I noticed a young girl with the word "Doubt" printed on her T-shirt. The word was circled in red with a slash through it, in a sense advocating the doubt-shunning view of faith we discussed in part 1. Underneath this symbol was a reference to James 1:6–8. This is not surprising, for this is a key passage frequently appealed to in support of the notion that doubt is the enemy of faith. This passage reads:

> But when you ask, you must believe and not doubt, because the one who doubts is like a wave of the sea, blown and tossed by the wind. That person should not expect to receive anything from the Lord. Such a person is double-minded and unstable in all they do. (James 1:6–8)

On the surface, it certainly looks as if this passage is advocating the very model of faith I spent three chapters trying to refute. "You must believe and not doubt." What could be clearer than this? Initial appearances notwithstanding, there are five considerations that demonstrate that this passage not only does not support a certainty-seeking model of faith; it actually *refutes* it.

What's This Passage About?

First, as is always the case, it's crucial that we read this passage in context. In the verse that immediately precedes this one, James says:

"If any of you lacks wisdom, you should ask God, who gives generously to all without finding fault, and it will be given to you" (James 1:5). James *then* continues, "but when you ask . . ."

This indicates that James is not promising believers they can expect to receive *whatever they ask for* if they simply "believe and not doubt." He's speaking specifically about asking God *for wisdom*. Hence, if this verse warrants the assumption that exercising faith involves suppressing doubt—a point I will in a moment argue against—it does so only with respect to our coming to God for wisdom.

What's the Wavering About?

Second, the word translated as "doubt" (*diakrinō*) in this passage literally means "to separate, distinguish, judge, or evaluate." When used to describe an activity that a person does in their own mind and heart, the word signifies they are *in the process of* evaluating or judging competing ideas, convictions, ambitions, or commitments. It thus signifies that the person is not yet resolved about a matter but is continuing to waver between various options. Indeed, some versions of the Bible appropriately translate the word simply as "waver" (e.g., NLT, KJV; WEB, "wavereth").

The wavering this word describes can justly be described as doubting *if* the person is wavering between competing beliefs or ideas, each of which claims to be true. In this case, the person is not yet convinced about the truth of any of these competing beliefs or ideas and thus can be said to be in a state of doubt. But a person can waver between other things in their mind and heart that we wouldn't say puts them in a state of doubt.

Suppose a father is wavering between whether he should obey his boss who has told him to work late or to leave on time so he can make it to his daughter's piano recital, as he had promised her? He's certainly wavering back and forth, but we wouldn't describe his wavering as doubting. He's simply conflicted over his loyalties.

Or imagine a person is wavering between competing options when one of the options is obviously right. For example, suppose a woman was wavering between whether she wants to honor her wedding vows and remain faithful to her husband or to run off with the man she's become enamored with at work. This woman is certainly wavering back and forth as she evaluates and judges her options, but we again wouldn't describe her as being in a state of doubt. I think we'd rather be inclined to say that the very fact that she is wavering about this matter reflects a lack of loyalty on her part.

I'm convinced that this is the sort of wavering James is describing. It's a sense that is captured well by the New Living Translation.

> But when you ask him, be sure that your faith is in God alone. Do not waver, for a person with divided loyalty is as unsettled as a wave of the sea that is blown and tossed by the wind.

If this translation is accepted, then James is not describing a person who is wavering between whether they believe they'll receive wisdom when they ask for it; James is rather describing a person who is wavering between whether they will remain loyal and seek wisdom from God alone, on the one hand, or whether they will be duplicitous by also trying to derive wisdom from the world.

Doubt that Threatens Covenant

Incidentally, I believe we should interpret the several other passages that stress the importance of *not* doubting along the same lines. When doubt is contrasted with covenantal faith, it must be understood in a *relational* rather than a *psychological* way. There is a type of doubt that betrays a covenant relationship, but this isn't about a lack of psychological certainty regarding a belief or a future event. It's about wavering in one's trust in another person or in God.

So, for example, when Jesus told his disciples they could move a mountain if they didn't doubt (Matt. 21:21), he wasn't sharing a sort of New Age mind-over-matter secret. In his typically hyperbolic manner (as we'll discuss below), Jesus was emphasizing the power that comes from placing complete trust *in God*. So too, when Jesus chided Peter for having little faith as he sank into the lake (Matt. 14:31), he wasn't talking about Peter's lack of psychological certainty that he wouldn't sink. He was talking about Peter's wavering confidence *in him*. The disciples got the point, for when Jesus got in the boat and the wind suddenly stopped, they worshiped him and proclaimed him to be the Son of God (Matt. 14:33).

The fact of the matter is that the certainty-seeking concept of faith that is practiced by so many Christians today, and that is most intensely advocated by New Age advocates and "Word of Faith" or "Positive Confession" Christians, illustrates how the concept of faith morphs when *a relationship with God is subtracted from it*.[1] Take God out of the picture, and faith becomes focused on what *our mind* can do if we make ourselves certain rather than what *God* can do if we simply trust him.[2]

Unstable Duplicity

Understanding the wavering James is talking about as a wavering between loyalties fits his description of the wavering person better than the doubt interpretation, and this is my third point. Why would James say that a person who is uncertain that God will grant their request for wisdom is "double-minded and unstable in all they do"? This is a description of a person with a conflicted frame of mind, resulting in an unstable lifestyle. This goes far beyond what a doubt about a specific prayer request would warrant. On the other hand, this description perfectly fits a person who is duplicitously relying on, and fusing together, two contrary sources of wisdom.

Competing Wisdoms

Fourth, the loyalty interpretation of the wavering James is talking about seems to be confirmed in the second half of chapter 3 of his epistle. He starts this section by noting that a "fig tree" cannot "bear olives," a "grapevine" cannot "bear figs," and a "salt spring" cannot "produce fresh water" (v. 12). James then makes the point that if anyone is going to be considered "wise and understanding among you," they must "show it by their good life" and "by deeds done in the humility that comes from wisdom" (v. 13). In other words, a person's lifestyle grows out of the kind of wisdom they have.

James then goes on to say that if a person has "bitter envy" and "self-ambition" in their hearts, they cannot "boast about it" or "deny the truth," for this reflects a kind of "wisdom" that "does not come down from heaven but is earthly, unspiritual, demonic" (vv. 14–15). This kind of "wisdom" can only bring forth "disorder and every evil practice" (v. 16). By contrast, "the wisdom that comes from heaven is first of all pure; then peace-loving, considerate, submissive, full of mercy and good fruit, impartial and sincere" (v. 17). And whereas the earthly and unspiritual wisdom produces "disorder and every evil practice" in a person's life, people who possess heavenly wisdom "reap a harvest of righteousness" (v. 18).

This passage indicates that James is passionate about highlighting two antithetical kinds of wisdom—the heavenly and the demonic— and about the two very different kinds of lifestyles they grow. It also reveals that James is emphatic about the need for believers to not confuse these radically different kinds of wisdom and instead to seek only the first. And this, I contend, provides strong support for the loyalty interpretation of the wavering James discusses in 1:6–8.

James is instructing disciples to not waver in their commitment to seek the wisdom from above that comes from God alone. People who waver in this commitment cannot expect to "receive anything" related to this wisdom "from the Lord." And since they are polluted by the unspiritual wisdom that brings forth "disorder and every evil practice," they will end up being "double-minded and unstable in all they do."

Wisdom to Persevere

Finally, this interpretation is further confirmed when we read verses 5–8 in the context of the three verses leading up to them. Here we find James encouraging his congregation to "consider it pure joy . . . whenever you face trials," and the reason is "because you know that the testing of your faith produces perseverance." Moreover, when they "let perseverance finish its work," James tells them they will be "mature and complete, not lacking anything" (1:2–4). It's with this in mind that James then says that if any "lack wisdom," they should ask God without wavering.

To me, this broader context strongly suggests that the wavering James is talking about isn't concerned with doubt: it's rather concerned with whether disciples will rely on God for the kind of wisdom that will enable them to find joy in trials and to persevere in their faith to become mature and complete, on the one hand, or whether they'll be polluted with the earthly wisdom that makes them "unstable in all they do," on the other.

In light of these five considerations, I trust it's clear that this passage provides no support for the notion that exercising faith involves suppressing doubt in order to convince ourselves that a belief is true. Indeed, far from supporting the carnal notion that God will give us anything we want if we convince ourselves he will do so, this passage actually teaches *the exact opposite*. For the sort of wisdom James encourages us to trust God alone for is a "heavenly wisdom" that finds joy in trials, perseveres, and is free of the "self-ambition" that is a characteristic of demonic wisdom of the world.

Believing You Have Already Received

Another verse that is among those most frequently cited in support of the common misconception that faith is as strong as it is free of doubt is found in Mark when Jesus says, "Therefore I tell you, whatever you ask for in prayer, believe that you have received it, and it will be yours" (Mark 11:24). As I argued throughout part 1 of this work, when this and several similar verses (e.g., Matt. 18:19; 21:21; Mark 11:23; John 14:13–14; 15:7, 16; 16:23) have been taken literally, it has consistently led to idolatrous, unhealthy, bizarre, and sometimes disastrous consequences. Fortunately, there are several telltale indications that Jesus did not intend his statement to be taken literally.

An Impossible Instruction

First, if we interpret Mark 11:24 literally, this instruction is simply impossible to obey. Think about it. We are instructed to believe we have already received what we ask for when we ask for it. But the very act of asking for something presupposes that we *don't* believe we've *already* received it. If we truly believed we'd already received what we're asking for, we obviously *wouldn't be asking for it*. Anytime the literal interpretation of a passage involves a self-contradiction such as this, it suggests that the passage was not intended literally.

Was Jesus a Hypocrite?

Second, if Jesus intended Mark 11:24 literally, then he's guilty of hypocrisy, for never do we find him encouraging people to convince themselves they'd already received what they asked for when they prayed or when he prayed for them. Indeed, we sometimes find him acting in ways that contradict this advice.

For example, Jesus once prayed for a blind man by spitting in his eyes. Why he resorted to this rather gross practice is not at all clear. What's important, however, is that after he did this, Jesus asked the man, "Do you see anything?" (Mark 8:23). If Jesus intended his instruction in Mark 11:24 to be followed in a literal way, he should never have asked this question. He should rather have encouraged the man to believe he had received the healing that Jesus just prayed for.

It turned out this man's eyes were not completely healed, for he replied that, while he could see people, "they look like trees walking around" (Mark 8:24). Significantly enough, Jesus didn't rebuke this man for lacking faith by admitting this, which is precisely what he should have done if he intended his instruction in Mark 11:24 to be taken literally. He instead prayed for the man again so his eyesight could be completely restored. If we assume, as we should, that Jesus was never guilty of hypocrisy, his behavior in this episode completely refutes the literal interpretation of the teaching in question.

Scripture Interprets Scripture

Third, a key principle of biblical interpretation is that "Scripture interprets Scripture." This means we must interpret every verse of the Bible in light of everything the Bible has to say on the subject matter of that verse.[3] Read literally and in isolation from the rest of the Bible, Mark 11:24 gives the impression that our level of certainty while praying is the only variable that affects whether we'll receive what we're asking for. But when we zoom out to get the bigger picture, we find the situation is a good bit more complicated than that.

For example, in Matthew 18:19, Jesus says, "truly I tell you that if *two of you* on earth *agree* about anything you ask for, it will be done for [you] by my Father in heaven" (emphasis added). Jesus is here indicating that the number of people agreeing about a prayer request is a variable that affects the outcome of a prayer, yet Mark 11:24 said nothing about this. So too, in 1 John 5:14 John says that, "if we ask anything *according to [God's] will*, he hears us" (emphasis added). John here indicates that God's will is an important variable affecting the outcome of prayer, but again, Mark 11:24 says nothing about this.

In fact, as I've argued at length elsewhere, Scripture indicates that there are a multitude of factors that affect the extent to which praying about a matter makes a difference.[4] An assortment of passages indicate that the faith of the person you're praying for, the persistence of your prayer, the fervency of your prayer, and the presence (as well as the number and strength) of spiritual forces working for or against you, all factor into the equation. Other passages indicate that the presence of sin in your life or the life of the person you're praying for, as well as the irrevocable influence of free decisions made by humans and angels, influences the outcome of prayer.

When you consider all the things that influence what comes to pass, you quickly come to realize that to know why *anything* happens the way it does, including why prayer has the effect it has (or doesn't have), you'd have to possess exhaustive knowledge about every single thing that has ever influenced the course of history, going back to the beginning of time. This is why we can never be certain ahead of time that our prayer will bring about the results we are praying for and why it's foolish mental gimmickry to pretend otherwise. As we earlier noted in relation to the book of Job (chap.4), this is also why we can never know, in any exhaustive sense, why good and evil seem to be meted out so randomly and why prayer produces miraculous results one moment and seems to accomplish nothing the next.[5]

Moreover, the unfathomably interconnected complexity of a world populated with free agents also explains why we should never assume either that God simply didn't want to answer a prayer, or that someone lacked faith when prayer isn't "successful." And, finally, it's why it's simply absurd to interpret Mark 11:24 literally.

The Nature of Hyperbole

If we aren't to interpret Jesus's statement in Mark 11:24 literally, how *are* we to interpret it? First of all, as I've previously noted, ancient Jews made extensive use of hyperbole (exaggerated expressions). We still use hyperbolic expressions, like when a frustrated mother says to her child, "I've told you a million times to hang your coat up!" The mother obviously isn't intending to suggest that she actually counted the number of times she's said this, with this being the millionth time. She's rather simply expressing her frustration by intentionally overstating the number of times she's told her child to hang up a coat.

Ancient Jews used hyperbole far more extensively than Western people do today. And this is why the Bible is packed full of it. Truths are frequently expressed in unqualified and extremely exaggerated ways to emphasize their importance. It's vitally important to remember this when you're reading Scripture because, as we'll explore more fully in the next chapter, few things have caused as much misunderstanding and have led to such damaging consequences as the tendency of modern readers to mistake hyperbolic expressions for literal statements.

Trusting Mistaken Promises

Several years ago I spoke with a dear woman who was profoundly angry with God and severely depressed because, she told me, "God didn't keep his promises." She had been taught that God promises that if we raise our young children with the right instruction, they will never reject it when they become adults. This is, after all, exactly what Proverbs 22:6 seems to say: "Start children off on the way they should go, and even when they are old they will not turn from it." She and her husband had done their best to raise their son this way, but the son ended up turning from their instruction and rebelling against them as a teenager. He moved out at the age of eighteen, soon became a meth addict, and before long was selling it to sustain his addiction. After a number of run-ins with the law over the next few years, this young man was tragically killed in a drug-related gang war.

On top of the terrible pain that would accompany the loss of a child under any circumstances, and on top of the pain of the divorce that ensued when her marriage couldn't bear the weight of this nightmare, this woman felt betrayed by God, who previously had been her source of strength and joy. To make matters worse, on the basis of this same literal interpretation of this same verse, some of her friends at the church she attended concluded that she and her ex-husband must have failed as parents. Had they raised their child properly, this group insisted, the Word of God promises that God would not have allowed their son to go wayward.

As happens all too often, the drama of the book of Job was once again being reenacted. This poor woman was blaming God for her tragedy, while her friends were blaming her. Like Job's friends, they "proved to be of no help" because they saw "something dreadful and [were] afraid" (Job 6:21). They clung to a belief system that made them feel secure, indicting their "friend" in the process. And, as also happens all too often, the point of this profound book was completely missed. For as we saw in chapter 4, when God finally speaks out of the storm (Job 38:1), his central point is that humans know far too little about the vast complexity of the war-torn creation they live in to ever point a finger at God or anyone else when tragedy strikes.

All of this was brought about because this woman and this church failed to realize that this proverb, like so many proverbs, was utilizing hyperbole. To drive home the importance of being diligent in raising young children in a godly way, the author expressed his teaching in an emphatic and unqualified way: "even when they are old they *will not* turn from it" (emphasis added)—no ifs, ands, or buts. But no ancient Jew would ever suspect he was claiming that raising children the right way *guarantees* that they'll never go astray, as though children raised correctly no longer possess free will or that others with free will cannot negatively influence them.

Whenever people interpret hyperbolic expressions in a literal way, they ignore the vast complexity of the world and transform the principles expressed in hyperbolic language into magical formulas. They find security in thinking that if they just do this or that they're guaranteed to magically receive whatever they believe the magic formula promises. But as happened with Job's friends, they purchase their magical security at the expense of all those for whom these "promises" have failed, and by the same token, this false security backfires with a vengeance if ever they or a loved one end up on the losing end of these "failed" promises.

Faith and Imagination

As a first-century Jewish teacher, Jesus made extensive use of hyperbole, and Mark 11:24 is a case in point. Jesus wasn't telling people to literally try to believe they'd received what they were asking for, nor was he guaranteeing that people always get what they ask for if they succeed at doing this. What he was doing, I will now argue, was emphatically stating an important point about how we are to exercise faith when we pray.

Reinforcing Covenantal Trust

First, it's clear that Jesus is giving a hyperbolic instruction about the importance of not doubting when we pray. But as we noted earlier, it's crucial we remember that we are talking about *covenantal* faith, and therefore *covenantal* doubt. This is one of the passages that Rhonda Byrne includes in her bestselling New Age manual *The Secret*. Byrne purports to let people in on the "secret" that if you visualize something and convince yourself you have it, you are guaranteed to actually receive it. Byrne can use this passage in this way, however, only because she has stripped it of its covenantal meaning and thus divorced it from a relationship with God. This psychologized, magical interpretation is impossible if we retain the covenantal framework of Mark 11:24, as we should. In this framework, Jesus is simply stressing, in a hyperbolic way, the importance of trusting God when we pray.

At the same time, as misguided as Byrne's psychologized concept of faith is, there is one aspect of this passage that I believe she almost gets right. When I interpret this passage in light of Hebrews 11:1, which we'll discuss below, I think we can discern that Jesus is not only stressing the importance of trusting God when we pray; he's also giving us an indication of what it looks like *from our side* when we do this. And the point Byrne almost got right is that this has a lot to do with our imagination.

As is clear from Byrne's abuse of this passage, when the role of imagination in faith gets severed from the more fundamental point about trusting God, faith is transformed into a self-centered, mind-over-matter gimmick. And because there's so much of this kind of talk going on today, many conservative Christians have understandably become rather paranoid about any talk of imagination. But the right response to this nonsense is not to throw out the imagination baby with the New Age bathwater: the right response is to take our imagination back for its God-intended use! As I hope to demonstrate throughout the remainder of this chapter, if we always remember that the purpose of imagination in prayer is to help us more effectively lean on God, it becomes a crucial, God-glorifying dimension of what covenantal faith is all about.

The Way We Think

To unpack the role imagination plays in Mark 11:24 and to lay the groundwork for our subsequent treatment of Hebrews 11:1, I'd like to spend a little time drawing our attention to something that is actually perfectly obvious, yet rarely noticed, about how we think. To some this may initially seem like I'm digressing from the topic of faith and doubt, but I assure you, when I'm finished you'll see that this discussion discloses an all-important and extremely empowering aspect of how we exercise faith. The perfectly-obvious-but-rarely-noticed fact I want to talk about is that we think, anticipate, and remember, not by reciting information in our minds, but by replicating our actual experiences of the world in our imagination.

When I think about my wife in her absence, for example, I don't think about facts about her—for example, that she is five feet four inches tall, has lovely oval eyes, gives our pet dog, Max, too much attention, and so on. I rather *envision her* in my "mind's eye"—my imagination—*as though* she is present with me. I represent her—I literally make her *present again* (re-present)—in my imagination by replicating actual experiences of her in my mind. So too, when I anticipate something I expect to happen, I don't think about facts pertaining to it. I rather represent it in my imagination by *envisioning* what I expect to see, and sometimes imaginatively *hearing* what I expect to hear or *feeling* what I expect to physically feel when the event takes place. And it's the same when I remember a past event. I make it present again by imaginatively reexperiencing what I saw, heard, and/or physically felt when I initially experienced the event. Sometimes my sense of smell or taste may also be involved in my imaginative representations of a present, future, or past person or event, if these senses are relevant to the person or event in question.

The Power of Imagination

This is how we all think. If you doubt this, take a moment right now and think about someone you love who is not with you now. As you do this, ask yourself; how do I know this thought is of the person I love *and not someone else*?

If you did this exercise, I'm sure you found that you distinguished this person from others in your thought by the same means you identify this person in your actual experience. This person *looks, sounds, feels*, and maybe even *smells* different from others. Though people differ over which sense gets emphasized when they represent reality in their imagination as they think about things in the past, present, or future, we all think by relying on our brain's capacity to entertain images of things that are not actually present to us. We all think by means of *imaginative representations* (making present again) of our actual experience of the world.[6]

Not only this, but the more concrete any particular imaginative representation is, the more it impacts us emotionally. If you merely give a passing thought to an upcoming event you're looking forward to, for example, you probably won't feel very different than if you hadn't had this momentary anticipation. But if you take the time to enter into your thought about this event, imaging it as vividly as you can, you'll likely find it affects your mood significantly. Your excitement (or dread) reflects the fact that you're bringing into the present—representing—some of the pleasantness (or unpleasantness) you expect to experience when the event actually happens.

Contemplating events we anticipate in a vivid way makes us long for them (or dread them), which in turn sometimes motivates us to do what is necessary to ensure the event happens (or to avoid the event). A wife and mother may have an aversion to putting in the extra hours she needs to work in order to afford taking her family to Disney World. But if she would spend some time vividly imagining how much fun it would be for her and her family to go on this vacation and how much good it would do her family to spend this enjoyable time together, she would find her imaginative representations of this event generating an excitement in her that might be sufficient to motivate her to make the sacrifice of working these extra hours.

Though most don't realize it, we are thinking, anticipating, and remembering all day long, and every single imaginative representation involved in this ceaseless mental activity carries an emotional component that to some degree affects us and motivates our behavior. The extent to which any representation impacts and motivates us depends on the degree to which it vividly replicates reality. *Everything* we feel and *everything* we do is a reflection of the mostly unconscious perpetual imaginative activity going on in our minds.

In this light, it's no wonder that the New Testament places so much emphasis on the need for believers to take control of their thoughts (e.g., Rom. 12:2; 2 Cor. 10:3–5; Phil. 4:8). Unfortunately, most people today assume this merely involves memorizing and reciting true information. This is certainly a good thing to do, but it alone won't significantly transform us because, as we've seen, we don't think with information, so information alone simply does not significantly impact us. In order to take thoughts "captive" to Jesus Christ (2 Cor. 10:5) and to be "transformed by the renewing of [our] mind" (Rom. 12:2), we instead need to change the concrete representations that automatically, and mostly unconsciously, pop into our brain, usually in response to external stimuli, throughout the day.[7]

Faith Motivation

The obvious but rarely noticed insight that we think with imaginative representations lies at the heart of the nature of faith, and I believe it's what Jesus is hyperbolically alluding to in Mark 11:24. We can't literally believe we have received what we're asking for when we pray, but we can, and should, mentally envision receiving what we're praying for *as though* it is present to us.

We earlier said that biblical faith is about a willingness to act in the face of uncertainty, and now we're learning how we can acquire the motivation to do this. When we imaginatively represent something we believe to be God's will in a vivid, real-seeming way, it impacts us emotionally, the way anticipating an upcoming vacation would.

This in turn creates the desire and motivation to do whatever is neces-sary—including engaging in passionate prayer—to bring about this aspect of God's will.

The Motivation behind Audacious Seeking

To illustrate, Jesus taught us that "the one who seeks, finds" and "to the one who knocks, the door will be opened" (Matt. 7:8). And we're to seek and knock, he said, like a woman who has the audacity to pester a neighbor in the middle of the night to get bread to feed unexpected guests (Luke 11:5–10) or like a widow who has the audacity to pester an unjust judge to get justice (Luke 18:1–8). Both parables are about what persistent, audacious, faith-filled prayer looks like (see Luke 11:1; 18:8). But when we recall that motivation is a consequence of the way we imaginatively represent things in our minds, I believe we can also see in each of these parables a reflection of how we too can engage in such faith-filled praying.

Neither woman could be certain she would receive what she was seeking; yet both were willing to engage in audacious behavior in the hope of getting it. What was it that gave the women the courage and strength to act so brazenly and with such persistence? The first woman was clearly anticipating the embarrassment she would feel if she had nothing to offer guests and/or the sadness she would feel if she had to turn them away hungry. The second was clearly anticipating the ongoing hardship she and perhaps her family would face if she never found justice. Unless these women were vividly experiencing *in the present* the pain that would come about if their requests were not honored, they couldn't possibly have had the motivation to act so audaciously and persistently.

So too, whether it concerns a negative situation we hope to avoid, as it was with these women, or something positive we hope to acquire, if it involves seeing God respond in radical ways to our prayer, we will need to exercise the audacious faith these women exercised and to therefore engage in audacious seeking and knocking the way they did. Yet, we can't hope to do this unless we first have the sort of pas-sionate motivation both of them displayed, which means we'll need to engage our imagination the way these women did.

What Jesus is teaching us in Mark 11:24, I believe, is that the way to acquire this motivation is by imaginatively representing what we are seeking and knocking for, *as though* it were already present before us, just as these women did. If we believe in a way that makes what we are asking for present to us, imagining that we have already received it, then (speaking hyperbolically, without any qualifications or nuances) it will be done for us.

If I'm correct about this, then Jesus's teaching in this passage is the *exact opposite* of what those who use it to support a certainty-seeking model of faith conclude. Whenever we interpret hyperbole literally, we turn it into magic, as I said above. Hence, those who interpret this passage literally think that if we can simply make ourselves psychologically certain about something we ask for, it will magically be done. Not only is no further work necessary, but no further work is even possible. For if we persist in asking for something, this is obviously evidence that we *don't* in fact believe we've *already* received it.

In the interpretation I'm offering, by contrast, the purpose for believing in a way that makes what we're asking for imaginatively present before us—*as though* we've already received it—is precisely to motivate us toward audacious persistence as we seek and knock—like a woman who won't leave an unjust judge alone until she receives justice.

Seeing Hope and Feeling the Unseen

I believe this understanding of what it means to exercise faith is reinforced in Hebrews 11:1. While this passage is uniformly understood to provide a definition of faith, I think it also offers us some instruction on how to *practice* faith.

A Question of Translation

To help us see this, I first need to weigh in on the translation of this passage. The different translations of the Bible available today usually differ from one another only in how they nuance the meaning of a passage. This is not the case with Hebrews 11:1, however. The slightly different way two Greek words in this passage can be translated give the passage a very different meaning, as we'll now see.

For reasons that will be clear in a moment, I prefer Darby's very literal translation, which reads, "Now faith is [the] substantiating of things hoped for, [the] conviction of things not seen." Coming in a close second, in my estimation, are the King James and Webster's translations, which read, "Now faith is the substance of things hoped for, the evidence of things not seen."

The Greek word translated as "substantiating" by Darby and as "substance" by the KJV and WEB is *hypostasis*. As we observed when we discussed what the Son reveals about God in Hebrews 1:3 (chap. 9), this word refers to a thing's "essence" or "substance." Now, the word was sometimes used to denote something solid that one could confidently stand or lean on, so most modern versions translate *hypostasis* as "being sure" (TNIV), as "confidence" (NIV, NLT), or as "assurance" (RSV, NASB, ASV, ESV). Unfortunately, by identifying a *feeling of confidence* as the essence of faith rather than the *substance* that gives confidence, these translations reinforce a certainty-seeking model of faith that we've seen is unbiblical and that leads to so many unfortunate consequences. For this and several other reasons that we're about to discuss, I think it is in this case better to stick as close as possible to the literal translation of *hypostasis* as "substance" or "substantiating."

The Greek word that is translated as "conviction" by Darby is *elegchos*. On the one hand, this word can refer to "evidence," as it's found in the KJV and the Webster Bible, with the connotation that this "evidence" leads to a particular conviction. On the other hand, *elegchos* can refer to the "conviction" that is *based on* evidence. A variation of this word is used in 1 Timothy 3:16 when Paul claims that Scripture is useful for (among other things) "rebuking" (*elegmos*). Paul is saying that Scripture can be used as the evidence by which a teacher brings *conviction* on another person. Since it's not clear how faith could function as the "evidence" of things not seen, many modern translators agree with Darby and translate *elegchos* as "conviction" (ASV, ESV, NASB, NRSV, YLT).

Unfortunately, however, some modern translations further reinforce certainty-seeking faith by specifying the kind of "conviction" that the author is talking about as the feeling of being "certain" (TNIV, Phillips, NIV 1984, GNT) or, even worse, as "knowing" (NCV), "convinces" (GW), or even as "proof" (CEB, HCSB). So far as I've been able to discern, while *elegchos* signifies a sense of confidence, in this context, I'm convinced it stops short of a feeling of *certainty*. Indeed, I will in a moment argue that the examples of faith that follow in Hebrews 11 preclude the suggestion that faith involves a feeling of certainty.

Envisioning and Longing for the Future

If we translate *hypostasis* as "substantiating" or "substance" rather than as a feeling of confidence that is a result of standing or relying on something solid, and if we translate *elegchos* simply as "conviction," with the connotation that it is a conviction that arises from evidence, then it's easy to discern in this passage the same instruction we found Jesus giving when he told us to believe we have received what we're praying for. That is, faith involves embracing a vivid vision of an anticipated future that in turn gives rise to a compelling conviction that moves us toward that future.

In the terms I used above, we exercise faith when we imaginatively represent, as a substantial reality, something in the future that we believe to be God's will. And just as evidence produces a conviction in a person, our imaginative representation produces in us a confident motivation to do what is necessary to bring this imaginative representation into reality.

I believe this interpretation finds support in the way the author talks about the heroes of faith throughout the remainder of this chapter. After talking about several heroes of faith, with an emphasis on Abraham and Sarah (vv. 8–12), the author says, "All these people were still living by faith when they died. They did not receive the things promised; they only *saw them* and *welcomed them* from a distance" (v. 13, cf. 39, emphasis added). Note the visual imaginative imagery in the faith these heroes exercised. So too, this author claims that the heroes of faith he's speaking of were "*looking for* a country of their own" (v. 14, emphasis added) and were "*longing for* a better country—a heavenly one," which he then identifies as a city that God prepared for them (v. 16, emphasis added). Note not only the imaginative seeing but the "conviction" this imagery produces as they longed for that which they imaginatively envisioned. Like Abraham, these heroes lived as foreigners and vagabonds in this world because they were "*looking forward* to the city with foundations, whose architect and builder is God" (v. 10, emphasis added).

It's evident that these heroes of faith were *looking for*, and *saw*, something they could not *physically* see. They were "substantiating," to use Darby's term, an anticipated future. And their imaginative, real-seeming vision produced a "conviction" of *longing* in them, which is what motivated them to sacrifice all this world had to offer to remain faithful to the One who called them as they moved forward into an uncertain future. Contrary to those above-mentioned versions that translate *elegchos* as "certain," these heroes of faith *couldn't* have been certain they would receive what they longed for, for as a matter of fact, "none of them received what had been promised" by the time they died. Yet, they were "all commended [by God] for their faith" (v. 39).

As I've repeatedly stated in this book, faith isn't about striving for certainty. It's about striving to remain faithful in the midst of uncertainty. And what this passage, as well as Jesus and our own experience, teaches us is that we exercise this faith by imaginatively embracing God's promises as a substantial reality (*hypostasis*) that in turn creates a conviction (*elegchos*) that it will be so, which motivates us to act in ways that we hope will bring what we imaginatively envision into reality.

Exercising Faith in My Marriage

Earlier in this book I mentioned that, while Shelley and I are happily married now, we had to go through hell together to get here. We were fortunate to come under a wise Christian counselor who helped us work through this troubled time and discover ways to understand each other's alien world. One of the things this counselor helped me to discover was that I wasn't being a faithful husband to Shelley. No, I wasn't having an affair! But I wasn't exercising the kind of faith in my wife and our marriage that would result in true faithfulness.

As is usually the case with spouses in difficult marriages, my mind often drifted toward the negative things I felt at this time about Shelley and our marriage. Without trying to do so, I would often find myself ruminating over the worst aspects of our relationship. And since we think with our imagination, this meant I was continually envisioning, in concrete, substantial ways—as a *hypostasis*—the things about our relationship that made me feel alone, misunderstood, unloved, and unappreciated. And each of these negative representations caused me to reexperience the pain that was associated with it and the conviction—the *elegchos*—that this is the way my marriage would remain.

My counselor helped me realize that I was *exercising faith* that my marriage would remain miserable. And by doing this, I was pretty much ensuring that it *would* in fact remain miserable. Each negative representation, and each experience of pain associated with the representation, motivated me to become more emotionally distant from Shelley, which in turn encouraged her to become more emotionally distant from me.

There were a number of practices Shelley and I were instructed to do, individually and together, to rebuild our marriage. But the instruction that had the most impact on me was to stop exercising faith in a miserable marriage and to begin exercising faith that Shelley and I were going to eventually enjoy a loving, fulfilling marriage together. To be honest, this was challenging inasmuch as there was, at this point in our marriage, no evidence that this could happen. But I knew this was God's will for us, and I believed God could work miracles in people's lives and in their marriages.

And so, out of sheer obedience to God, I began to intentionally envision, in concrete, vivid, real-seeming ways, what it would look like if God's will for our marriage became a reality. And whenever I caught myself drifting back into negative ruminations, I would stop and replace them with the positive imaginative representations that I was convinced reflected God's will. I was, in effect, taking every thought "captive" to Christ (2 Cor. 10:5). I was being transformed by the renewing of my mind (Rom. 12:2).

I was amazed at how quickly this changed my disposition, which in turn began to bring about positive changes in our marriage. When I would concretely envision Shelley and me walking around the block with our arms around other and smiles on our faces, or when I would vividly imagine us happily engaging in a project together, it produced a longing for this in my heart and, over time, a conviction that this would become a reality. (And it has become a reality!) Whatever we hold as a *hypostasis* in our mind creates an accompanying *elegchos* that it will be so, which in turn moves us in that direction. And this works whether what we're imagining is positive or negative, in line with, or out of sync with, God's will.

As I was exercising this newfound faith in my marriage, was I *certain* our marriage was going to become a loving, fulfilling marriage? Not at all. To be honest, I struggled with no small amount of doubt, especially in the early weeks we were in counseling. But I had *enough* confidence in God and just *enough* hope in my marriage to begin to walk, by faith, in this direction. And as is always the case when we embark on a new direction in our lives, my walk had to start by bringing my imagination into alignment with God's will (cf. Phil.4:8).

The Place for Setting Aside Doubt

This is the one context in which it is appropriate, and even necessary, to set aside doubt. Whereas doubt is necessary and healthy when deciding what we believe is true, and while doubt can play a healthy, beneficial role as we work to integrate our faith with our expanding worldviews, there is no positive role it can play when faithfulness requires us to resolve to be steadfast as we move toward something we are confident is God's will. In these contexts, we of course can't be certain things will turn out the way we believe God wants them to turn out. But faithfulness requires us to not dwell on this uncertainty and to instead envision, as concretely as possible, the future we hope for, and to experience the conviction that it will be so.

"According to your faith it will be done," Jesus said. It is magical to think this hyperbolic teaching guarantees we'll receive whatever it is we're exercising faith for. Yet, while there are multiple variables that affect what comes to pass, Jesus is emphasizing that the faith we practice day in and day out, usually without noticing it, is the most important of them. Because Shelley and I both chose to have faith and to be faithful to each other, and because we were willing to put a lot of work into our relationship (how nice it would be if magic *was* real!), we have been blessed to receive what our faith was pointing us toward. But we never would have received this *in reality* if we had not first envisioned ourselves receiving this *in our imagination*.

You need not be certain that a belief is true or that something you believe to be God's will is going to come to pass in order to have faith. You need merely be confident enough to commit to a course of action. And the first act of faith we take, and the act that builds motivation for all subsequent actions, is the act of imagining. Envision the world *as if* your belief is true, and then experience the conviction (*elegchos*) that motivates you to act in the world *as if* your belief is true. We are living as faithful disciples to the extent that we do this throughout each day, all the while purging from our mind and behavior everything that is inconsistent with what we believe to be God's will.

And this has nothing to do with how relatively certain or doubtful we are that our belief is *in fact* true.

Conclusion

Faith is the substantiating of things hoped for and the conviction of things not yet seen. I encourage you, therefore, to be aware of what you are representing in your mind when you pray, and to take care to align it with what you believe to be God's will. When you pray for someone who is sick or suffering some other infirmity, I encourage you to imagine God's will being done "on earth as it is in heaven" by envisioning the person being healed. As you align your vision with God's vision, you'll find your heart gets aligned with God's heart as you long to see his will come to pass and as you partner with God by pushing in this direction in passionate prayer.

So too, when you pray for a couple in a bad marriage, ask the Holy Spirit to help you concretely envision the marriage being restored and encourage this couple to do the same. When you pray for someone in bondage to something, ask the Spirit to give you a faith-filled vision of that person being set free. And when you obey Jesus by praying a blessing on your enemies, ask God to help you imaginatively represent his love flowing over them, to see them being freed from their anger, their hostility, their pettiness, or whatever bondage they may be under.

I encourage you as well to use any means possible to remind yourself throughout the day to observe the faith movies and faith soundtracks that are playing in your imagination. These concrete representations, which are automatically activated when triggered, usually go unnoticed, though we on some level feel their emotional component. Once activated, these imaginative reenactments of past experiences determine how we interpret, feel about, and respond to our moment-by-moment experiences. And in this subtle and usually unnoticed way, they each influence the direction, quality, and kingdom significance of life.

And yet, for most people, the vast majority of these images communicate messages that are not in line with truth, as revealed by God. People may consciously affirm all true beliefs while unconsciously exercising a faith that is largely conformed to the "pattern of the world" (Rom. 12:2) and that is therefore pulling them in a direction that is contrary to their beliefs. This is why so many people are puzzled about the perpetual stark mismatch between their beliefs and their actual life. According to our *faith*, Jesus said, not our *beliefs*, it is done to us.

And when you wake up to the way you unconsciously and automatically practice false faith, I encourage you not to get angry with yourself (which is always unhelpful) but instead to ask God to help you calmly set aside the false things you were envisioning and to instead envision truth as a vivid, substantial reality. It might be helpful to structure into each day several five- to fifteen-minute breaks in which you simply run vivid, lifelike, imaginative videos and soundtracks that represent truth—the truth about God, you, your marriage, your friends, and your enemies, as well as God's will for every other aspect of your future.

You don't need to try to pretend you're certain about anything to do this. So long as you are *confident enough* that God is fully revealed in Christ that you are willing to commit to living for him, you are able to exercise a faith that will transform you while positioning you to be used by God to help transform the world.

Stumbling on the Promises of God

Half the promises people say were never kept, were never made.

—EDGAR WATSON HOWE

Has his unfailing love vanished forever?
Has his promise failed for all time?

—PSALM 77:8

We've seen that the biblical model of faith is premised on a commitment to authenticity, to trust and to be trustworthy in our relationship with God. And we've seen that the way we exercise faith in our mind is by imaginatively representing what we believe to be God's will as a substantial reality, accompanied with the conviction that it is so, which motivates us to take action to turn our vision into reality. These real-seeming imaginative representations with their accompanying motivating convictions are generated in our minds all day long, and while most people are conscious of very few of them, they exert the single greatest influence in the direction our lives take—hence the truth of Jesus's teaching, "According to your faith it will be to you."

This brings us to this very important question: If faith is about trusting God, what is it that we are supposed to trust God for? It's fairly clear what covenantal trustworthiness looks like from *our* end of the relationship. In essence, we're to simply imitate God by living in love as Christ loved us and gave his life for us (Eph. 5:1–2). But what does trustworthiness look like from *God's* end of the relationship?

A Foggy Faithfulness

A Sincere—and Sincerely Confused—Brother

Remember Brother Jacobson, the elderly man who testified about his unwavering faith almost every Sunday night in the church I served during seminary? In the course of sharing his heart, this dear man would almost always say things like, "My God is so faithful," "God has never failed me," or "Our God has never broken a promise." This is the way Christians typically talk about God's faithfulness, but I have to honestly confess that I rarely had a clue what exactly this dear brother meant by these phrases.

I remember one particularly baffling Sunday night service. As he usually did, Brother Jacobson was the first to respond when I asked if anyone had a testimony to share. After once again declaring his unshakable faith in God's Word, Brother Jacobson praised God for healing his wife of a potentially fatal bout of pneumonia twenty-some years earlier. "I stood on his Word that tells me, 'By his stripes we are healed,'" he said, "and as he always does, God faithfully honored his Word!"[1] And as they always did, the congregation responded with a hearty "Amen!"

Then, three or four sentences later, this precious elder again shared an episode demonstrating God's faithfulness. Two years after being healed of pneumonia, he said, his dear wife was diagnosed with breast cancer. This time, however, God didn't heal her. Brother Jacobson testified that God instead proved his faithfulness by taking his wife with merciful speed, thereby sparing her a lot of pain. Yet, he added, "The good Lord left her just enough time to resolve a grievance between her and her sister that goes back decades." Holding up his Bible once again, he proclaimed, "God is so faithful!"

A Vacuous Praise?

As the congregation again responded with a loud "Amen," I wondered if anyone else had noticed the obvious question posed by this testimony. If 2 Peter 2:24 is really a promise of God to always heal, as Brother Jacobson claimed, and as this congregation seemed to agree, then how can we avoid the conclusion that God did *not* honor this promise when this man's wife was *not* healed? If her healing is evidence of God's faithfulness, how can her failure to be healed not count as evidence of his *unfaithfulness*?

It's an important question because if nothing is allowed to count as evidence *against* our belief in God's faithfulness, one has to wonder if we're really asserting anything meaningful when we point to events as evidence *of* God's faithfulness. It's generally accepted in philosophy that a concept that contrasts with nothing is a vacuous concept—that is, a concept devoid of meaning, which means it is actually a pseudo-concept. So if nothing could possibly count *against* God's faithfulness, then it would seem to logically follow that we are not really asserting anything meaningful when we claim that certain events *demonstrate* God's faithfulness. In this case, if the concept of God's faithfulness retains any meaning at all, it could only be to express a pious commitment to find the silver lining in every cloud and to credit it to God.

To be frank, as I have listened over the years to the way Christians typically talk, and especially to the lyrics of many popular Christian songs, I have to confess that I harbor a deep suspicion that this is, in fact, often what our faithful-God talk amounts to.

Chloe's Dilemma

Despite how I may sound to some readers right now, I want you to know that, as a matter of fact, I passionately believe that *God is faithful*! But I also am convinced that belief in God's faithfulness should amount to more than just a piously optimistic way of looking at the world. For the concept of God's faithfulness to mean more than this, however, we need to get clear on what it is that we're supposed to trust God for and, just as importantly, what it is we're *not* to trust God for. And I believe we need to do this not just so our concept of divine faithfulness can become more coherent, but also because our lack of clarity often ends up hurting people badly.

A Secret Uncovered

Chloe was a smart, personable, and devoted Christian student from South America whom I had the pleasure of teaching in several theology classes. Despite a gregarious demeanor, however, this young woman had a number of secrets that weighed heavily on her heart. For whatever reasons, I turned out to be the first person in her life she trusted enough to share her darkest one with.

Chloe was the daughter of a missionary couple. Toward the end of the semester of her first class with me, this nineteen-year-old woman shared with me that a well-respected missionary friend of her family had sexually molested her when she was just nine years old. Despite the man threatening her if she ever told anyone, Chloe immediately told her parents.

Instead of going to the police, her parents decided to report their fellow missionary to their superiors within their missionary organization. The organization immediately removed the man from the mission field—though, to her dismay, Chloe learned several years later that he had before long been allowed to reenter the field in a different location.

Chloe remembered her parents trying to console her by assuring her that God would heal her wounds and that the blood of Jesus could make her feel clean again. She also remembered being told that "even good men of God sin," and that since God forgave this man, she and her parents needed to forgive him as well. This they did in a single prayer before going to bed the night after the molestation. Chloe was unfortunately also told that, since Scripture teaches that "God casts our sins from us and remembers them no more," Chloe also needed to forget about this man's sin against her. They said, "No good purpose would be served by bringing this matter up again."

And it never was! As with most religious households where a premium is put on keeping up appearances, this was a family with a lot of secrets. And as is invariably the case with children raised in such households, Chloe's upbringing taught her how to appear healthy while concealing emotional sickness. It also made her hesitant to share anything. Indeed, she told me she felt as if she were dishonoring her parents by letting me in on her secret.

Noticing the Obvious

Chloe and I spoke sporadically over the next year and a half. Soon after the second class she took from me, Chloe made an appointment to talk about another matter that was bothering her tremendously.

In this meeting, Chloe confessed that, despite the confident appearance that she projected, she actually lived with a sense of guilt and had never felt like a good Christian. In fact, Chloe said she had never been confident she was "truly saved." She knew that salvation is based on our faith, and she knew that the essence of faith is trust. But trusting God was something Chloe said she always struggled with. "Everyone else at this college seems to trust God for everything in their life," she said, "but I just can't!"

Chloe seemed baffled when I asked her what she felt she was supposed to trust God for. I had taught evangelical college students long enough to know what her answer would likely be, which is precisely why I asked it. "You know," she said, "I'm supposed to trust God to bring the right man into my life to be my husband, and I'm supposed to trust that he'll lead us into the right ministry together and that he'll bless and protect our family."

"Protect?" I asked. "As in, protect *your children*?" We sat in silence for a moment before I continued. "You're having trouble trusting God to protect your children . . . as in, protect them from things like child molesters?" Tears began to well up in Chloe's eyes. I leaned forward, grabbed Chloe's hand, and said in a soft voice, "Chloe, maybe it's time to stop beating yourself up for not trusting God for something you already *know* he can't be trusted for. If God didn't protect you when you were nine, it's little wonder you have trouble trusting him to protect you and your future children when you're twenty."

Chloe was stunned. I had broken an unacknowledged rule among Christians like Chloe who try to find security in the magical promise that, if they can just "trust and obey," God will bless them and protect them and their children. The unspoken rule is, *don't notice the obvious*. And the obvious reality no one is supposed to notice is that this magical formula *contradicts the way the world actually is.*

At one point in Job's dispute with his "friends," Eliphaz rhetorically asks Job, "Who, being innocent, has ever perished? Where were the upright ever destroyed?" (Job 4:7). Only a person who wore magical glasses that deleted out innocent people perishing and upright people being destroyed could ever say something so absurd. Anyone looking at the world with any degree of objectivity sees that innocent and righteous people perish and are destroyed as routinely as guilty and unrighteous people.

This is a scary world to confront, however. We would all feel more secure if we could trust that the world is actually fair and that we will be spared its random nightmares if we just "trust and obey." The faith of Eliphaz, Chloe, and multitudes of others is anchored in the irrational insistence that *this* is how God runs the world—which, ironically, is exactly the charge Satan leveled against God in the beginning of this book: God manipulates people to serve him by promising them protection and other blessings (Job 1:9–10). This faith makes some feel secure, but the price we must pay to live in it is that we must never notice the obvious.

Faith versus Reality?

Chloe's story illustrates the downside of this magical sort of faith. In sermons, songs, books, and the comments of friends, Christians are routinely encouraged in times of trouble to alleviate their worries by entrusting their children, marriages, careers, finances, and health to God. I completely agree that we should place all these things in God's care. But I don't believe this means we should think of this as a *guarantee* that we'll always enjoy protection in these areas.

To anyone who is not wearing Eliphaz's magical glasses, it's obvious that godly people who trust God have their children abducted, just as ungodly people do. It's obvious as well that Christians have their marriages fall apart as regularly as non-Christians, that disciples lose their jobs and lose their savings and possessions in catastrophes just as people who aren't disciples do. And to all who simply open their eyes, it's obvious that the righteous suffer debilitating and fatal diseases the same way the unrighteous do.

Living under the illusion that trusting God about such matters ensures our safety allows some people to enjoy a false sense of security, but as Chloe's story illustrates, it can also be a source of tremendous pain. Many struggle, as did Chloe, with guilt and doubt simply because their own experience refutes this magical worldview. Though they may not break "the rule" by admitting the obvious, they know, on some level, that there are a multitude of variables other than God's will or our faith that influence what happens to children, marriages, careers, finances, health, and every other aspect of our lives.

As much as we might wish it were otherwise, the truth is that in an unfathomably complex world in which every human and angelic decision ever made exercises an ongoing influence on what comes to pass, there is no magical formula that can guarantee things will turn out one way rather than another. As I argued in chapter 4, the book of Job was written to teach Eliphaz-type believers this very point.[2]

A Misguided Search

Random Promise Grabbing

In the Pentecostal church where I first found Christ, we used to sing a hymn called "Standing on the Promises of God." The hymn itself isn't bad, for it focuses entirely on our relationship with God. But in this church, as well as throughout the broader evangelical Christian culture, I've found this phrase applied in ways that express, and reinforce, the magical kind of faith I'm refuting in this chapter. Yes, we should stand on the promises of God. But the all-important question, once again, is this: *What has God actually promised us?*

Over my years of ministry, I've discerned a tendency among conservative Christians to assume that anything in Scripture that *looks like* a promise is in fact something that God promises *them*. Sometimes driven by a need to find some security in a world that can be very scary, and paying little attention to the context or original meaning of passages, Christians tend to randomly cling to verses that seem to promise what they're looking for.

To give just a few examples, as we saw Brother Jacobson do, many Christians who are in pain or who have a loved one in pain latch onto verses like 2 Peter 2:24 and conclude that God promises to heal them or their loved one. Similarly I've encountered many who stood on verses that they sincerely thought promised them wealth (Deut. 5:33; 29:9), protection and a long life (Ps. 91), and happiness (Ps. 16:11). Along the same lines, I've encountered loving and concerned parents who, on the basis of verses like Proverbs 22:6 and 29:17, believed God would make sure their children turned out well if they raised them correctly. And I've known several infertile couples who stood on several randomly grabbed verses with the conviction that, through these verses, God promised to bless his faithful people with children (Deut. 28:4; Pss. 84:11; 127:3–5).

More often than not, the thing that led these people to share their convictions with me was that the promise they were clinging to had failed them. While some folks, like Brother Jacobson, could look past such failures and praise God for whatever silver lining they could find in the cloud, many others could not. And some of their stories were frankly heart wrenching. On top of the pain anyone would feel in the wake of a tragedy, these sincere people had the even greater pain of either feeling betrayed by God or feeling the promise was not honored because they lacked faith or did something wrong.

As with Chloe's story, these sad accounts are the result of the church's lack of clarity about what it means to trust that God is faithful. In the following chapter I'll outline what I believe we *should* trust God for, but for the remainder of this chapter I'd like to clarify what we are *not* to trust God for. And I'll start by explaining how these sincere believers got it wrong.

Treating Principles Like Formulas

There are a number of interpretive mistakes that people commit when they pull "promises of God" from the Bible, but for our present purposes, we need discuss only two of them.

First, I've found that people who search Scripture for random promises tend to treat hyperbolic statements as though they were literal. As we pointed out in chapter 2, this causes people to treat biblical *principles* as if they were *magical formulas*. So, for example, while it's a sound *principle* that if you "start children off on the way they should go, . . . even when they are old, they will not turn from it" (Prov. 22:6), this is not a *magical formula*. Raising children the right way does not take away their free will or collapse all other influences in their life. And this is why parents whose older children decide to walk away from God and/or to make poor decisions need not think God betrayed them or that they didn't do a good enough job raising their children.

As I pointed out in the previous chapter, whenever we come upon unqualified promises or instructions in Scripture, whether in the Old or the New Testament, we should consider it likely that we are dealing with hyperbole, especially if the promises or instructions contradict reality or are otherwise absurd.

The "Where" Determines the "What"

Second, we've seen that the Bible is not a mere collection of revealed truths, but a story with a surprising twist in the final chapter—the coming of Christ—that reframes everything (chap. 9). *Where* a passage is found, and *the way* the passage relates to the story *as a whole*, determines *what* the passage means to us.

Most of the promises that people today stumble over are part of God's covenant with Israel. In the early stages of his dealing with humans, God had to condescend to a system of immediate rewards and punishments as a means of teaching them the importance of walking in his ways (see, e.g., Deut. 28). When Jesus shows up on the scene to reveal what God is really like, however, we learn that God condescended to this way of relating to people only as a concession to their fallen, immature condition.

And so, with the coming of the new covenant, anchored in the revelation of God's true character, this system of immediate rewards and punishment is done away with. This is very similar to the way that we raise our own children. We rely on immediate punishments and rewards with young children that are no longer appropriate when they are grown.

In fact, as part of the surprise ending of the biblical narrative, Jesus actually turned the Old Testament's system of rewards and punishments *on its head*. For example, while Yahweh promised people under the old covenant that he would bless them with financial prosperity if they trusted and obeyed him, Jesus said the poor were blessed while he pronounced warnings against the rich (Luke 6:20, 24). So too, while Yahweh promised people under the old covenant that they would be blessed by being well fed if they trusted and obeyed him, Jesus said that the hungry were blessed while he pronounced warnings against the well fed (Luke 6:21, 25). And while Yahweh promised protection from enemies and even victory over enemies as a blessing to obedient people under the old covenant, Jesus taught that we are blessed when persecuted by enemies (Matt. 5:10) and that we are to love and do good to our enemies and to never try to be victorious over them (Matt. 5:39, 43–45; Luke 6:35).[3]

The Reason for the Reversal

Why did Jesus reverse these Old Testament blessings and curses? There are several possible reasons, but the clearest and most important one is directly related to the revelation of God's true, self-sacrificial, character on the cross. While God stooped to give immediate rewards and punishments in the Old Testament, sometimes taking on the appearance of a rather typical ancient Near Eastern tribal deity in the process, Jesus revealed that God's true character is other-oriented love. Moreover, Jesus calls and empowers his people to *imitate* this other-oriented love in their own lives.

So too, while God patiently allowed people in the Old Testament to continue to think in self-centered ways, putting the concerns of their own nation over others, in the New Testament God empowered his people to individually and collectively place the concerns of others over their own interests (Phil. 2:3–4). Rather than seeking to be "blessed" in this present world, we are to seek to bless all others, including our enemies. We're to consider nothing to be our own private possession (Luke 14:33) and are therefore to be willing to give it away freely (Luke 6:30–35; cf. Matt. 19:31). And we are to do this with the confidence that, when the kingdom is fully established at the end of the age, we will "inherit the earth" (Matt. 5:5) and reign with Christ forever (2 Tim. 2:12; Rev. 20:6). We might say that the Old Testament reflects God's dealings with humanity when we were in the early childhood stages of his plan of salvation, while the New Testament reflects his dealings when we had arrived at a more mature stage of development within this plan.

In this light it should be clear that *where* a promise is found makes all the difference in the world in terms of how the passage is to be interpreted and applied today. And as we discussed in chapter 9, we who follow Jesus are to consider his teachings and example, as well as his revelation of God's character, to carry far more weight than everything that preceded him. He alone is the exact representation of God's very essence (Heb. 1:3). And this simply reiterates the point that there is no justification for Christians to ever jump over Jesus, as it were, to stand on promises that were made under the old covenant.

Framing the Question Correctly

To bring this chapter to a close and set up the final one, I want to probe more deeply into the nature of the question, what are we supposed to trust God for? More specifically, I want to probe into the nature of the "what" in this question, with the hope that we will notice how this word takes on a different meaning and character depending on *how the question is framed*. And while I may risk readers tiring of this analogy, I honestly don't know any better way to embark on this question than to return, once again, to my marriage to Shelley.

The Core Problem

The problem we're wrestling with is that the church has become confused about what it is that God promises us. It's no longer clear what we are to trust God for. And the thing that gives this question special urgency is that we live in a scary world that is oppressed by the one who "comes only to steal and kill and destroy" (John 10:10). Children get kidnapped, loved ones die or forsake us, and thieves or catastrophes steal our possessions, our security, and sometimes our lives. In this threatening world, we desperately want to know, what can we confidently trust God for?

If the Eliphaz-type believers who cling to random verses are going about answering this question in the wrong way, what is the right way? I'll share my perspective on this in the next chapter, but to lay the groundwork for doing so, I want to suggest that the problem with the Eliphaz-type random-promise grabbers is not merely that they have misinterpreted the verses they treat as promises. The problem, and therefore the solution, goes much deeper than biblical interpretation.

The core problem, I submit, is the same problem we've been addressing throughout this book: namely, we tend to identify faith with belief and tend to frame every theological issue within a legal paradigm. This causes us to, among other things, confuse covenants with contracts.

Contractual versus Covenantal Promises

In contracts, we've seen, parties place their trust in a *legally binding document* that holds each party to the terms of a deal. In covenants, by contrast, parties place their trust in *the character* of the other party. I contend that the practice of combing through the Bible in search of promises to stand on and to feel secure in is reflecting a contract mind-set more than a covenant mind-set. While their motives are perfectly sincere and their desire for security understandable, people who do this are, in fact, acting a bit like lawyers scanning a legal document to see if there may be hidden clauses they could seize on and benefit from.

But as we've repeatedly said, God doesn't want to make a *deal* with us: he rather wants a *marriage-like covenantal relationship* with us. He has completely poured himself out to us in the hope that we will reciprocate and pour ourselves completely out for him and for one another. He thus wants our trust to be placed solely *in his character*, not in *a legally binding document*—not even in his inspired Word, treated like a legal document.

Everything I promised Shelley and asked Shelley to trust me for when I took my marriage vows was about *my character*. I could not, in fact, promise her anything else. This is precisely why my vows

included—and I believe all marriage vows should include—the promise to be faithful in sickness and in health, in good times and in bad,
whether we are joyful or sorrowful, and whether we become wealthy
or become poor.

In this light, it would reflect a lack of understanding and trust if
Shelley were to treat her life circumstances as evidence for or against
my faithfulness. And it would reflect a similar lack of understanding
and trust if Shelley were to comb through my vows, or our marriage
certificate, or any other written document related to our marriage, to
try to find hidden clauses that could perhaps benefit her by promising
wealth, or health, or constant good times. In short, it would reflect a
misunderstanding, and would be unfaithful, if Shelley were to treat
my *covenantal promises* as if they were *contractual deals*.

What Is the "What" We Are to Trust God For?

So too, when Jesus died on the cross on our behalf, he was not trying
to make a deal with us; he was inviting us into a covenant. And it is
vital that we remember this as we ask the question: *what* can we trust
God for? If we were involved in a contractual arrangement, such as
pagans have always made with their gods, the "what" in this question
would be specific things that benefit us, and it would be appropriate
to comb through the Bible looking for hidden clauses that benefit us.
But since we are invited into a covenant, not a contract, the "what"
in this question is *all about God's character*.

And what is true of Shelley in our marriage is also true of all of
us in our betrothal to Christ. To try to find security in anything outside God's character is to reflect both a lack of understanding and a
lack of trust. It is to treat God's *covenantal promises* as if they were
contractual deals.

And so we now turn to once again ask, what are we to trust God
for? But we are now framing this question in a covenantal rather than
a contractual framework. Hence, the question now becomes, what
kind of character are we to trust God for? And as we'll see, to answer
this, we need not, and should not, comb through the Bible and involve
ourselves in questionable exegesis. To answer this question, we need
only, and must only, keep our eyes fixed on the cross.

The Promise of the Cross

God, hold us to that which drew us first,
when the Cross was the attraction,
and we wanted nothing else.
> —Amy Wilson-Carmichael

For no matter how many promises God has made, they
are "Yes" in Christ.
> —2 Corinthians 1:20

In this final chapter I'll argue that all we can and need to trust God for is found in the cross. To set this up, however, I first need to help us appreciate how thoroughly the kingdom revolves around the cross.

The Cross-Centered Kingdom

An Invitation without Clutter

In an earlier chapter I noted that the way to know what a person or people group really believes is not to ask them but to watch. Christians frequently say, "It's all about Jesus," but our actions betray us. Judging by the amount of time, energy, and emotion that many put into fighting a multitude of battles, ranging from the defense of the literalness and inerrancy of the Bible to the war against gay marriage or universal health care, one easily gets the impression that Christianity is about a lot of different, equally important, things.

This unfortunately sends the message to the broader culture that becoming a follower of Jesus requires a person to embrace all of this. It's a "package deal," as I've said, and, frankly, it's a package that is for many quite unattractive.

This is, to me, profoundly sad, for it causes multitudes of hungry people to be unnecessarily barred from the "one thing [that] is needful" (Luke 10:42 KJV)—a *life*-giving and life-transforming relationship with their Creator whose unsurpassable love and beauty is revealed on Calvary. Everything the kingdom of God is about revolves around, and is an expression of, the *life* that flows out of this relationship. And compared to the breathtaking revelation of this magnificently beautiful God and the profound relationship we're invited to have with him, everything else we might be concerned about or interested in is of minor importance, at best.

While it's good to debate any number of issues from the inside of the faith, my conviction is that there is no issue—absolutely *none*—that is worth debating with a non-Christian if it could possibly hinder them from entering into this relationship. What difference does it make what a person believes about this or that story of the Bible, or how they vote, or whether they're gay, straight, or transgender, or whether they're a patriot of our country or of a country that is an enemy of ours, if they're not yet in a relationship with Christ?

The relationship with the God whose character is revealed on the cross is everything, and anything that could possibly prevent a person from coming to this is simply clutter. And to allow clutter to get in the way of a person finding the *life* God offers them on the cross is simply irresponsible and unloving. There are many things to be discussed, debated, and confronted in our relationships with one another as we together follow Christ. But as I said toward the end of chapter 8, we should never make resolving any of these issues a precondition to joining us on the journey.

The Proposal of the Heavenly Bridegroom

Strip away all clutter, and what is left is simply the cross, where God reveals his true character and invites us to be transformed into his likeness through the power of his love. We trust that our fallen and self-oriented character will be transformed into God's cruciform character. *That* is the kingdom, pure and simple.

The central significance of the cross is reflected in the fact that the sign of our covenant relationship with Christ is communion, as we noted in chapter 6. When we look to the cross, we see the heavenly bridegroom wooing us, as his prospective spouse, by opening up his heart and unveiling his true character. On the cross we see the heavenly bridegroom demonstrating his perfect love for his prospective bride—all of humanity—even while she had assumed the posture of an enemy toward him (Rom. 5:10). On the cross we see the heavenly bridegroom paying the required dowry to acquire his bride and to free us from our self-inflicted bondage to sin and to the powers of darkness.[1] And on the cross we see the heavenly bridegroom imploring every human being to accept his marriage proposal and to become his bride who is making "herself ready" for his return, when the wedding supper of the lamb will be celebrated and she shall begin her eternal reign with him (Rev. 19:7–9).

We say "yes" to this proposal when we exercise faith, which is why Paul says we are saved and reconciled to God through faith (e.g., Rom. 3:22–28; Eph. 2:8). We've seen that faith involves trusting God to be faithful in his relationship with us as well as pledging ourselves to be faithful in our relationship with God. And the cross defines what this covenantal faithfulness looks like for both God and us. By taking the bread and cup in fellowship with others, therefore, we are reminded of the love and faithfulness God demonstrated and pledged toward us on the cross, and we are reminded of our call to imitate the love and faithfulness to God and our neighbor that was modeled for us on the cross.

The Cross Is Everything

One of the most remarkable expressions of the all-encompassing nature of the cross is reflected in an incidental, but extremely important, comment that Paul made in his First Letter to the Corinthians. He noted that when he brought "the testimony of God" to Corinth, he hadn't come "with eloquence or human wisdom." He instead "resolved to know nothing . . . except Jesus Christ and him crucified" (1 Cor. 2:1–2).

While this statement may be somewhat hyperbolic (did Paul really resolve to know absolutely *nothing* except Christ crucified?), it clearly implies that, for Paul, the entire gospel was found in the message of the cross. It implies that, when we understand what took place through the "foolishness of the cross," we understand all we need to know about God and about other humans. When you know the character of God revealed on the cross and what he thinks about us as revealed on the cross, you've got the essence of all you need to know about anyone.

And this is why I contend that *everything* we are to trust God for is found in the cross. We are not involved in a contract that would require us, or even just allow us, to comb the Bible to latch onto this or that particular passage as a kind of insurance policy that God will come through for us. We are rather in a covenant in which it is not particular things we trust God for; our trust is rather in *God himself*. As we'll explore further below, we trust God to be who he reveals himself to be on the cross and trust that his moment-by-moment attitude toward us is what he reveals it to be on the cross.

As Paul said, when we place our trust in the character of God revealed in the crucified Christ, we are saying "Amen" to every one of God's promises, for they are all embodied and confirmed in him (2 Cor. 1:20). The love of God revealed on the cross is the summation of all God's promises, for the love of God revealed on the cross is God himself being poured out for us.

To tie this in with other aspects of faith developed throughout part 3 of this book, it should be clear that I am proposing that we anchor our understanding of *what we should trust God for* in the same revelation that serves as the *intellectual foundation* of our faith, the same revelation that serves as the *center of our interpretation of Scripture*, and the same revelation that serves as the *center of our theology*. Every aspect of faith, in short, is centered on "Jesus Christ, and him crucified."

Trusting God's Word *about* God

In the remainder of this chapter I will unpack three pledges that I find God making on the cross and that constitute the essence of all we are to trust God for. While I will discuss these as three distinct pledges, however, they are in fact three aspects of one pledge, which is that God pledges to faithfully demonstrate toward us the kind of character he displays on the cross. For our purposes, however, it will be helpful to treat this as the first pledge, followed by a second pledge that concerns what the cross reveals about God's attitude toward us, as well as by a third pledge that follows from the first and second and concerns what the cross reveals about our future with him.

The Root of Our Bondage

The first word of promise that God speaks on the cross—and, as I've said, it's the word that encompasses the following two words—is a word *about him.*

Whether we're talking about our relationship with God or with other people, the quality of the relationship can never go beyond the level of trust the relating parties have in each other's character. We cannot be rightly related to God, therefore, except insofar as we embrace a trustworthy picture of him. As we noted in chapter 3, to the extent that our mental picture of God is untrustworthy, we will not rely on him as our sole source of *life.* This is why the first thing that Satan went after, according to the Genesis narrative, was Eve's conception of God. The story reflects the truth that the root of our alienation from God and our bondage to fallen powers is our untrustworthy and unloving mental pictures of him.

This is as true today as it was in the garden. Paul tells us that the gospel continues to be "veiled . . . to those who are perishing" because "the god of this age has blinded *the minds* of unbelievers, so that they cannot see the light of the gospel that displays the glory of Christ, who is the image of God." And notice, the *seeing* Paul is talking about is a seeing *in our mind* (cf. 2 Cor. 3:14–15, emphasis added). Nor can those who are yet under Satan's blinding oppression receive the "light" that God wants to "shine in [their] hearts to give

[them] the light of the knowledge of God's glory displayed in the face of Christ" (2 Cor. 4:3–4, 6).

Only when the Spirit lifts the veil from our minds and hearts can we form and embrace a truly accurate picture of God. This is to say, only when the Spirit frees us from the blinding oppression of "the god of this age" can our hearts and minds see the glorious beauty of the God revealed in Christ. And only as we "with unveiled faces contemplate [or imagine, *katoptrizō*] the Lord's glory" can we be "transformed into his image with ever-increasing glory" (2 Cor. 3:17–18).

The Foundation of the New Covenant

What this shows is that the revelation of God in Jesus, most clearly reflected on the cross, is the foundation of the new covenant because it is God's definitive refutation of all false images of him. Jesus described himself as the "the way and the truth and the life" (John 14:6). The Greek word for "truth" (*alētheia*) is the combination of the prefix *a*, which is a negation, and *lathanō,* which means to "cover" or "conceal." So the word has the connotation of something "uncovered" or "not concealed." While we've been, to one degree or another, blinded by our sin and the "god of this age" from seeing the true, glorious character of God, he is finally fully unveiled in Christ. As John earlier wrote, no one had "ever seen God" or really known God up to this time. But the Son, "who is himself God . . . has made him known" (John 1:18).

This is why Jesus is also the "way" to the Father as well as the "life" of the Father. We can only experience the *life* that God wants for us when we know and trust his true character as it's unveiled in Christ. Hence Jesus later prays, "Now this is eternal life: that they know you, the only true God, and Jesus Christ, whom you have sent" (John 17:3).

And we are making the same point from the opposite direction when we point out that, when Jesus fully unveiled the true character of the one true God on the cross, he "disarmed the powers and authorities," vanquished Satan and his minions (Col. 2:14–15; cf. Heb. 2:14; 1 John 3:8), and thereby set free all who would accept this truth. On the cross, the light expelled the darkness, the truth vanquished all deception, and the beauty of the true image of God destroyed the ugliness of all false images. And so now, for all who will yield to the Spirit, as the veil over our minds is removed, we can see "God's glory displayed in the face of Jesus" (2 Cor. 4:6) and be set free to enter into the loving, trusting, and transforming relationship God has always wanted to have with his people.

Understood in a covenantal context, therefore, the cross is first and foremost the full disclosure of the true character of our heavenly bridegroom and his pledge to demonstrate this loving, self-sacrificial character in all his dealings with us. And the first and most important responsibility of all who say, "I do," to this proposal is to take him at his word and to reciprocate by pledging to cultivate this same character in our relationship with him and all others. And, as we just read, we acquire this image "with ever-increasing glory," according to Paul, not by striving in our own effort, but simply by gazing on his beauty with our hearts and minds open to the Spirit.[2]

Specific Applications of Our Trust

There are a number of ways that trusting in the character of God as revealed on the cross can be applied to our lives. To mention just a few, since the cross reveals what God is always like while revealing that God did everything possible to restore us into a relationship with himself, we can trust that God continues to do everything possible to enter into a relationship with people. As Paul told the Athenians, at all times, in all places, through all circumstances, God is working to get all people to "seek him and perhaps reach out for him and find him," though, in fact, "he is not far from any one of us" (Acts 17:27).

Moreover, because God experienced God-forsakenness on our behalf on the cross, we can trust that God will never abandon us, condemn us, or allow anything to separate us from his love. Terrible things can happen to us, as is the common lot of humans in the fallen war zone in which we find ourselves. But even when we undergo "trouble or hardship or persecution or famine or nakedness or danger or sword" (Rom. 8:35), Paul assures us that nothing "will be able to separate us from the love of God that is in Christ Jesus our Lord" (8:39). And this is why he can proclaim that in all these things "we are more than conquerors through him who loved us" (8:37).

Hence, when we find ourselves in the midst of radical suffering—our child dies, our marriage dissolves, cancer strikes, a tornado wipes out all we held dear—we should not infer anything about God's character from this. The only one from whom we should ever draw conclusions about God's character is *Jesus*. In all situations we must trust that when we look upon Jesus we are seeing the character of the Father and that we need not, and cannot, look anywhere else to learn about this (John 14:7–9). And, in any case, we've seen that Jesus put an end to the fallen tendency to discern the hand of God behind "natural" disasters (Luke 13:1–5).

So long as we keep our eyes fixed on Jesus (Heb. 12:2), we can and should trust that God is for us, never against us. In the fog of war that we find ourselves in, it is vitally important for us to discern what is and is not of God. A central strategy of Satan has always been to do terrible things or to motivate others to do terrible things and then try to deceive us into attributing these terrible things to God. To the extent that he succeeds, he compromises the beauty of our mental image of God, which in turn compromises our trust in him and hinders our capacity to experience true *life* and to therefore be transformed into his image.

Though I know some will disagree with me, I implore people to trust that the cross reveals what God is really like and to therefore use this as the criteria by which we access what *is* and *is not* of God in the world. If we trust that the cross reveals what God is really like, I don't see that we have any other choice but to conclude that every aspect of our circumstances that fails to reflect the loving character revealed on the cross is traceable back to wills *other than God*, whether human or angelic or both. If we know the good farmer plants only wheat, then when we find weeds, we ought to conclude, "an enemy has done this" (Matt. 13:28 RSV; cf. John 10:10).[3]

Turning Evil to Good

At the same time, because God outwitted his enemies on the cross as he turned the evil they intended into the ultimate good—namely, the liberation of humanity and all creation—we can trust, along with Paul, that "in all things God works for the good of those who love him, who have been called according to his purpose" (Rom. 8:28). Paul isn't saying that God *causes* all things, for this would make God responsible for evil. Paul is rather saying that *in* all circumstances—regardless of who or what is responsible for them—God is working to bring good *out of* evil.

It is also significant, I believe, that the word that the NIV translates "works," *synergeō*, has the connotation of working *in sync with* or in *cooperation with* another. We get the term "synergy" from this word. The synergy spoken of in this passage can refer to the *things* that God works together or to the people God works with. The latter option is taken, for example, by the *Good News Translation*, which has "in all things God works for good *with those* who love him" (emphasis added).

If this translation is accepted, it would explain why Paul specifies that God works for the good of those "who have been called according to his purpose." The God who suffered death for all people (1 John 2:2) would love to bring good out of evil for *all* people. But only those who have accepted the call to align their lives with his purpose are willing to *cooperate with him* to do this. As in so many other areas, God relies on created agents to freely choose to do their part to see his redemptive will accomplished "on earth as it is in heaven" (Matt. 6:10).

Trusting God's Word *about Us*

The Manifestation of Our Alienation

The second word of promise God speaks on the cross (and as I've said, it's a word that is implicit in his first word) is a word about us.

As we noted in chapter 3, when Eve embraced Satan's lie and stopped trusting God for *life*, she viewed herself as deficient and in need of something she currently lacked—namely, the kind of wisdom that belongs to God alone. No longer leaning on God for *life*, she was no longer content to simply be a human *being* who fellowshipped with God. Eve unfortunately now believed she needed to *do something* and *acquire something* to complete her.

This was the first human *being* to become a human *doing*—namely, a human whose identity, worth, significance, and security were wrapped up in what she could possess, who she could impress, what she could achieve, and so on. And we've pretty much been human *doings* ever since. If the root of our alienation from God and our bondage to the fallen powers is our false mental pictures of God, then our perpetual hunger-driven activity to acquire and protect idolatrous forms of *life* is its *primary manifestation*.

A Love That Knows No Limits

Just as Jesus's sacrificial death is God's definitive response to all false images of him, so too is the cross God's definitive response to all false ways of getting *life*. For the cross reveals not only the full truth about God; it also reveals the full truth *about us*. And for reasons that will now become clear, this reconnects us with our true source of *life*, which in turn heals our idol addictions. This dimension of the cross is frankly so breathtakingly beautiful that, so far as I can tell, very few followers of Jesus have ever really grasped it.

You know what something is worth to someone by what they are willing to pay for it. Consider, then, what our heavenly bridegroom was willing to pay to redeem us and make us his bride. Out of his love for us, the all-holy God was willing to do nothing less than to go to the extremity of *becoming* our sin (2 Cor. 5:21) and *becoming* our God-forsaken curse (Gal. 3:13). Which means, as we noted in chapter 5, that God's love for us led him to the extreme of somehow *becoming his own antithesis*. It means, in other words, that God gave us the perfect revelation of his true loving nature as well as the perfect revelation of his love for us by somehow *becoming anti-God*!

I know it sounds insane, but it is an undeniable truth that is insanely beautiful!

Whatever else we think about this paradoxical revelation, it clearly means that God *could not have gone further* than he in fact did to free us from our bondage and make us his bride. And if the worth of something or someone to another is determined by what they are willing to pay to acquire it, then the fact that God was willing to pay the greatest price that could possibly be paid can only mean that we have the greatest possible worth to God. The *unsurpassable price* God paid for us, in other words, means that we have *unsurpassable worth* to God.

Which means God could not possibly love us more than he actually does, and we could not matter more to God than we actually do. Reflect on that for a moment. It's breathtaking.

Caught Up in the Love That Is God

Another way of saying this is to say that God loves us with the *very same love that God eternally is*. Calvary is what the love of the Trinity looks like when it encompasses us. Jesus reflects this truth when he prays that we would know that the Father loves *us* with the *very same love* he has for his own eternal Son (John 17:26). Paul reflects this truth when he declares that God, out of love, gives us "his glorious grace . . . in the One he loves" (Eph. 1:4–6). And Peter touches on this profound truth when he teaches that we are able to "participate in the divine nature" (2 Pet. 1:4), for as we've seen, God's nature *is* his love (1 John 4:8)—the very love that is expressed on Calvary (1 John 3:16).

In this light, we aren't going too far if we conclude that God loves us with the same love he has *for himself* as Father, Son, and Spirit. When we say, "I do," in response to God's marriage proposal, we are incorporated into Christ and therefore into the eternal triune community so that we receive and reflect the very same perfect love that unites God throughout eternity![4] The God whose love led him to go to the infinite extreme of offering up his Son to become our sin and our God-forsakenness also gives us, as a result of this unsurpassable sacrifice, "*all* things"—including, we now see, full participation in the loving community that God eternally is (Rom. 8:32, emphasis added). It's no wonder Paul declares that God's love for us in Christ "surpasses knowledge" (even as he paradoxically prays that we may "grasp how wide and long and high and deep" this love is [Eph. 3:18–19]).

All of this is part of the magnificent revelation and promise of the cross. On the cross God reveals his true character and promises to be this kind of loving husband to his bride. On the cross God reveals his perfect love for us and reveals our unsurpassable worth to him. And on the cross God promises to always love us like this and to always ascribe this worth to us. All of this, we've seen (chap. 3), means that on the cross, God promises to always be our source of *life*, for *this* is what the vacuum in our soul longs to be filled with.

A Love That Is Conditioned on Nothing

The most remarkable aspect of God's promise to always ascribe unlimited worth to us and to be our source of *life* is that God promises this "while we were still sinners" and were positioning ourselves as his enemy (Rom. 5:8, 10)! In fact, God made this promise precisely by *becoming* our sin and by standing in our place as a God-forsaken enemy! This clearly demonstrates that the unsurpassable worth God ascribes to us isn't based on anything positive he finds in us, and it can't be lessened by anything negative he finds in us. The cross rather demonstrates that God's love for us, and our priceless worth to him, are *completely* based on *God's* character, not *ours*. Even when we are in bondage to sin and are thinking, feeling, and/or acting like God's enemies, we can trust that it remains as true as ever that we could not be loved more than we actually are, and could not matter more to God than we actually do.

I don't know about you, but there is nothing that fills my heart with a greater sense of joy, peace, and confidence than the realization that God's perfect, unsurpassable, unwavering love for me is also unconditional. The person who has allowed this unconditional love to form the core of their self-identity is a person who will remain unshakable in their sense of being fully alive, regardless of what life in this war zone may throw their way.

Trusting God's Word about Our Future

The Cross and the Resurrection

The third and final word of promise that God speaks through the cross (and as I said, it's a word that is implicit in the first and second words) concerns our future with him.

Now, to appreciate this promise, it's first of all important to remember that the cross cannot be understood apart from the resurrection, just as the resurrection can never be understood apart from the cross. They are, in fact, two sides of the same event.

If we consider the cross apart from the resurrection, the crucified Christ becomes nothing more than one among the many thousands of people who were tortured and executed as criminals by the first-century Romans. And if we do not keep the resurrection closely connected to the cross, it can easily become a triumphant explosion of supernatural power that not only *lacks* the enemy-loving, self-sacrificial character of the cross; it actually *subverts* it!

Indeed, there's a strand in Western theology that implies that God merely used the humble, self-sacrificial approach reflected through Jesus's life leading up to the cross because it was necessary to get Jesus crucified to atone for human sin. Once this was accomplished, this misguided line of thinking goes, God could return to using his superior brute force to get his will accomplished on earth and to defeat evil, which, in this view, is what the resurrection signifies. This line of thinking allowed theologians to assure Christian rulers, soldiers, and others that God didn't intend all Christians to follow the enemy-loving, nonviolent example and teachings of Jesus. It was a line of thinking that was unfortunately very convenient whenever Christians felt the need to set Jesus's teaching and example aside to torture heretics, massacre enemies, or take over countries.

Though it was never openly acknowledged, this perspective implies that Jesus's humble, servant lifestyle, his instructions to love and bless enemies, and especially his self-sacrificial death *conceal* rather than *reveal* God's true character! If we're totally honest about it, it implies that God was only *pretending* when he assumed a humble posture in Christ. His true character is displayed when he acts more like a cosmic Caesar than the crucified Christ, accomplishing his plans and achieving his purposes by flexing his omnipotent muscle rather than by picking up the cross.

But think about it. Any suggestion that Jesus's humble, servant, self-sacrificial life and teachings were a temporary means to an end has the effect of making Jesus into a liar when he said, "Anyone who has seen me has seen the Father" (John 14:9). In fact, it would pretty much undermine the truthfulness of all the material we covered in chapter 9 about Jesus being the revelation that trumps all other revelations—material that I argued was the central point of the New Testament. On the other hand, if we remain steadfast in holding that the material covered in that chapter is true, then we must dismiss out of hand any suggestion that the resurrection in any way qualifies, let alone replaces, the character of God revealed on Calvary.

Against this way of thinking, I contend that the cross and resurrection must be considered as two sides of one event. When emphasizing this aspect of the promise of the cross, therefore, I like to speak of the cross-resurrection event. And when we view the cross and the resurrection this way, it becomes clear that the resurrection confirms not only *that* the Son of God was victorious over sin, death, and the powers of hell, it also confirms that *the way* the Son defeated evil is *God's* way of defeating evil. It thus confirms that Jesus's humble, servant lifestyle, his instructions to love and bless enemies, and especially his self-sacrificial death *reveal* rather than conceal God's true, eternal character. The humble character of Christ wasn't something God adopted for utilitarian purposes, as though it were foreign to him. Christ rather displayed this character because this is "the exact representation of [God's] being" (Heb. 1:3).

This is why the New Testament teaches that all who are "raised with Christ" (Col. 3:1; cf. Col. 2:12; Eph. 2:6) and who therefore share in his resurrected life are called and empowered to respond to evil *the way Jesus did*. The power of the resurrection is the power to "be imitators of God," which means we are able to "walk in the way of love, just as Christ loved us and gave himself up for us" (Eph. 5:1–2). It's the power to overcome our fallen self-oriented instincts and to instead love, serve, bless, and pray for enemies, just as Jesus did (Rom. 12:17–21). It's the power to rise above the brute retaliation game that has fueled the mindless merry-go-round of bloodshed that largely defines history by choosing to turn the other cheek and to refrain from violence, even if it may result in our suffering or being executed, as it did Jesus.

This is part of what Paul was referring to when he said he and his coworkers shared "abundantly in the sufferings of Christ" (2 Cor. 1:5) and "always carry around in our body the death of Jesus" (2 Cor. 4:10). Paul understood it was "the power of God" that empowered him to suffer for the gospel (2 Tim. 1:8). And in this light, it is clear that the power that raised Jesus from the dead and that is at work in all who have been raised with him (Eph. 1:17–23) isn't a power that *contrasts* with the cross; it's the power that *leads to* the cross and that *confirms* the cross as God's way of responding to evil, even as it confirms that the cross reflects the kind of God that the true God is.

The Victory of the Cruciform Life

When understood in this light, we can discern in the cross-resurrection event God's promise, reiterated throughout the New Testament, that, if we "participate in the sufferings of Christ," we will also "be overjoyed when his glory is revealed" (1 Pet. 4:13). "If we endure," Paul says, "we will also reign with him" (2 Tim. 2:12). Now, if you interpret this within the kind of legal paradigm that was discussed in part 1, you'll be inclined to read promises like this in a contractual way. In this case, the contractual interpretation would be that Paul is stipulating a "deal" God made with us: namely, if you want the reward of reigning with Christ, you have to first pay the price of suffering.

As we've seen, however, the New Testament works with a covenantal rather than a legal paradigm. And in a covenantal context, it's clear that Paul is simply describing what those who share in Christ's life and who are on their way to reigning with Christ look like. When Christ is your life, Paul is teaching, you will be in the process of being transformed into his likeness. You will be on your way to becoming your own unique version *of him*. You will be growing in your capacity to love like Jesus, serve like Jesus, forgive like Jesus, and yes, to *suffer* like Jesus. So, if you endure suffering as a consequence of living like Jesus, Paul is saying, you're on the way that will take you to the throne, where you will, as part of the bride of Christ, reign with him.

What Kind of Suffering Is Suffering with Christ?

The suffering Paul is referring to when he talks about "suffering with Christ" is not the kind we experience when we lose a loved one, are told we have a terminal illness, and so on. In other words, though many today seem to misinterpret Paul to be saying this, our "suffering with Christ" doesn't refer to the "normal" kind of suffering we experience by virtue of being born into a fallen race on a fallen planet.

We should of course offer up all our suffering to God so that God can work with us to bring good out of it, as we said above. But the specific kind of suffering Paul and others in the New Testament identify as "suffering with Christ" is suffering that is unique to followers of Jesus, for it's the suffering we experience only because we are following him. As we learn to yield to Christ within us and he increasingly forms his character in us, we find ourselves in conflict with the ways of the world, as Christ was. And this is the cause of the distinctive kind of suffering that the New Testament means by "suffering with Christ."

All true disciples must "suffer with Christ" at least in the sense that they experience the pain of regularly crucifying their old self. Most will also experience, to one degree or another, the pain of social rejection as they are marginalized, looked down upon, or rejected for failing to conform to people's "normal." And, in certain contexts, some will suffer from overt persecution, torture, or even death, as did Christ, Paul, and multitudes of others in the early church. Regardless of the nature and severity of this kind of suffering, *this* is what it means to "suffer with Christ."

The cross-resurrection event is thus God's promise that, however much we may suffer, we who have chosen to walk in the way of Christ will eventually overcome and reign victorious with him. Moreover, the cross-resurrection event is the promise that, however otherwise it may now appear, the Jesus way of responding to evil will win in the end. Indeed, it's the promise that God is using our Jesus way of fighting evil to advance his cause now. However counterintuitive it may feel to our fallen common sense, we can be confident that God is using our decisions to love rather than hate, to serve rather than retaliate, and to be killed rather than to kill to move the world closer to the time when God will fully reign on the earth. So with our eyes fixed on the cross-resurrection event, we can trust, and we must trust, that God will win the day in the end by our refusal to try to win by relying on the typical coercive and violent ways of the world.[5]

The Assurance of the Bride

I find it helpful to also think about the word of promise that God speaks about our future through the cross within the framework of God's marriage-like covenant with us. I've said that the cross, which reveals the true character of the bridegroom, is God's proposal of marriage and pledge to always demonstrate this kind of character to his bride. When we understand the cross in connection with the resurrection, as well as with the sending of the Spirit, we can also see in the cross his promise to return.

As we noted in chapter 6, we are presently in the betrothal period of ancient Jewish marriages, during which time a couple was legally married but did not live together or become "one flesh." As was common with first-century Jewish husbands, our heavenly bridegroom has gone away "to prepare a place" for us, promising us, "if I go and prepare a place for you, I will come back and take you to be with me that you also may be where I am" (John 14:2–3). Not only this, but as we've also seen was common for Jewish husbands of this time, Jesus has given us a betrothal gift to reassure us of his return. And this gift, we have seen, is none other than the Holy Spirit.

When placed in this context, the pledge of God to us on the cross reiterates these points. The one "who did not spare his own Son, but gave him up for us all" will surely not stop there, as Paul notes. Having done this much, he will, "along with him, graciously give us all things" (Rom. 8:32). If God has already given us that which is most precious, Paul is saying, how could anyone imagine he would fail to fulfill the reason he gave us this most precious gift, which is to glorify us by incorporating us into the never-ending triune fellowship?

This is the same assurance we should have as we contemplate the cross. Even beyond the fact that Jesus promised that he's preparing a place for us, and even beyond the fact that he's given us the Spirit as a promissory betrothal gift, the very fact that God went to this infinite extreme to demonstrate his love for us is more than enough for us to have complete confidence that, however bleak things may seem as we carry out his work in this fallen war zone, Jesus is most certainly going to return for us.

He Will See It Through to the End

Keeping our eyes steadfast on the cross-resurrection event, where God poured himself out as a proposal and promise to his bride, we can have complete confidence that God will not stop until we, together with all God's people and the heavenly hosts, sit down to celebrate the "wedding supper of the Lamb" (Rev. 19:9). Knowing that God was willing to become our sin to free his bride from sin, and knowing that God was willing to experience separation from God in order to incorporate his bride into his own loving fellowship, we can have total assurance that he will not fail to bring his courtship with us to a glorious and never-ending finale.

Similarly, when we contemplate the event by which God ascribed unsurpassable worth to us and by which he bequeathed to us a new, Christlike nature, can we imagine that he would fail to see this through until we perfectly manifest this new nature? If he raised Christ from the dead as the "firstborn" of his new creation, we can be assured that he will not fail to raise all others who trust in him, "that he might be the firstborn among many brothers and sisters" (Rom. 8:29; cf. Col. 1:18; Rev. 1:5). With Paul, we can be "confident of this, that he who began a good work in [us] will carry it on to completion until the day of Christ Jesus" (Phil. 1:6).

The Hope That Is True Already

In fact, in the bizarre and beautiful world of the realized eschatology of the New Testament, the truth is that, in a very real sense, God has *already* "raised us up with Christ and seated us with him in the heavenly realms" (Eph. 2:6). And while "we do not see everything subject to [us]," the truth of the matter is that, in Christ, we have *already* been restored to our rightful place as corulers with Christ. Indeed, it is already true that God has "left nothing that is not subject to [us]" (Heb. 2:8). It is in this same sense that we have already been made "holy" and "blameless" and have been "blessed . . . with every spiritual blessing" (Eph. 1:3–4).

It's evident, therefore, that we aren't so much called to work to complete God's redemptive work in creation as we are called to work to get creation to line up with the redemptive work God has *already completed*. The whole "creation waits in eager expectation for the children of God to be revealed" so that all things can be "brought into the freedom and glory of the children of God" (Rom. 8:19, 21). But the children are children *already*. We simply are waiting for the day when all that was made true when Christ died and rose will be perfectly manifested. We don't yet see it manifested, but as the author of Hebrews says, "we do see Jesus" (Heb. 2:9), in whom the old has passed away and in whom everything is already a "new creation" (2 Cor. 5:17).

John makes the same point. Because of the cross-resurrection event, we can affirm "what great love the Father has lavished on us" when he made us "children of God." And however much we may yet think, feel, and behave in ways that are contrary to the true nature of a child of God, John reminds us that the Father calls us children because "that is what we are!" regardless of how we may now appear (1 John 3:1). He then goes on to say that "what we will be has not yet been made known" (v. 2). Our feeble and fallen imaginations cannot even conceive of what "we will be." But John proclaims the glory of the assurance we receive from the cross-resurrection event when he continues, "But we know that when Christ appears, we shall be like him" and "we shall see him as he is" (1 John 3:2).

While our present sin-struggling condition may conceal more than it reveals of the truth of who we are in Christ, we must fix the "eyes of [our] heart" (Eph. 1:18) (our imagination) on the truth that we will someday look like him, for we shall be like him. He is our *life* already, but our old self with its habituated fallen thoughts, feelings, and actions conceals this truth, to one degree or another. If our imaginative eyes stay fixed on him, however, we can trust that we will continue to grow in our capacity to manifest our Christ *life*, and trust that someday we will be exactly like him. As we saw in chapter 10, and in accordance with Hebrews 11:1, this imaginative envisioning of our true self in Christ, as a substantial reality (*hypostasis*), is simply how we exercise faith in God's word about our true self. And it is this imaginative envisioning that generates the "conviction" (*elegchos*) that motivates us to move in this direction.

When the time for the wedding festival arrives and the groom returns, his bride, who is now still muddied, will appear radiantly beautiful and wearing the "fine linen" of her "righteous acts," as John depicts her (Rev. 19:8). We will appear with Christ "in glory" (Col. 3:4), with all that obstructs the truth of our union with Christ done away with. Every member of the bride will perfectly display, in our own unique way, the brilliance of God's beauty and love that is, even now, our true nature. All this is true already, but how glorious it will be when this truth is finally fully manifested!

The End

We cannot know, and need not know, any of the details of what this never-ending wedding feast will be like, still less when or how it will occur. The many symbolic images we're given in Scripture are intended not to satisfy our curiosity but to excite our imagination, thereby intensifying our faith.

As we look to the cross-resurrection event, it is enough to know that the *Sehnsucht* in our heart will be fully healed and our hunger for *life* permanently satisfied. It is enough for us to feel assured that all wrongs will then be made right and all wounds will then be healed. It is enough to know there will be no more curse, no more tears, no more despair, no more injustice, no more violence, no more death, no more loss, and no more evil (Rev. 21:4; 22:3).

As we wait for the return of our Lord, with our vision yet blurred by the fog of war, it is enough to know that, when the glorious never-ending finale takes place, we will see God face to face, as he truly is (1 John 3:2; Rev. 22:4). And we will see God's will fully done "on earth as it is in heaven," with every square inch of the cosmos reflecting the radiant beauty of the other-oriented love of God—the love that radiates like ten thousand suns from the cross, reflecting the true eternal nature of the God who gave his life for all and who defeated all evil, by selflessly submitting to the torture of the cross.

You may feel quite certain that all I've just shared is true, or perhaps you are filled with doubt and can at present merely entertain a glimmer of hope that it is true. This is of no consequence. Your relative level of certainty and doubt does not improve or diminish God's love for you, manifested on Calvary, one iota. The only relevant question is, are you *confident enough* of the truthfulness of this glorious gospel to say "yes" to God's marriage proposal and to begin to be transformed by the love of this heavenly bridegroom by committing to living your life *as if* it is true?

If so, then I encourage you to step out, just as you are, and offer yourself up to Christ, without any thought of hiding your doubt, confusion, sin, woundedness, fear, or anger. For as we have seen throughout this book, biblical faith has nothing to do with trying to pretend we're something we're not, but everything to do with trusting God to transform us into who he created us, and saved us, to be—the radiant bride who endlessly participates in and reflects the rapturous love of the triune community.

Concluding Word
How I Live by Faith

Inasmuch as this book has been somewhat autobiographical, it seems fitting to end on an autobiographical note. And I'll start by asking the question, once again: Am I *certain* that history will wrap up with the glorious finale I just outlined in the concluding chapter? And the answer, you should by now expect, is *of course not*.

I confess there are times when I *feel* certain. In fact, the longer I live out my faith, the more frequently, and the more deeply, I feel this way. There are actually moments when Macbeth's suggestion that life might be "a tale, told by an idiot, full of sound and fury, signifying nothing," strikes me as utterly preposterous.[1] In these moments, even apart from any considerations of the reliability of the New Testament, it seems intuitively obvious to me that we are each characters in an unimaginably beautiful love story that, though it is full of drama and pain, is destined to have a glorious climactic ending, which in fact will never end.

I cherish these moments, but I don't *seek* them. If moments of certainty come, they are a gift. But I don't believe it is ever appropriate or healthy to engage in psychological self-manipulation by *trying* to make ourselves feel certain. And, as I argued throughout part 1, if a person feels a *need* to try to make themselves feel certain, it indicates to me that they are operating with a misguided, unhealthy, and certainly unbiblical understanding of faith.

While there are times I feel certain, however, I must in honesty confess there are other times when the vision of a beautiful finale feels too good to be true. In these moments, I wonder to myself if I might be engaging in wishful thinking. It's a perfectly reasonable suspicion. If the suspicion persists, I simply step back and reexamine the question I've explored so many times before: *Why do I believe what I believe?* Doubt isn't a problem that needs to be overcome; it's an *invitation that needs to be explored.* It is not the enemy of faith, but a friend.

In any case, as I now bring this book to a close, I trust it is clear why my feelings of certainty or doubt are completely irrelevant to my faith walk, *so long as* I continue to remain *confident enough* that Jesus is the supreme revelation of God that I'm willing to commit to living my life *as if* this belief is true.

Making this commitment does not mean I have shut the door on this or any other matter. To the contrary, an important part of my calling has been to continually seek out objections to my faith in order not only to reexamine my faith for myself, but also to help others who may struggle with these objections. But this commitment *does* mean that I will passionately live each day on the assumption that my faith in Christ is true until I am given convincing reasons to think otherwise, which, obviously, I have thus far not found.

We've seen that biblical faith is first of all based on a commitment to be ruthlessly honest before God (chaps. 4 and 5). So for me to live as if it's true that Christ is the definitive revelation of God means that I on a daily basis place my trust in his love and grace and bare my soul before him. For me personally, this commitment has led me, in this season of my life, to spend the first twenty minutes or so of every day opening up my heart and allowing the Holy Spirit to reveal to me what is there. And almost invariably, this means I must confess sin and receive his eager forgiveness.

We've also seen that the first movement of faith is a movement in our imagination (chap. 10). To be a disciple is first and foremost about being disciplined in one's thought life. I'm always aware that, if my goal is to live as if it's true that Christ is Lord, I must first learn to *imagine myself* living as if it is true that Christ is Lord. My faith commitment thus leads me to strive in the power of the Spirit to "take captive every thought and make it obedient to Christ" (2 Cor. 10:5).

This means I regularly make time to imaginatively gaze upon "God's glory displayed in the face of Christ," as Paul instructs us to (2 Cor. 4:6; see 3:17–4:6). I therefore regularly carve out time to sit alone in a darkened room, put on the classical music that is best able to soften my heart and open up my imagination, and ask the Holy Spirit to open up the eyes of my mind and heart (2 Cor. 3:14–15) to envision Jesus. I see, hear, and sense, as vividly as possible, Jesus personally telling me all the things that the New Testament reveals are true about me, because of what Christ has done for me. He tells me he is overjoyed that I am his child, for example, and that he loves me with a perfect, everlasting love and has made me holy and blameless. Beyond the sheer enjoyment of encountering Jesus in this way, I and many others have found this traditional form of prayer, called "cataphatic" or "imaginative" prayer, to be the single most effective way to experience the fullness of *life* we've been created and saved to experience.[2] I also will sometimes converse with Jesus, "face to face," as my friend (Exod. 33:11) during these encounters. I will sometimes share things that weigh heavy on my heart and receive the wisdom he sometimes offers in response. Often he has brought healing to my heart by revising the lying message embedded in a wounding childhood memory. But often we just sit together and enjoy each other's company.

Reflecting this same understanding of imaginative faith, I try to always remember that I won't ever be able to *actually* manifest all that God says is true about me if I can't first envision myself manifesting all that God says is true about me. So throughout the day, I try to imagine, as a substantial reality, who I really am as a person whose *life* is Christ (Col. 3:3) and who is "in Christ" (e.g., Rom. 6:11; Eph. 2:6). And I try to always stay mindful of the fact that I am at every moment enveloped in the perfect love of Christ.[3]

Along the same lines, I aspire to be compelled by "Christ's love" as the apostle Paul was, by remaining "convinced that one died for all and therefore all died" (2 Cor. 5:14). I therefore try to no longer see any human being "from a worldly point of view," but to rather envision them in light of the "new creation" (2 Cor. 5:16–17), as Paul did. Whoever I come upon throughout the day, I try to look past whatever my physical eyes may notice and to instead envision them enveloped and transformed by God's love while praying that they someday come to realize and accept this. I am continually amazed how viewing people with the eyes of faith allows you to experience God's heart toward them. And when I throughout the day notice thoughts and attitudes in my mind that are not consistent with the truth in Christ (something that happens all the time, by the way), I simply set these deceptive images and feelings aside and turn my mind back to things that are "true, . . . noble, . . . right, . . . pure, . . . lovely, . . . [and] admirable," as Paul encourages us to do (Phil. 4:8).

At the same time, we've seen that faith is always visible (chaps. 6 and 7), for it is impossible to live as if Christ is Lord and not have it impact every area of one's life. My faith commitment thus leads me to try to converse with God throughout the day, inviting this conversation into everything I do. It leads me to regularly assess, in dialogue with others in my kingdom community, my priorities, as evidenced by how I spend my time, energy, and money, to discern if I am in fact reflecting the priorities of the kingdom or if I've inadvertently been unduly influenced by the priorities of my fallen culture. And my faith commitment leads me to live each day with my eyes open to opportunities to bless, serve, and express love to others. In fact, I've learned that every single encounter I have with another person throughout the day is such an opportunity, if only to whisper a quiet blessing over them.

Along the same lines, we've seen that our covenant relationship with Christ is inseparable from our covenant relationships with other disciples. So for me to live as if Christ is Lord means I make time to fellowship within the bride of Christ and to engage in various ministries within the body of Christ. And it means I take the time and effort to cultivate a deep, intimate relationship with a small group of people in which it is appropriate to "[speak] the truth in love" (Eph. 4:15), as we help one another mature in Christ and prepare for the return of our Lord.[4]

The final thing I'll say about how I live out my faith brings me back to the foundational aspect of biblical faith discussed in chapters 4 and 5: namely, the commitment to authenticity and the willingness to wrestle with God. For I must end by openly confessing that I continue to fail quite miserably at consistently thinking and living as if Christ is Lord. In fact, as people throughout the ages have discovered, I feel the closer I grow to Christ, the more fine-tuned my awareness of my sin becomes. I am acutely aware of how much of my moment-by-moment thinking and living is actually more reflective of a person who lives as though it were *not* true that Christ is Lord—what Paul calls living in "the flesh." And this intensifying awareness consistently brings me back to my foundational trust in the character of God, revealed on Calvary.

I am always brought back to my need to trust that God's love is infinitely greater than my sin. So I offer up my sin, receive his forgiveness, and bask in his loving embrace. And as I behold the beauty of his magnanimous, relentless, unfathomable love and grace, flowing from Calvary, I am transformed "from one degree of glory to another" (2 Cor. 3:18 ESV). Though I don't consistently manifest it, I know that I *am*, by the grace of God, a child of God. And as John so beautifully puts it, while I can't imagine how I will appear when God has completed his gracious work in me, I know I shall "see him as he is," for I "shall be like him" (1 John 3:1–3).

Correction: I don't actually *know* this. I can't be certain. But I'm confident enough to live *as if* it's true, with the confident *hope* that it's true, and with a profound *longing* for the glorious day when, I trust, it will be proved to be true.

Acknowledgments

At the risk of sounding cheesy, I want to begin my list of people who have helped bring this work into being by mentioning Jesus Christ. Obviously, my existence and salvation and every single positive thing I have is a direct reflection of his love toward me. I love you! Not only this, but I would of course *like* to believe that Jesus has been the strongest influence on the theology reflected in this book, and in all my writing and speaking. I do honestly seek his will and his mind in all my endeavors, but whether readers think he actually influenced me will obviously depend on whether they find this work to be insightful and helpful, or unhelpful, if not heretical. Either way, I owe it all to Jesus!

Neither this nor any other writing of mine would likely have come into being were it not for my lovely wife, Shelley (a.k.a. "Beso"), mentioned so warmly throughout this book. Shelley deserves a Nobel Prize of some sort for her remarkable patience in allowing this quasi-Asperger's bookworm to regularly be locked in his office, writing away at times for up to twelve hours straight. As I think is evident throughout this book, our life together has far and away taught me more about the nature of covenantal love, conflict, faith, and faithfulness than any book I've ever read. Thank you, Beso! I love you!

I also want to express my profound gratitude to my precious friend for over thirty-five years, Terri Churchill. Terri is a beautiful poet,

artist, and all-round human being, and she spent endless hours edit-
ing this work, offering masterful, creative suggestions at numerous
points. Terri's heart and mind permeate every page. Terri is part of
the kingdom house-community that Shelley and I have belonged to for
almost twenty years, and our extraordinary life together has impacted
my mind and heart in profound ways that are reflected throughout
this book. Alex, Greg, Dave, Julie, Marcia, and, again, Terri and my
Beso—I love you guys!

My many discussions about the nature of faith with my good friend
and member of my ReKnew Board, Brett Strand, have contributed
enormously to this work. In fact, *Brett* is the one who came up with
the über-clever title, *Benefit of the Doubt*. Thank you, Brett! So too,
as usual, I also need to give a shout out to my close covenant bro Paul
Eddy. We have always been each other's theological confidants, for
better or for worse. And it was Paul who first convinced me several
years ago that covenant is a centrally important concept for understanding the biblical narrative. Thank you, bro!

I would also like to express my profound appreciation for the be-
loved kingdom people of Woodland Hills Church, including our ten
to fifteen thousand regular "podritioners." I love you folks, and it's an
honor to serve you and to test out all my new theological "insights"
on you. Most of what eventually finds its way into one of my books
was first "floated" in a sermon or sermon series, and *Benefit of the
Doubt* is certainly no exception. Something similar goes to the growing
community of folks around ReKnew (reknew.org), an exciting ministry
that exists to help serve as a catalyst for the kingdom revolution that is
rising up out of the rubble of the collapsing religion of Christendom.
Thank you for all your love and support!

I don't for a moment doubt that there are others with whom I have
spoken, written, and debated and whose influence is, in one way or
another, reflected in this book. In the flow of life, it's impossible to
accurately parse out what idea originated where and in whom and by
whom, and so on. So all I can do is say, if you see something in this
book, or any other book or article of mine, that you think you may
have influenced, then assume you have, feel good about yourself, and
receive my sincere and warm appreciation. Thank you!

Notes

Introduction

1. For those who may not know, the "rapture" is the belief that Christians will literally ascend into the sky when Jesus returns. It's based on a literal interpretation of 1 Thess. 4:16–17. It's a belief that has been made popular by the bestselling *Left Behind* series by Tim LaHaye and Jerry Jenkins. I have since come to side with the majority of scholars who believe Paul was using apocalyptic imagery in this passage that his original audience would not have interpreted literally. For an insightful critique of this doctrine and the harmful ramifications it can have, see B. R. Rossing, *The Rapture Exposed: The Message of Hope in the Book of Revelation* (Boulder, CO: Westview, 2004).

2. As I'll discuss in chapter 8, my faith in Christ *does* presuppose that the Gospels are substantially reliable. But this is not because I hold these writings to be inspired. As I'll argue in that chapter, it is rather because the demonstrable substantial reliability of these writings constitutes one of the main reasons (but not the only reason) I believe that Jesus Christ reveals all I need to know about God, myself, my neighbors, and our world. As will become clear in that chapter, I don't believe in Jesus because I first believe in the inspiration of Scripture. I rather believe in the inspiration of Scripture because

I first believe (on historical-critical grounds as well as on philosophical, existential, and personal grounds) in Jesus, and he in turn leads me to believe in Scripture. For the issue of the reliability of the Synoptic Gospels, see P. Eddy and G. Boyd, *The Jesus Legend: A Case for the Historical Reliability of the Synoptic Tradition* (Grand Rapids: Baker Academic, 2007). For those less academically inclined, see our popularized version of this work, titled *Lord or Legend: Wrestling with the Jesus Dilemma* (Grand Rapids: Baker Books, 2007; Eugene, OR: Wipf & Stock, 2010). On the general reliability of the Gospel of John, see C. I. Bloomberg, *The Historical Reliability of John's Gospel: Issues and Commentary* (Downers Grove, IL: InterVarsity, 2001); and P. N. Anderson, *The Fourth Gospel and the Quest for Jesus: Modern Foundations Reconsidered* (New York: T&T Clark, 2006).

Chapter 1: Embracing the Pain

1. With the exception of my son, Nathan, and my wife, Shelley, I will throughout this book protect people's anonymity by altering in my accounts the names as well as any details that could possibly allow anyone to identify them.

2. I will put "scare quotes" around "saved" or "salvation" throughout this book

whenever these terms are used to refer to the guarantee to avoid hell. The reason is that avoiding hell is not the focus of the biblical concept of salvation, as I'll discuss in chapter 6.

3. I was reading S. Kierkegaard, *Training in Christianity*, trans. W. Lowrie (Princeton: Princeton University Press, 1941); and S. Kierkegaard, *Concluding Unscientific Postscript*, trans. W. Lowrie (Princeton: Princeton University Press, 1968).

Chapter 2: Hooked on a Feeling

1. See D. Kinnaman, *You Lost Me: Why Young Christians Are Leaving the Church . . . and Rethinking Faith* (Grand Rapids: Baker Books, 2011).

2. See D. Kinnaman and G. Lyons, *Unchristian: What a New Generation Really Thinks about Christianity . . . and Why It Matters* (Grand Rapids: Baker Books, 2007).

3. If you're curious about this group, see my *Oneness Pentecostals and the Trinity* (Grand Rapids: Baker Books, 1992).

Chapter 3: The Idol of Certainty

1. The concept of *Sehnsucht* permeates Lewis's writings, so much so that the C. S. Lewis Society titled its annual journal *Sehnsucht: The C. S. Lewis Journal*. For an overview of the concept in Lewis and the various roles it plays, see Dave Brown's essay "Real Joy and True Myth" at http://www.oocities.org/athens/forum/3505/LewisJoy.html. For a scientific account of *Sehnsucht*, see D. Kotter-Grühn, M. Wiest, P. Zurek, and S. Scheibe, "What Is It We Are Longing For? Psychological and Demographic Factors influencing the Contents of Sehnsucht (Life Longings)," *Journal of Research in Personality* 43 (2009), 428–37; and D. Kotter-Grühn, S. Scheibe, F. Blanchard-Fields, and P. B. Baltes, "Developmental Emergence and Functionality of Sehnsucht (Life Longings): The Sample Case of Involuntary Childlessness in Middle-Aged Women," *Psychology and Aging* 24 (2009): 634–44.

2. I've elsewhere argued that various aspects of the longings in the human heart provide a compelling reason for believing in a personal God. See G. Boyd and E. Boyd,

Letters from a Skeptic, 2nd ed. (Elgin, IL: David C. Cook, 2008), 62–71. C. S. Lewis argues along somewhat similar lines in book 1, "Right and Wrong as the Clue to the Meaning of the Universe," in *Mere Christianity* (New York: Macmillan, 1943).

3. W. H. Lewis, ed., *Letters of C. S. Lewis* (New York: Harcourt Brace & World, 1966), 289.

4. C. S. Lewis, *The Weight of Glory* (Grand Rapids: Eerdmans, 1949), 12.

5. *The Confessions of Augustine*, trans. S. E. Wirt (Grand Rapids: Zondervan, 1971), 1.

6. See J. Edwards, "Dissertation concerning the End for Which God Created the World," in Jonathan Edwards, *Ethical Writings: The Works of Jonathan Edwards*, vol. 8, ed. Paul Ramsey (New Haven: Yale University Press, 1989).

7. Well, to be honest, I should say he is *almost* on the money. As a staunch Calvinist, Edwards believed God only created some people—the "elect"—with the goal of having them share in his eternal love. All others were created with the goal of having them somehow "glorify God" by suffering in hell for eternity. In my mind, this completely ruins the otherwise beautiful portrait of God and his creation that Edwards painted. I'm personally convinced God creates every human with the hope that they would forever share in his fullness of *life* and that Jesus died for every human with this same hope (e.g., 2 Pet. 3:9; 1 Tim. 2:4; 4:10; 1 John 2:2). See F. Guy, "The Universality of God's Love," in *The Grace of God and the Will of Man: A Case for Arminianism*, ed. C. Pinnock (Grand Rapids: Zondervan, 1989), 31–50; and T. Miethe, "The Universal Power of the Atonement," in ibid., 71–96.

8. See esp. M. Gorman, *Cruciformity: Paul's Narrative Spirituality of the Cross* (Grand Rapids: Eerdmans, 2001); T. Caroll and J. B. Green, "'Nothing but Christ and Him Crucified': Paul's Theology of the Cross," in *The Death of Jesus in Early Christianity* (Peabody, MA: Hendrickson, 1995), 113–32. Several other more general treatments are C. Cousar, *A Theology of the Cross: The Death of Jesus in the Pauline Letters* (Minneapolis: Fortress, 1990); and R. Bauckham, *God Crucified: Monotheism*

and Christology in the New Testament (Grand Rapids: Eerdmans, 1998).

9. M. Kähler, *The So-Called Historical Jesus and the Historic Biblical Christ*, trans. C. E. Braaten (1896; Philadelphia: Fortress, 1964), 80n11. Dodd forcefully argues that the basic structure of the passion-centered Gospel narratives predates the writing of Mark. See C. H. Dodd, "The Framework of the Gospel Narratives," in *New Testament Studies* (New York: Scribner, 1952), 1–11.

10. See the discussion in A. Moody, "That All May Honour the Son: Holding Out for a Deeper Christocentrism," *Themelios* 326, no. 3 (2011): 403–14.

11. Gorman, *Cruciformity*, 75–94; John T. Carroll and Joel B. Green, "Nothing but Christ and Him Crucified: Paul's Theology of the Cross," in *The Death of Jesus in Early Christianity* (Peabody, MA: Hendrickson, 1995), 123–32.

12. I defend the view that violence in nature reflects the corrupting influence of Satan and other fallen powers as was championed by the early church fathers in G. Boyd, *Satan and the Problem of Evil: Constructing a Trinitarian Warfare Theodicy* (Downers Grove, IL: InterVarsity, 2001), esp. 29–49. I integrate this thesis into an evolutionary framework to account for prehuman animal suffering in "Evolution as Cosmic Warfare: A Biblical Perspective on Satan and 'Natural' Evil," in *Creation Made Free: Open Theology Engaging Science*, ed. T. J. Oord (Eugene, OR: Pickwick, 2009).

13. I say "glimpse" because it's important to remember that many biblical narratives are more like expressionistic portraits than literal snapshots, which is why they communicate truths more profoundly and in ways that people from every culture throughout history can potentially understand and be impacted by.

14. Had I the space, I would also talk about how this leads to our internalizing a self-serving version of "the knowledge of good and evil." On this, see G. Boyd, *Repenting of Religion: Turning from Judgment to the Love of God* (Grand Rapids: Baker Books, 2004).

15. For a fuller discussion of this, see ibid., 157–70.

Chapter 4: Wrestling with God

1. As is usually the case with name changes in the Old Testament, the association of *Yiśrā'ēl* with "struggling with God" is based on popular associations at the time, not on the actual etymology of the word. The actual etymological history of "Israel" is disputed by scholars. If you're interested in this sort of thing, see the discussions in H.-J. Zobel, "*yiśrā'ēl*," in *Theological Dictionary of the Old Testament*, ed. G. J. Botterweck and H. Ringgren, trans. D. E. Green (Grand Rapids: Eerdmans, 1990), 6:397–401; and S. S. S. Apóstolo, "On the Elusiveness and Malleability of 'Israel,'" *Journal of Hebrew Scriptures* 6 (2006), available at www.jhsonline.org/Articles /article_57.pdf.

2. I want to thank my dear friend Terri Churchill for drawing my attention to the connection between the name "Jacob" and certainty-seeking faith.

3. On this motif, see J. Sanders, *The God Who Risks: A Theology of Divine Providence*, rev. ed. (Downers Grove, IL: IVP Academic, 2007); G. Boyd, *God of the Possible* (Grand Rapids: Baker Books, 2000).

4. As I'll argue in my forthcoming book, *The Crucifixion of the Warrior God: A Cruciform Reinterpretation of Divine Violence in the Old Testament* (Downers Grove, IL: IVP Academic, forthcoming), it's important to always remember that, because they wrote prior to the full revelation of God in Christ, Old Testament authors frequently reflect a penultimate perspective on God's character and activity. They therefore frequently attribute to God violent activity that he in fact merely allowed, though this distinction is only clear to us when we interpret their writings from the perspective of the cross. I'll share a brief overview of this perspective in chap. 9.

5. While the degree to which Job may reflect historical events is debated, all agree that the author's *intended purpose* is theological rather than historical in nature. Most scholars also agree that the genre of this book is along the lines of an epic poem and/ or epic drama and that the prologue (chaps. 1–2) is a literary fiction that sets up the drama that follows by letting the audience in on a secret (namely, why Job is suffering)

that the characters in the dramatic poem know nothing about.

6. The original Hebrew refers to "the satan" (*ha satan*, meaning "the adversary") rather than to "Satan" as a proper name. It's my conviction that, at this early stage in the progress of biblical revelation, Satan was viewed as an agent who had a degree of power to oppose God, but he was not yet known as the embodiment of pure evil and the "god of this age" (2 Cor. 4:4) that we find him in the New Testament. Nevertheless, because this is the same agent who is later identified by the name "Satan," and because I'm writing from the perspective of the New Testament, I will continue the traditional practice of referring to this agent as "Satan." For my argument against scholars who posit that "the adversary" in the prologue of Job and elsewhere in the Old Testament is simply one of the heavenly beings comprising Yahweh's council, see G. Boyd, *God at War: The Bible and Spiritual Conflict* (Downers Grove, IL: InterVarsity, 1997), 143–54.

7. I discuss this at length in G. Boyd, *Is God to Blame? Moving beyond Pat Answers to the Problem of Suffering* (Downers Grove, IL: InterVarsity, 2003); and *Satan and the Problem of Evil: Developing a Trinitarian Warfare Theodicy* (Downers Grove, IL: InterVarsity, 2001).

Chapter 5: Screaming at the Sky

1. Some argue Jesus was citing the whole of Psalm 22 by quoting its first verse. Since this Psalm ends with a proclamation of confidence in God's deliverance, these scholars argue that Jesus was also proclaiming his confidence that the Father would ultimately deliver him. I side with those scholars who think this interpretation is unlikely. Among other things, it requires us to believe that Jesus engaged in a rather sophisticated literary technique at the pinnacle of his suffering on the cross. See C. Bloomberg, "Matthew," in *Commentary on the New Testament Use of the Old Testament,* ed. G. K. Beal and D. A. Carson (Grand Rapids: Baker Academic, 2007), 100; D. Hagner, *Matthew 14–28,* Word Biblical Commentary 33B (Dallas: Word, 1995), 844–45; L. Morris, *The Gospel according to Matthew,* Pillar

New Testament Commentary (Grand Rapids: Eerdmans, 1992), 720–21; R. T France, *The Gospel of Mark,* New International Greek Testament Commentary (Grand Rapids: Eerdmans 2002), 653. The debate is important primarily because the view that Jesus had deliverance in mind when he quoted the first verse could have the effect of minimizing, if not undermining, the reality and horror of Jesus's experience of God-forsakenness. For several strong statements, see A. Lewis, *Between Cross and Resurrection: A Theology of Holy Saturday* (Grand Rapids: Eerdmans, 2001), 324–25; C. Evans, *Mark 8:27–16:20,* Word Biblical Commentary 34B (Nashville: Thomas Nelson, 2001), 507; L. Morris, *The Gospel according to Matthew*, Pillar New Testament Commentary (Grand Rapids: Eerdmans, 1992), 721.

Chapter 6: From Legal Deals to Binding Love

1. I need to acknowledge my profound indebtedness to my friend Paul Eddy, whose expertise on the biblical concept of covenant, combined with his willingness to be an intellectual sparring partner over two decades of friendship, has helped formed my convictions about the centrality of covenant in Scripture and for theology in general.

2. In his excellent work on the topic, Stephen Travis notes that, while there are judicial elements to the language of salvation and punishment, the dominant language is organic and relational. See S. Travis, *Christ and the Judgment of God: The Limits of Divine Retribution in New Testament Thought* (Peabody, MA: Hendrickson, 2009).

3. This is the view that Jesus had to be punished by the Father in our place so that the Father's wrath could be satisfied and humans forgiven. For a discussion of this view, often referred to as "the penal substitution" model of the atonement, along with three other models, including the "Christus Victor" model that I espouse, see P. Eddy and J. Bielby, eds., *The Nature of the Atonement: Four Views* (Downers Grove, IL: IVP Academic, 2007).

4. I discuss this in G. Boyd, *The Myth of a Christian Nation* (Grand Rapids: Zondervan, 2005).

5. The two exceptions might be Jesus's claim that Judas was "doomed to destruction" (John 17:12) and Jesus's reference to the rich man being tormented in flames (Luke 16:19–31). Concerning Judas, the Greek text literally says that Judas was the "son of destruction," and the concept of "son" in this context refers to one whose nature is suited for something. So Jesus was simply stating that Judas, in his present condition, had made himself fit to be destroyed. This leaves open the possibility that Judas would later repent, as the Eastern Orthodox Church has always taught. (For an excellent work on issues surrounding the possible salvation of Judas, see W. Klassen, *Judas: Betrayer or Friend of Jesus* [Minneapolis: Fortress, 2005].) Regarding Jesus's reference to the rich man, it's important to remember that Jesus was telling a parable that shouldn't be interpreted literally, and, in any case, this parable doesn't say the rich man was lost forever. But even if one insists Jesus *did* know two individuals were lost, this does not provide any precedent that we should ever claim such knowledge since, after all, Jesus was the Son of God.

6. For representative arguments on both sides of this debate, see G. Boyd and P. Eddy, *Across the Spectrum: Understanding Issues in Evangelical Theology* (Grand Rapids: Baker Academic, 2002), 165–77.

7. For an overview of the way every aspect of Jesus's life waged war against principalities and powers, as well as the way we are to follow this example, see G. Boyd, *The Myth of a Christian Religion* (Grand Rapids: Zondervan, 2009).

8. Two very good books on prayer as an exercise of the bride who co-rules with Christ are P. Billheimer, *Destined for the Throne* (Minneapolis: Bethany, 1975); and W. Nee, *The Prayer Ministry of the Church* (Anaheim, CA: Living Stream Ministry, 1993). For a book that aims at empowering people to be able to make thoughts and emotions "obedient to Christ" (2 Cor. 10:5), see G. Boyd and A. Larson, *Escaping the Matrix: Setting Your Mind Free to Experience Real Life in Christ* (Grand Rapids: Baker Books, 2005).

Chapter 7: Embodied Faith

1. C. S. Pierce, "How to Make Our Ideas Clear," in *Charles S. Pierce: Selected Writings: Values in a Universe of Chance*, ed. P. Wiener (New York: Doubleday, 1958), 121.

2. See, for example, George Barna's book, *The Second Coming of the Church* (Nashville: Word, 1998).

3. I discuss this further in G. Boyd, *Repenting of Religion: Turning from Judgment to the Love of God* (Grand Rapids: Baker, 2004), chap. 12. There are, of course, rare occasions when one may have to intervene to protect someone, though even this requires no judgment on our part of the person in question.

4. As I said in chap. 4, if we doubt that God's character is revealed on the cross to the point that we are no longer confident enough to get our *life* from this source, then the answer is not to try to suppress this doubt, but to reevaluate the grounds for believing this. I will outline some of my reasons in chap. 8.

Chapter 8: A Solid Center

1. See C. Pinnock, "From Augustine to Arminius: A Pilgrimage in Theology," in *The Grace of God, The Will of Man: A Case For Arminianism*, ed. C. Pinnock (Grand Rapids: Zondervan, 1989), 15–30.

2. A number of impressive photos can be found simply by using a Google image search. See, for example, http://www.trevorshp.com/creations/cards.htm (accessed February 19, 2013).

3. C. S. Lewis, "Myth Became Fact," in *God in the Dock: Essays in Theology and Ethics*, ed. W. Hooper (Grand Rapids: Eerdmans, 1970). J. R. R. Tolkien espoused similar insights in "On Fairy Stories," in *Leaf and Tree* (Boston: Houghton Mifflin, 1965).

4. P. Eddy and G. Boyd, *The Jesus Legend: A Case for the Historical Reliability of the Synoptic Jesus Tradition* (Grand Rapids: Baker Academic, 2007). I should add that I am well aware of the complexity of every person's "web of beliefs," and aware of how this affects how they assess not only historical evidence but every truth claim made from every field. Some of this is discussed in chap. 1 of *The Jesus Legend*. Entering into

this complexity would take us far outside the focus of this book. A classic, insightful, succinct, philosophically sophisticated introduction to the issue is W. V. Quine and J. S. Ullian, *The Web of Belief* (New York: Random House, 1970).

5. On the reliability of the Gospels, see Eddy and Boyd, *Jesus Legend*. On Jesus's view of the Old Testament, see B. B. Warfield, "The Biblical Idea of Inspiration," in *The Inspiration and Authority of the Bible*, ed. S. Craig (Phillipsburg, NJ: Presbyterian and Reformed, 1976), 131–65. See also Warfield, "'It Says,' 'Scripture Says,' 'God Says,'" in *Inspiration and Authority*, 299–348.

6. The vast majority of biblical prophecies were not predictions of a settled future but warnings to motivate people who were headed down a path that would lead to disaster. As I'll discuss in the next chapter, when Gospel authors say Jesus "fulfilled" various passages, they don't mean these passages *predicted* an event in Jesus's life. They rather simply testify that an event in Jesus's life parallels and fills out the *full meaning* of the passage. On the flexible nature of biblical prophecy, see C. Pinnock, *Most Moved Mover: A Theology of God's Openness* (Grand Rapids: Baker Academic, 2001), 47–54; J. Sanders, *The God Who Risks: A Theology of Divine Providence*, rev. ed. (Downers Grove, IL: IVP Academic, 2007), 72–92, 131–39; G. Boyd, *Satan and the Problem of Evil: Constructing a Trinitarian Warfare Theodicy* (Downers Grove, IL: InterVarsity, 2001); G. Boyd, *The God of the Possible* (Grand Rapids: Baker Books, 2000), 75–85, 93–100.

7. This is the central theme of G. Boyd, *Repenting of Religion: Turning from Judgment to the Love of God* (Grand Rapids: Baker Books, 2002).

8. I am indebted to my friend and former colleague Roger Olson for the labels I attach to each of the circles in my paradigm. My thoughts on this paradigm have also been refined by many discussions with my friend Paul Eddy.

Chapter 9: The Center of Scripture

1. You can see this reversal, for example, in Jesus's hometown inaugural sermon in Luke 4:18–23. Jesus was reading Isa. 61:1–2, but he stopped after announcing the day of the Lord's favor, leaving out the second half of verse 2, which refers to "the day of vengeance of our God." The crowd was irritated because this was, to many of them, the best part, for to them it meant the defeat of the Romans and the liberation of Israel. But Jesus made matters worse by moving on to tell two Old Testament stories in which Jewish heroes bypassed their fellow Jews to minister to non-Jews (Luke 4:24–27). He was suggesting that the kingdom was going to bypass many who thought they were on God's side because of their Jewish nationality, but would be accepted by many whom these people thought were against God. No wonder his people wanted to kill him (vv. 28–29).

2. I will defend the supremacy of the revelation of God in Christ at much greater length and develop a cross-centered way of interpreting violent portraits of God in the Old Testament in my forthcoming book, *The Crucifixion of the Warrior God: A Cruciform Interpretation of Divine Violence in the Old Testament* (Downers Grove, IL: IVP Academic, forthcoming).

3. There are a multitude of other examples of Jesus making claims that force us to accept that he is either the embodiment of God or a lunatic. To give just one more example, Jesus taught that he came so that "all may honor the Son *just as* they honor the Father. Whoever does not honor the Son does not honor the Father, who sent him" (John 5:23, emphasis added). For an excellent book demonstrating the truth that Jesus's disciples claimed he was fully God, see R. Bowman Jr. and J. Komoszewski, *Putting Jesus in His Place: The Case for the Deity of Christ* (Grand Rapids: Kregel, 2007). I should acknowledge that my argument in this paragraph assumes that the Gospels more or less reflect the sayings of the historical Jesus. On the case for this, see chap. 8, note 4. As a final word, it's worth mentioning that the outlandish claims of Jesus, combined with the many other ways he failed to conform to people's expectations (e.g., getting crucified!), are themselves compelling evidence against the Gospel's portrait of Jesus being substantially legendary. Legends

generally *reinforce* cultural and religious assumptions; they don't generally *overturn them*, the way the Gospels do.

4. "The Law and the Prophets" was often a shorthand way of referring to the whole Old Testament (e.g., Matt. 7:12; 22:40; Luke 24:27; John 1:45; Acts 26:22; Rom. 3:21).

5. See, e.g., M. Wilkins, *Matthew: The NIV Application Commentary* (Grand Rapids: Zondervan, 2004), 240.

6. So argues, e.g., D. R. A. Hare, *Matthew: Interpretation: A Bible Commentary for Teaching and Preaching* (Louisville: John Knox, 1993), 50; and W. D. Davies and D. C. Allison, *The Gospel according to Saint Matthew: A Critical and Exegetical Commentary* (Edinburgh: T&T Clark, 1988), 1:506.

7. Against the common claim that the *lex talionis* was intended merely to limit the amount one can retaliate, see J. Nolland, *The Gospel of Matthew: A Commentary on the Greek Text* (Grand Rapids: Eerdmans, 2005), 256.

8. This may on the surface seem to contradict Jesus's teaching that he didn't come to do away with the law but to fulfill it (Matt. 5:17). But there is no inconsistency on the part of Jesus once we understand that Jesus fulfilled the law by embodying its ultimate intent, which was to foster a faithful covenantal relationship with God. See, e.g., M. E. Boring, "Matthew," in *The New Interpreter's Bible*, vol. 8., ed. L. Keck (Nashville: Abingdon, 1995), 188; and U. Luz, *Matthew 1–7: A Commentary*, trans. W. C. Linss (Minneapolis: Augsburg, 1989), 277–79.

9. I will offer an explanation for how an Old Testament hero could have performed a supernatural feat that Jesus would have regarded as ungodly, if not demonic, in my forthcoming *Crucifixion of the Warrior God*. I will attempt to demonstrate that throughout Scripture God uses evil to punish and ultimately destroy evil and that Old Testament authors frequently ascribe to God activities that he merely allowed, including violent actions of humans and even spirit-agents, when the violence of these agents serves God's punitive purposes.

10. I should also note that the church has traditionally taught that passages can have a fullness of meaning—a *sensus plenior*—that goes beyond their "original intended meaning." The idea that interpreters should stick to the "original intended meaning" of a passage only arose when, in the wake of the Enlightenment, academics in the seventeenth and eighteenth centuries began to adapt a secular "historical-critical" approach to Scripture that insisted on treating the Bible the same way scholars treat any other ancient book. Many Christian scholars today are calling for a return to a more traditional, and more Christ-centered, way of interpreting Scripture. This is now customarily referred to as the TIS ("Theological Interpretation of Scripture") movement. For a good introduction, see D. J. Treier, *Introducing Theological Interpretation of Scripture: Recovering a Christian Practice* (Grand Rapids: Baker Academic, 2008).

11. Boyd, *Crucifixion of the Warrior God* (forthcoming). A great deal has been written recently about the way violent images in sacred literature have often been used to justify and motivate violence throughout history. Several examples that I have found helpful are J. J. Collins, "The Zeal of Phineas: The Bible and the Legitimization of Violence," *Journal of Biblical Literature* 122 (2003): 3–21; B. E. Schmidt and I. W. Schröder, "Violent Imaginaries and Violent Practices," in *Anthropology of Violence and Conflict*, ed. B. E. Schmidt and I. W. Schröder (London: Routledge, 2001), 1–24; H. Avalos, *Fighting Words: The Origins of Religious Violence* (Amherst, NY: Prometheus, 2005); J. Nelson-Pallmeyer, *Is Religion Killing Us? Violence in the Bible and the Quran* (Harrisburg, PA: Trinity, 2003); C. Selengut, *Sacred Fury: Understanding Religious Violence* (Lanham, MD: Altamira, 2003); and the four-volume work edited by J. H. Ellens, *The Destructive Power of Religion: Violence in Judaism, Christianity, and Islam* (Westport, CT: Praeger, 2004).

12. Some may argue that the book of Revelation contains a violent portrait not only of God but of Christ. Others argue that Jesus acted violently when he cleansed the temple. And some even argue that God acted violently when Jesus died on the cross. For my part, I agree with the expanding rank of scholars who argue that the apparent violence

of Revelation is all symbolic and is actually intended to motivate believers to engage in nonviolent warfare against the powers of darkness through self-sacrificial love, as Jesus did. Also, there is no indication in the Gospels that Jesus inflicted any harm on people or animals when he cleansed the temple. He simply cracked a whip to drive the animals out. And, finally, it's important to notice that all the violence Jesus suffered on the cross was done by wicked humans under the influence of fallen powers, *not by God*. For a balanced response to all allegations of violence in the New Testament, see T. Neufeld, *Killing Enmity: Violence and the New Testament* (Grand Rapids: Baker Academic, 2011). A popular-level defense of a nonviolent interpretation of Revelation is V. Eller, *The Most Revealing Book of the Bible: Making Sense out of Revelation* (1974; repr., Grand Rapids: Eerdmans, 1982). Other excellent works defending a nonviolent, and even *anti*violence, interpretation of Revelation are R. Bauckham, *The Theology of the Book of Revelation* (Cambridge: Cambridge University Press, 1993); M. Bredin, *Jesus, Revolutionary of Peace: A Nonviolent Christology in the Book of Revelation* (Waynesboro, GA: Paternoster, 2003); and L. L. Johns, *The Lamb Christology of the Apocalypse of John* (Tübingen: Mohr Siebeck, 2003).

13. A classic recent example is P. Copan, *Is God a Moral Monster? Making Sense of the Old Testament God* (Grand Rapids: Baker Books, 2011). It's as good an attempt to minimize the horror and make Yahweh appear just as possible. But it frankly does very little to demonstrate how these violent portraits point to the cross, where God reveals that he's a God who would rather die out of love for his enemies than to crush them.

Chapter 10: Substantial Hope

1. The "Word of Faith" or "Positive Confession" movement refers to Christians who believe that if Christians believe without doubting and confess it fervently, they have a divine "right" to health, wealth, and prosperity. For a balanced critical review, see R. Bowman, *The Word-Faith Controversy: Understanding the Health and Wealth Gospel* (Grand Rapids: Baker Books, 2001).

2. The most recent example of the New Age mind-over-matter distortion of faith is Rhonda Byrne's best-selling book *The Secret* (New York: Simon & Schuster, 2008).

3. At the same time, it's important to remember, as I argued in the previous chapter, that not everything in Scripture carries equal weight.

4. G. Boyd, *Is God to Blame? Moving beyond Pat Answers to the Problem of Suffering* (Downers Grove, IL: InterVarsity, 2003); G. Boyd, *Satan and the Problem of Evil: Developing a Trinitarian Warfare Theodicy* (Downers Grove, IL: InterVarsity, 2001).

5. A point that has significant ramifications for the problem of evil, as argued in the works cited in the previous note.

6. It might seem that thinking about abstract concepts (e.g., truth, time, justice) does not involve representations of our actual experience of the world, but there is widespread agreement among specialists in the field this is in fact not the case. For a fascinating academic exploration of this topic with an emphasis on its implications for philosophy, see G. Lakoff and M. Johnson, *Philosophy in the Flesh: The Embodied Mind and Its Challenge to Western Thought* (New York: Basic Books, 1999). Also of interest is M. Tye, *The Imagery Debate* (Cambridge, MA: MIT Press, 1991).

7. For techniques on becoming aware of, and then changing, our mental representations, see G. Boyd and A. Larson, *Escaping the Matrix: Setting Your Mind Free to Experience Real Life in Christ* (Grand Rapids: Baker Books, 2005).

Chapter 11: Stumbling on the Promises of God

1. Brother Jacobson was loosely quoting 1 Pet. 2:24 (KJV).

2. I discuss this at length in G. Boyd, *Is God to Blame? Moving beyond Pat Answers to the Problem of Suffering* (Downers Grove, IL: InterVarsity, 2003), and even more extensively, and more academically, in *Satan and the Problem of Evil* (Downers Grove, IL: IVP Academic, 2001).

3. In *The Crucifixion of the Warrior God* I attempt to demonstrate that, while God

sometimes stooped to allow his people to view him as a violent ancient Near Eastern warrior deity as he fought on their behalf in the Old Testament, we who read these narratives in light of the cross can discern that God's way of fighting on behalf of his people never actually involved him acting violently.

Chapter 12: The Promise of the Cross

1. We miss the point of the dowry or ransom analogy if we worry about *who* God paid the dowry *to*—himself or Satan? Both answers are highly problematic, but neither is necessary. The dowry or ransom price simply represents God's willingness to pay whatever price was necessary, which is to say, to make whatever sacrifice was necessary to acquire this fallen race of people as his bride.

2. This is why I believe that the practice of imaginative prayer and meditation (usually called "cataphatic spirituality" in the church tradition) is a foundational kingdom discipline. See G. Boyd, *Seeing Is Believing: Experiencing Jesus through Imaginative Prayer* (Grand Rapids: Baker Books, 2004).

3. See G. Boyd, *Is God to Blame? Moving beyond Pat Answers to the Problem of Suffering* (Downers Grove, IL: InterVarsity, 2003).

4. Since God loves all people, shows no partiality, desires everyone to be part of his bride, and gave his Son for all people (see chap. 3, note 7), we must assume that God has an unsurpassable love for *all* people. But since a love *relationship* requires love to be freely reciprocated, only those who say, "I do," to God's love benefit from it. While I can't go into it now, I'm inclined toward the view that the fire of God's love is experienced as wrath by those who refuse it, and while this love-experienced-as-wrath will refine those who repent, it will destroy those who will not and who become irrevocably hardened in their opposition. The best defense of this view, usually referred to as "annihilationism," that I have found is E. Fudge, *The Fire That Consumes: A Biblical and Historical Study of the Doctrine of Final Punishment*, 3rd ed. (Eugene, OR: Cascade, 2011).

5. This is a central theme of the book of Revelation as it extols those who "triumphed . . . by the blood of the Lamb and by the word of their testimony" and who "did not love their lives so much as to shrink from death" (Rev. 12:11). The motif is captured well by Vern Eller, *The Most Revealing Book of the Bible: Making Sense out of Revelation* (1974; repr., Grand Rapids: Eerdmans, 1982); and, in a more academic way, by Richard Bauckham, *The Theology of the Book of Revelation* (Cambridge: Cambridge University Press, 1993); as well as Michael Bredin, *Jesus, Revolutionary of Peace: A Nonviolent Christology in the Book of Revelation* (Waynesboro, GA: Paternoster, 2003).

Concluding Words

1. Shakespeare, *Macbeth*, act 5, scene 5, lines 26–28.

2. I flesh out this practice in *Seeing Is Believing: Experiencing Jesus through Imaginative Prayer* (Grand Rapids: Baker Books, 2004), as well as in G. Boyd and A. Larson, *Escaping the Matrix: Setting Your Mind Free to Experience Real Life in Christ* (Grand Rapids: Baker Books, 2005).

3. This is known as "practicing the presence of God," a spiritual discipline made famous by a humble seventeenth-century monk named Brother Lawrence, but also espoused by a twentieth-century mystic missionary named Frank Laubach and a fiery seventeenth-century priest named Jean. P. de Caussade. See Brother Lawrence and F. Laubach, *Practicing His Presence*, Library of Spiritual Classics 1 (Jacksonville: Seed-Sowers, 1988); and J. P. de Caussade, *The Sacrament of the Present Moment* (New York: HarperCollins, 1989). I have discussed this foundational discipline and offered reflections and strategies surrounding it in G. Boyd, *Present Perfect: Finding God in the Now* (Grand Rapids: Zondervan, 2010).

4. I unpack the community aspect of the kingdom, together with the revolt against the idolatry of modern Western individualism that it entails, in G. Boyd, *The Myth of a Christian Religion: Losing Your Religion for the Beauty of a Revolution* (Grand Rapids: Zondervan, 2009), 67–76.

Also Available from
Gregory Boyd

Connect with

BakerBooks
Relevant. Intelligent. Engaging.

Sign up for announcements about
new and upcoming titles at

www.bakerbooks.com/signup

 ReadBakerBooks

 ReadBakerBooks

Sample Our Newest Releases!

Videos

Book
Samples

Made in United States
Orlando, FL
20 February 2022

15007117R00168